D1267208

John Barth

An Introduction

JOHN BARTH

An Introduction

David Morrell

The Pennsylvania State University Press

University Park and London

Library of Congress Cataloging in Publication Data

Morrell, David.
    John Barth: an introduction.

    Bibliography: p. 176.
    1.   Barth, John—Criticism and interpretation.
PS3552.A75Z8   813'.5'4   75-27284
ISBN 0-271-01220-X

To Philip Young:
the better maker

It comes to me again and again . . .
that one's bag of adventures, conceived
or conceivable, has been only half-emptied
by the mere telling of one's story. . . .
There is the story of one's hero, and then,
thanks to the intimate connexion of things,
the story of one's story itself. I blush
to confess it, but if one's a dramatist
one's a dramatist, and the latter imbroglio
is liable on occasion to strike me as really
the more objective of the two.

(Henry James, the Preface
to *The Ambassadors*)

Contents

List of Figures

Acknowledgments

The author wishes to express his thanks to the following persons. To John Barth for allowing access to those manuscripts of his on file at the Library of Congress, for permission to reproduce pages of those manuscripts and to quote from various unpublished essays, for the time he gave to answering questions and correcting factual errors in the biographical sections of this project's typescript. To Philip Young, Research Professor in Residence at The Pennsylvania State University, a former colleague of Barth, for more encouragement and guidance than can possibly be here described. To Barth's agent, Lurton Blassingame, his present editor, Anne Freedgood, and his former editor, Timothy Seldes, for the information they provided about Barth's relationship with his publishers. To Charles W. Mann, Curator of the Rare Book Room at the Pattee Library of The Pennsylvania State University, for permitting access to the Barth correspondence on file there. To Professor Bernard Oldsey for several afternoons of conversation about Barth that helped ease the author into the present study.

Foreword

"The best writer of fiction we have at present, and one of the best we have ever had": that is how critic Robert Scholes has described John Barth.[1] Another critic, Leslie Fiedler, has maintained that Barth's *The Sot-Weed Factor* is "closer to the 'Great American Novel' than any other book of the last decades,"[2] while still another, Granville Hicks, has called Barth's *Giles Goat-Boy* "one of the most important novels of our time."[3] There are some who disagree, and in the course of this study their opinions will be noted, but these three critics fairly represent a good many others who are impressed by Barth's work. In 1965 *Book Week* conducted an extensive poll that ranked *The Sot-Weed Factor* among the twenty best American novels since 1945. The American Library Association voted *Giles Goat-Boy* one of the Notable Books of 1966. The National Book Committee nominated his first novel, *The Floating Opera*, for its 1956 award. It nominated him again for his 1968 collection of short fiction, *Lost in the Funhouse*, and it awarded him half of its 1972 fiction honors for his collection of novellas, *Chimera*. *Giles Goat-Boy* attracted enough readers to become a best seller. After a slow start his other books have become widely read as well, especially at universities, and various English departments have on occasion made *Lost in the Funhouse* required reading for their majors.

Yet, despite Barth's considerable reputation and his large readership, few extended efforts to group his work and try to understand it have appeared. To be sure, he has been the subject of several scholarly articles, but most of these deal with some one feature of his work. He has also been the subject of Gerhard Joseph's 1970 pamphlet, but for reasons of space that provides only a swift, condensed analysis of each of Barth's first five books. There has been one full length study of him, Jac Tharpe's *The Comic Sublimity of Paradox* (Southern Illinois University Press, 1974), but as that title indicates, Barth's work is there approached from a very localized and limited point of view, and indeed the term "full length" misleads since the text itself is only roughly twice as long as Joseph's pamphlet. Certainly Barth's books, their sentences, structures, and themes, are extremely complex, deserving of more wide and varied attention. Accordingly the present study is an attempt to provide some part of the extensive commentary that the novels and stories invite but have not yet received.

With that said, however, it is necessary to make a disclaimer: the intent here is to exhaust neither the subject nor the reader. A volume could be written on Barth's use of metaphor, or of myth, history, eighteenth-century literary conventions, and many other devices. Indeed, full treatment of either *The Sot-Weed Factor* or *Giles Goat-Boy* might require an effort every bit as long as the present one. But this study has been written to introduce the reader to its subject as a whole, encompassing a variety of such topics, so that he will have a reasonably complete insight into the general nature of Barth's fiction and hopefully will be both stimulated and prepared to investigate the subject in detail for himself once he has been led into it. As a rule, of course, a study of this sort is written for a group of specialists in a rather small and well-defined area of knowledge, but that is not exclusively the audience this book addresses. It is directed as well toward an audience of educated but non-specialist readers—lay people as opposed to academics— who are interested enough to want to read Barth and learn about him.

The method is threefold. First, the story behind each book is told: how Barth got the idea for the book, how he researched and developed the idea until he made it into a fully integrated art work. Next the book's reception by its publisher and reviewers is detailed. Finally the book itself is analyzed and interpreted. The advantage of the first is that we understand what each book is by understanding how it came to be. The advantage of the second is that we are able to consider a number of different attitudes toward Barth without deciding on any one, pro or con, which our closeness in time to Barth, our inescapable lack of aesthetic distance, prevents us from legitimately taking. The advantage of the last is that by analyzing each book we simplify, though not necessarily distort, its complexity in order to facilitate an understanding of it.

But "I think that to understand any one thing entirely . . . requires the understanding of every other thing in the world," says Todd Andrews, the narrator of *The Floating Opera*.[4] So with Barth's fiction: we understand a little more about what is going on in one book after we have examined the others and have tried to achieve a coherent view of them put together. As a result, each chapter in this study tends to build on the chapter that came before. What is said about *The Floating Opera* is relevant to what is said in the next chapter about *The End of the Road,* and what is said about *The End of the Road* is relevant to what is said in the next chapter about *The Sot-Weed Factor.* And so on. No chapter is self-sufficient; to help tie things together, information about one book is frequently withheld from the chapter about that book and inserted in a later chapter in connection with a different book. The last word about any of them never comes until the last word.

The subject matter is presented, then, chronologically and organically; and with any luck the presentation will turn out to be a little like *The Floating Opera,* full of "curiosities, melodrama, spectacle, instruction, and entertainment" (p. 7). The various chapters discuss *The Floating Opera* and *The End of the Road* and their respective themes of relativism and nihilism; Barth's research of early Maryland history and his incorporation of that history into *The Sot-Weed Factor; The Sot-Weed Factor* itself and its theme of innocence versus experience; *Giles Goat-Boy,* its mythic structure, its themes of mysticism and tragedy; *Lost in the Funhouse,* its reliance on the unique properties of print, tape, and live voice; *Chimera,* its novella format, its spiral metaphor. In one chapter the books are considered as a corpus and as their themes and techniques relate to each other. In another Barth's life is recounted as completely as seems pertinent. The bibliography is extensive—of Barth's work, of important reviews and scholarly studies of his work.

"I have mixed feelings about narrative writing," Barth once said.

> Contemporary writers can't go on doing what's been done, and done better. I revere Flaubert and Tolstoy, Hemingway and Faulkner; but they're finished as objects of interest to the writer. My God, we're living in the last third of the twentieth century. We can't write nineteenth-century novels.
>
> Joyce and Kafka bring the novel to one kind of conclusion. So do Beckett and Borges. From both, I get pure esthetic bliss. It's an

esthetic of silence. Beckett is moving toward silence, refining language out of existence, working toward the point where there's nothing more to say. And Borges writes as if literature had already been done and he's writing footnotes to imaginary texts.

But my temperament is entirely different. The future of the novel is dubious. OK. So I start with the premise of the "end of literature" and try to turn it against itself. I go back to Cervantes, Fielding, Sterne, the *Arabian Nights*, to the artificial frame and the long connected tales. I'm interested in the *artifices* of narrative, in what can be done with language.[5]

What *can* be done with language, at any rate what Barth does with it, is a story in itself and the progress of this book.

1

The Life and Opinions
of Todd Andrews,
Ex-Suicide

It is not things themselves which
disturb men, but their judgments
about those things.
                    (Epigraph to vol. 1 of *Tristram Shandy*)

By the time John Barth was twenty-four, he had put in five years of
hard work writing and had seen only three small stories make it into
print. His master's project, a novel titled *Shirt of Nessus*, was of
interest to no one, not even himself ("a neo-primitive miscarriage"
he called it); and his half-finished cycle of tales imitating the *Decameron* was, he feared, too bawdy to be published.[1] Then, in 1954,
he happened upon a photograph of an old showboat that used to
tour up and down the Chesapeake Bay in Maryland: he had seen
that showboat at the dock of his home town, Cambridge, Maryland,
when he was around seven, and now, remembering, he decided to
use it in the climactic scene of another novel he was going to write.[2]

   That novel was eventually christened *The Floating Opera*. As
though making up for lost time, Barth wrote it very fast, from early
January to late March of 1955, and the theme he chose was one
which had been fascinating him since at least 1953: nihilism. "I
thought that I had invented [it]," he said.[3] So fascinated was he in
fact that, having finished this book about it, he planned to write a
series of them dramatizing various nihilistic attitudes. The plot of
one would not be continued exactly into the plot of another, he explained in a letter to the *Library Journal*, nor would they have any
specific characters in common. But they would, he went on in the
letter, all have one *similar* character, "some sort of bachelor, more
or less irresponsible, who either rejects absolute values or encounters

1

Figure 1. *The Original Floating Theater.* Barth found this photograph
in A. Aubrey Bodine's collection of photographs about Maryland,
Chesapeake Bay and Tidewater (New York, 1954), p. 18. There is a
caption that reads: "This 'floating theater' sailed up and down the Bay
for 25 years. It had a seating capacity of about 500 (reserved seats cost
40 cents), and a repertoire that included such favorites as 'Smilin'
Through' and 'Ten Nights in a Barroom.' Edna Ferber spent a summer
aboard soaking up background for her famous novel, 'Show Boat.'" (The
photograph is reproduced through the courtesy of Mr. Bodine.)

their rejection." The flagship of the series, *The Floating Opera*, he said was his "nihilistic comedy," and the bachelor he presented in it was Todd Andrews—a fifty-four-year-old Maryland lawyer "characterized mainly by his opinions, like Tristram Shandy," who one day plays with those opinions until he reasons himself into attempting suicide.[4]

As it happens, Barth was not directly influenced by *Tristram Shandy* at the time he wrote the book, however. "I've never been a great admirer of Sterne, although he's certainly an interesting figure," he later said.

> But when I wrote *The Floating Opera*. . . , I was very much under the influence of a Brazilian novelist whom I'd just come across, Machado de Assis—who in turn, though he wrote at the end of the 19th century and the beginning of the 20th, was very much under the influence of *Tristram Shandy;* the same kind of technical playfulness and similar view of the world. So I got my Sterne by way of Brazil.[5]*

In particular, he liked the way the narrator of one book by de Assis, *Dom Casmurro*, introduced himself directly at the start, explained the title of his book and the purpose of the book itself, and then went on to digress freely as the dictates of his interest overwhelmed the chronological development of his plot. These devices Barth incorporated fully.

At the same time his reference to *Tristram Shandy* was not just second thought. His character resembles Tristram in other ways besides his playing with opinions. Both, for example, are in imminent danger of death: Tristram from consumption and Todd from heart disease. They both look back over their lives and write about them, and they both have no wish to stay on any subject very long. What is more, they both engage in extensive mock-dialogue with the

---

* De Assis (1839–1908) is extremely well-known in his native Brazil, but only since 1955 or so has he begun to attract much attention elsewhere. A prolific writer of novels, stories, plays, poems, criticism, and journalism, he was elected president of the Brazilian Academy of Letters when it was first established in 1897, and he was re-elected ever after until his death when, by order of the nation's Chamber of Deputies, he was buried in a state funeral with full military and civilian honors.

reader, and while Tristram employs such typographical devices as blank, inked, and marbled pages, Todd reproduces in full the handbill for a minstrel show, provides a double column of narrative, and ends two chapters with the same paragraph.

There is one main difference between them, however. Tristram never tries to kill himself: he is too absorbed in life, or at least in writing about it, to want to leave. But then he is a notoriously sentimental eighteenth-century Englishman. He relishes emotion, and laughter is for him a drug to pain. Todd, on the other hand, is an intensely rational twentieth-century American, a detached observer who is almost always conscious of observing. Only five times in his life has he experienced great emotion, and when he laughs (which is surprisingly seldom, considering how funny the book often is), the laughter is no drug at all, but a hysterical reaction to the absurdity he believes is everywhere around him.

That he is writing about himself is the result of his father's hanging himself on Ground-Hog Day, 1930, in the basement of the family home. The ostensible motive for the suicide was that his father had gone bankrupt in the crash of 1929 and could not face his creditors. But Todd did not accept that as the actual reason, and so he began preparing to write an inquiry into the death of his father, a project that soon blossomed into a second inquiry, this one investigating the life of his father and the relationship between his father and himself. He had also another inquiry to make, a self-inquiry that took the form of an autobiographical letter to his father. He had been drafting it since 1920, and even though his father was now dead, he still continued. In it he left out nothing of importance about himself, and because every thought and action seemed important, the letter grew extremely long. The older he got, the more material there was to add, so the letter grew longer yet; and eventually his life outdistanced his writing: he could never catch up to the point where he would be writing about the events of the day when he was writing.* At any rate, *The Floating Opera* is a part

---

* Tristram Shandy is in the same position. "I am this month one whole year older than I was this time twelve-month; and having got, as you perceive, almost into the middle of my fourth volume—and no farther than to my first day's life—'tis demonstrative that I have three hundred and sixty-four

of that self-inquiry. He is composing it in 1954 in his room in the Dorset Hotel, Cambridge, Maryland, and his topic is a June day in 1937 when he decided to kill himself and then changed his mind.*

He tried to kill himself, he explains, because "it is my bad luck that I tend to attribute to abstract ideas a life-or-death significance."[6] When, that is, an Army doctor casually informed him in 1919 that he had a heart condition which could kill him at any second, Todd commenced assuming various poses to help him hide his heart from his mind and his mind from his heart. First he became, he says, a rake, then a saint, then a cynic, and at last in 1937 he found the mask of cynicism gone and despair in its place. Since it was his habit to justify on philosophical grounds his every attitude, he investigated the several reactions he could have to despair. Turning to God was out of the question: Todd did not believe in Him, and he refused to sacrifice his integrity by pretending to believe in Him. "There is no way to master the fact with which I live," he concluded (p. 241; rev. ed. p. 226), went to sleep with that conclusion, woke up in the

---

days more life to write just now, than when I first set out. . . . It must follow, an' please your worships, that the more I write, the more I shall have to write" (vol. 4, ch. 13).

* There are two items of interest here. First, Barth is not a very biographical writer; hence it is worth noting where he does occasionally adapt his own experiences into his fiction. Just as Todd is writing in 1954 about 1937, so in 1954 Barth got the idea for *The Floating Opera* because he was reminded of an old showboat he had seen in 1937.

The other item concerns the novel's publication history. It is a complex history and will be gone into shortly, but for now the reader should know that there are two principal versions of the book: the original edition (New York: Appleton-Century-Crofts, 1956) and the revised edition (Garden City, N.Y.: Doubleday, 1967). The revised edition is in parts substantially different from the earlier one, in both chronology and the wording of certain passages; and these differences make it necessary to cite both texts when quoting. Occasionally a passage exists in only one of the editions, and only one page reference can then be provided. All this is mentioned now because that June day in 1937 which Todd cannot date exactly is an instance of Barth's revision. In the first version, Todd says the day was either June 23 or 24; in the second, he says it was either June 21 or 22. This change has puzzled many readers and at least one critic, Gerhard Joseph, who in his pamphlet on Barth finally decided that Barth changed the dates to June 21 or 22 because the Zodiacal calendar changes then from Gemini to Cancer. Actually Barth's reason for the change was "to bring the dates closer into line with the summer solstice" (John Barth to D.M., 23 March 1970).

morning, splashed cold water on his face, and decided to kill himself. The next twelve hours he spent gathering philosophical support for his decision.

I. Nothing has intrinsic value. Things assume value only in terms of certain ends.

II. The reasons for which people attribute value to things are always ultimately arbitrary. That is, the ends in terms of which things assume value are themselves ultimately irrational.

III. There is, therefore, no ultimate "reason" for valuing anything.

IV. Living is action in some form. There is no reason for action in any form.

V. There is, then, no "reason" for living. (Pp. 238, 243; rev. ed. slightly different, pp. 223, 228)

That closed the inquiry as far as he was concerned. All that remained was to close his life. But of course he did not succeed; otherwise he would not have been able to write about the attempt. And what he added to his premises afterward is the main point of the novel.

> To realize that nothing has absolute value is, surely, overwhelming, but if one goes no further from that proposition than to become a saint, a cynic, or a suicide on principle, one hasn't gone far enough. If nothing makes any final difference, that fact makes no final difference either, and there is no more reason to commit suicide, say, than not to, in the last analysis. (P. 270; rev. ed. slightly different, p. 251)

The corollary is that "it is one thing to say 'Values are *only* relative'; quite another, and more thrilling, to remove the pejorative adverb and assert 'There *are* relative values!' " (p. 271). And so *The Floating Opera* comes to a stop, somewhat optimistically, as a thunderstorm in the distance breaks the heat that gathered in the day.

For the sake of perspective, it should be noted that there are many other engines of narrative which help to move *The Floating Opera* along, and they will be examined shortly. But the story of Todd's suicide attempt is the main one, and there is a relevant story about it that must be recounted before going any farther. In 1955, when Barth was working on the novel, he arranged for Todd to try to kill himself in a dramatic and grisly fashion. He had him board a showboat where during a minstrel show Todd slipped backstage, switched on some gas jets, and then returned to watch the players and to wait for the explosion that would blast apart himself and 699 fellow townspeople, many of them his friends. On stage was an act imitating the explosion of the sidewheeler *James B. Taylor,* and Todd clearly thought it would be apt for the two to blast as one. But no such luck. Just the act was a bomb, rather impressive to some of the audience; and Todd shrugged his shoulders, figuring disinterestedly that a stage hand must have found the open jets and closed them.

Barth wanted him to try it that way, but several publishers were not enthusiastic—five of them, to be exact. Most liked the book as a whole, but they all felt that it had too grim an ending to attract many readers. Finally a sixth publisher, Appleton-Century-Crofts, agreed to market the book, but there was a condition: Barth had to take some of the shock out of the climax. "They were sure Todd Andrews loved life so much that he wouldn't want to kill himself or anyone else in that particular way," Barth later said,[7] and their request for a change understandably bothered him. He was after all a young writer with no major credit to his name, and he welcomed the chance to be published. Yet he did not know if he could make the change and still contend that he had written an honest, uncompromising novel that remained true to its character and its theme. After much thought, he decided that he could.[8]

So when the novel appeared on August 24, 1956, it concluded this way: Todd went backstage and switched on the gas jets as before, but then he remained backstage waiting to die of asphyxiation. Barth had literally fixed the book so that it ended not with a bang but a whimper: as Todd sat listening to the gas and smelling it, he was distracted by muffled voices in the next room. It seems a little girl who was perhaps his daughter had taken a convulsion while watching the show and was being carried backstage; and in his concern for her safety, Todd found a reason to keep himself alive.

Reviewers wished that Todd had found a different reason, though. Like the publisher, they were quite impressed by the book as a whole—"a delightful *tour de force* by a new author who, if this is a true measure of his talent, is going to become well known," one of them wrote, for example.[9] But they were equally unimpressed by the end, charging that it was badly sentimental, that the action was turgid, that Todd shifted too fast from being detached to being involved, that attention was wrongly directed away from Todd and

toward the child.[10] The criticisms were enough for Barth to regret
with bitterness ever having listened to Appleton-Century-Crofts. "I
learned a boatwright little lesson," he later said. So he gritted his
teeth and bided his time, and when in 1967 another publisher,
Doubleday, arranged to reissue the book, he was more than happy
to change back to the original ending.[11]

He made other alterations as well. Some of them involved
merely cutting words that seemed redundant or that impeded the
flow of a sentence. Todd's opening remarks, for example, are like
this in the 1956 text:

> To someone like myself, whose literary activities have been confined
> since 1920 mainly to such pedestrian *genres* as legal briefs (in
> connection with my position as partner in the firm of Andrews,
> Bishop, & Andrews) and *Inquiry*-writing (which I'll explain
> presently), the hardest thing about the task at hand—*viz.*, the
> explanation of a day in 1937 when I changed my mind—is getting
> into it.

But in the revised text of 1967, all the matter in parentheses has been
removed along with the reference to "pedestrian *genres*," so that the
book gets under way far more smoothly.

> To someone like myself, whose literary activities have been confined
> since 1920 mainly to legal briefs and *Inquiry*-writing, the hardest
> thing about the task at hand—*viz.*, the explanation of a day in 1937
> when I changed my mind—is getting into it.

Barth also cut one brief chapter of philosophy titled "Another
premise to swallow" (repetitive and overly didactic), and then rearranged several incidents in the last quarter. The best way to
illustrate this is to set some of the chapter headings side by side.

	1956		*1967*
XXII.	A tour of the opera	XXII.	A tour of the opera
XXIII.	Another premise to swallow		(omitted)
XXIV.	So long, so long	XXIII.	So long, so long
XXV.	Three million dollars	XXIV.	Three million dollars
XXVI.	The Inquiry	XXV.	The Inquiry
XXVII.	Will you smile at my rowboat?	XXVI.	The first step

With section 23, "Another premise to swallow," removed from the revised edition, the succeeding chapter has taken its place and its number; the other chapters have been renumbered accordingly; and the last chapter has been split in two. Thus one section has been taken away, another has been added later, and there are still twenty-nine chapters.

What all this means in terms of specific events has been conveniently summarized by a reader for *Publishers' Weekly*.

> In the original 1956 version the central character tries to commit suicide and is thwarted. In the 1967 version he tries not only to commit suicide but to blow up the whole "Floating Opera" boatload of actors and audience. He is thwarted here, too. In the new version Mr. Barth also fills us in on his character's relations following the suicide attempt with his friends the Macks. Another section of the novel [an old man swallows an overdose of sleeping pills] remains about the same but is now placed as occurring after the suicide attempt rather than before it.[12]

And the important consequence of all these changes is that Todd Andrews becomes a more consistent and convincing character who now at last does indeed "attribute to abstract ideas a life-or-death significance." He has been apparent friends with Jane and Harrison Mack. He has even been making love to Jane with Harrison's permission, and perhaps is the real father of Jeannine, Jane's daughter. Yet when he realizes that the whole family may be blown up with him on the showboat, he does not particularly care.

> Calmly I thought of Harrison and Jane: of perfect breasts and thighs scorched and charred; of certain soft, sun-smelling hair crisped to ash. Calmly too I heard somewhere the squeal of an overexcited child, too young to be up so late: not impossibly Jeannine. I considered a small body, formed perhaps from my own and flawless Jane's, black, cracked, smoking. (Rev. ed. p. 243)

"It made no difference, absolutely," he decides. Nor does it make any difference to him that his friendship with the Macks dissolved, that they soon moved away and he saw them and their (perhaps his) daughter seldom again. It just does not matter. *Nothing* matters. Absolutely. Including suicide. And that is why in the revised edition the old man who swallows the overdose of sleeping pills is discovered not before Todd's own suicide attempt, but after. The logic of the drama demands that sequence. Todd has to fail to kill himself and then conclude that, if there is no final reason to go on living, there is no final reason to commit suicide either. And only then should he come upon someone else who has tried to kill himself. The sequence must be that way because in Todd's view the old man has not investigated the problem of suicide as thoroughly as he should have, and hence the old man's shortcoming serves to make Todd's own conclusion all the more valid. Todd goes on to say that the old man somehow recovered from his overdose but that he tried again and was successful. Although the moral of that part of the story is never given, at least two come to mind. Either some people never learn from their mistakes, or else life is too much for them and, philosophy be damned, suicide is all that is acceptable.

So, then, the main plot line is a bit different in the two versions of *The Floating Opera*, both incidentally and in tone. The 1967 text provides a more effective, more grimly dramatic climax, and it alters Todd's character so that he is almost totally a man of intellect, disinterested, uncaring. Where before he laughed, now he smiles; where he smiled, now he shrugs. And where at the very end he had friends to go to, now he is alone. A comparison between the last paragraph of both editions illustrates the difference.

1956

I made a note to intercept my note to Jimmy Andrews, stubbed out my cigar, and without hesitation went downstairs to telephone the Macks, ignoring with a smile the absurd thunderstorm that just then broke over Cambridge.

1967

I made a note to intercept my note to Jimmy Andrews, stubbed out (after all) my cigar, undressed, went to bed in enormous soothing solitude, and slept fairly well despite the absurd thunderstorm that soon afterwards broke all around.

Enormous soothing solitude. That is as close as Todd will ever come to feeling joy.

Yet Barth called his book a comedy, and if only that day in 1937 is examined, it is hard to see why: broodings over death do not have much hilarity in them. There *is* comedy in the book, however— in the wealth of secondary narratives that Todd supplies and that remains alike in both editions. He thinks that everything is related to everything else, and he structures the novel accordingly. One detail frequently suggests another to him and then another and then he sets aside the main story to take up small associated ones. Thus on that June morning in 1937 Jane Mack was naked in his bed. How did she get there? Well, that's a tale in itself and must be gone into. So the reader is treated to the wonder of how the Macks were so much in love with each other and such good friends with Todd that they were certain Jane could seduce him "just for the pleasure of it, without a lot of complications" (p. 36; rev. ed., p. 28). The pleasure and the complications that ensue anyway last over fifty pages and are worth all the space devoted to them. Several chapters later Todd is describing how he came to be a lawyer, and that prompts him to clarify his attitude toward the law, and that in turn occasions the marvelous story of a contested will, three million dollars, and 129 jars of human excrement, most of which are dumped upon a bed of zinnias.

But not all the extra stories are so comic; some in fact are serious and horrid. The five times Todd felt strong emotion illustrate both extremes: his mirth when he made love for the first time and saw what the act looked like reflected in a mirror; his fear in the First World War when he befouled himself, hugged and kissed a German soldier and bayoneted him; his frustration when he could not understand why his father had hanged himself; his surprise when Jane seduced him; and his despair when he could no longer be cynical about his heart condition. The list is a fair sample of how different sorts of incident are juxtaposed in *The Floating Opera;* and it demonstrates that the book can be called a comedy only in part.

Barth has supplied one other phrase, though, which does adequately describe the book. He has said that, when in 1954 he happened to see the photograph of the old showboat, his intention was to write something unique and special: "I thought it would be a good idea to write a philosophical minstrel show. I wasn't going to write a novel at all; I was going to write a minstrel show, only it was going to be a work of literature."[13] He ended up writing a novel anyhow; nevertheless he was able to salvage a great deal of minstrel show—to such an extent that Todd Andrews can claim the book is "a floating opera, . . . chock-full of curiosities" (p. 14). There is something for everyone: blood and gore, fun and games; tales of suicide, war, fornication, adultery, excrement, and Morton's Marvelous Tomatoes; periodic philosophic edification; a grand finale in which nearly every character appears on the boat to watch the minstrel grand finale on the stage. And it all floats willy-nilly, as Todd says, on the tide of his vagrant prose. "You'll catch sight of it, then lose it, then spy it again; and it will doubtless require the best efforts of your attention and imagination . . . to keep track of the plot as it sails in and out of view" (p. 14; rev. ed. pp. 7–8). The image applies not only to the form of the book but also to its view of life; for Todd has always favored the notion of building a showboat with just one big flat open deck and a play going on forever.

> The boat wouldn't be moored, but would drift up and down the river on the tide, and the audience would sit along both banks. They could catch whatever part of the plot happened to unfold as the boat floated past, and then they'd have to wait until the tide ran back again to catch another snatch of it, if they still happened to be sitting there. To fill in the gaps they'd have to use their imaginations, or ask more attentive neighbors, or hear the word passed along from upriver or downriver. Most times they wouldn't understand what was going on at all, or they'd think they knew, when actually they didn't. . . . Need I explain? That's how much of life works. (P. 13; rev. ed. slightly different, p. 7)

"They wouldn't understand what was going on at all." If Barth had here treated that notion in a somewhat comic fashion, he was to do quite otherwise very shortly.

2

The Immobilization of Jacob Horner

The figure of Jack Horner has frequently
been used metaphorically, as by Swift in
"A Christmas Box," by Byron in *Don Juan*. . . .
Thomas Love Peacock (*Melincourt*, 1817)
described the rhyme as "one of the most
splendid examples on record of the
admirable practical doctrine of 'taking
care of number one.' "
  (*The Oxford Dictionary of Nursery Rhymes*)

The year 1955 ended up symmetrical for Barth. Having written
The Floating Opera in the first three months, he waited six, during
which he changed the *Opera* to suit Appleton-Century-Crofts, then
wrote another novel in the last three months. As of May 27, he was
twenty-five. His new book was *The End of the Road*, the second in
his announced series "about" nihilism (a "nihilistic tragedy" he
labeled it, as opposed to *The Floating Opera*, which he called a
"nihilistic comedy").[1] And the speed at which he had produced the
two excited him. Indeed he later told Philip Young, his friend and
colleague at The Pennsylvania State University where Barth taught
from 1953 to 1965, that back then he believed he could write novels
as fast as his publisher could bring them out, it taking about half a
year for the publisher to do so. Both his muse and his editor reckoned
otherwise, though. He was never again to write as much in one year
as he did in 1955. Nor was his then-publisher, Appleton-Century-
Crofts, very eager to print his books at the pace he wanted.

  The reason for Appleton's reluctance was at bottom the same
one that had made them ask Barth to change the climax in *The
Floating Opera*—fear of insufficient sales. Earlier they had maintained that readers would be repelled by Todd Andrews's attempt

to blow up 699 townsfolk aboard a showboat, and this time they were equally certain that critics would attack *The End of the Road* and thus sabotage the novel's selling power on the basis that *The Opera* and *The Road* are similar in plot.[2] To be sure, there is a similarity: each book depicts a triangle in which a bachelor makes love to a married woman with the husband's consent (more or less), and in which a pregnancy results with neither man knowing for certain who is the father. But the similarity is not as great as the difference: the affair in *The Floating Opera* takes up less than one-third of that book and is played for laughs, whereas the affair in *The End of the Road* is the action of the entire book and is not finally played for laughs at all. Specifically, in the first, Jane Mack survives and lives content with her husband and her daughter, but in the second, Rennie Morgan panics while having an abortion, vomits her supper of hot dogs and sauerkraut, and chokes to death. Regardless of this sharp difference, Appleton was determined to wait before marketing *The End of the Road*. Their plan was to shelve the book until they had put out some totally unlike work of Barth and *then* publish *The End of the Road*. Presumably they felt critics and readers would by that time have forgotten the parts of *The Floating Opera* that reappear, magnified and transformed, in *The End of the Road*. Barth, however, was not willing to go along with their plan. After all, he had no other novel for them, and at the moment he was interested in seeing this one in the book stores. So he instructed his agent, Lurton Blassingame, to seek out another publisher, and Blassingame showed it next to Knopf where the editors wanted to buy it but the owners did not.

Then Ed Aswell, who had been Thomas Wolfe's editor when that novelist had decided to do without Maxwell Perkins's help, and who was now an advisory editor at Doubleday, phoned Blassingame, explained how much he liked *The Floating Opera,* and asked to see some of Barth's work.[3] Doubleday had been specializing in commercial fiction, he said, but they were also trying somewhat to alter their image by promoting fiction of a more literary quality, and *The End of the Road* turned out to be just what they were looking for. They made only two suggestions. First, they felt that it was impolitic to have a Negro doctor perform an abortion on a white woman during which she dies, and they wondered, not strongly, if perhaps the Doctor could be white—to which Barth said *no*.[4]

Second, they felt that the novel's suggested title, *What To Do Until the Doctor Comes*, would make readers think that the novel was a first-aid book, and they asked that Barth change the title—which he did to the present one.[5] In August 1958, almost two and a half years after Barth finished it, *The End of the Road* was finally published, and although it sold very poorly, Doubleday further agreed to publish his later work, valuing his reputation more than the money he lost them.

The End of the Road at least had this measure of success: it attracted more buyers (3000) than did *The Floating Opera* (1682),[6] and at the outset it prompted more and influential reviews. *Time*, for example, led off a book section with over two columns devoted to *The Road* and concluded: "Barth is clearly one of the more interesting of younger U.S. writers and he has produced that rarity of U.S. letters—a true novel of ideas."[7] The *New York Herald Tribune Book Review* described the novel's theme as "profound and timely" and went on piling up such adjectives as "imaginative, unconventional, penetrating and entertaining."[8] Both *The Chicago Review* and *The Massachusetts Review* were also full of praise and, what is more, they both contended Barth had journeyed into unexplored novelistic territory:

> It is an original, entertaining, and timely novel, and it is even rarer than *Time* said, for its genre has yet to be named. . . . *The End of the Road* is of a special type, that may be called *ideological farce.*[9]

> We may be seeing here the emergence of a new genre—the serious farce. Comedy, tragedy, epic—for Mr. Barth the old tags no longer apply.[10]

Yet laudatory as these last two reviews are, they are not completely satisfying. If, as they propose, no old tag applies to *The End of the Road*, the new tags, "ideological farce" and "serious farce," themselves seem not to apply: they place too much emphasis on the farcical whereas there is nothing farcical about the novel's climax, Rennie Morgan's shocking death. At the beginning there is no doubt some farce, in the accepted sense of broad, often ribald comedy (Jacob Horner dancing manically nude about his bedroom; Joe Morgan spied picking his nose with one hand, masturbating with the other, and humming a sprightly tune throughout), but almost halfway into the book these farcic elements leave off and deadly serious ones take over. Barth's own tag for *The End of the Road,* a "nihilistic tragedy," is not accurate either: it does not account for the book's initial conspicuous humor. More likely the book is not of a new genre, but of a type that is already familiar and for which an acceptable tag already exists—what *Time* proposed from the start, a novel of ideas, one which strikes its readers as fairly unique because its author, unlike most other novelists of ideas, has learned to make *his* ideas dramatically intriguing. He develops his action by means of lengthy exposition of philosophy, he posits his conflict between characters who steadfastly maintain opposing philosophies, and he manages at first to amuse, later horrify, nearly always fascinate. "To the extent that [my novels] are novels of ideas—and that's a very limited extent—they are that because they dramatize alternatives to philosophical positions," Barth has said.[11] It should be emphasized here, however, that *The End of the Road* is Barth's only primary novel of ideas. The rest are similar to it inasmuch as parts of the action are based on philosophical debate. But they also have extravagant plot-structures and self-conscious artifices that make them more than novels of ideas, a topic that will be discussed in later chapters.

The ideas in this case are developed out of those in *The Floating Opera.* There Todd Andrews convinces himself that nothing has intrinsic value, including life, hence that suicide is the only logically valid act. But when he does not succeed in killing himself, he rethinks his notions and finally decides that if there is no reason to stay alive there is no reason to commit suicide either. That conclusion is crucial in understanding not only *The Floating Opera* but also *The End of the Road,* because as Barth explained to a reviewer: "I deliberately had [Todd Andrews] end up with that brave ethical subjectivism in order that Jacob Horner might undo that position in #2 and carry all non-mystical value-thinking to the end of the road."[12] Barth meant by "non-mystical value-thinking" a system of values that has no recourse to the rationally indefensible absolutes of religion, and that is based instead on other, non-religious values. But since nothing has intrinsic worth, since a thing's worth is always given to it from outside, the only values that have any validity are relative ones, peculiar to each person and not necessarily upheld by any other. That is what Todd Andrews at last believes.

And that is what Joe Morgan, a central character in *The End of the Road,* continually insists upon. His relative value is his marriage with Rennie.

> Certainly I'm not sold on marriage-under-any-circumstances, and I'm sure Rennie's not either. There's nothing intrinsically valuable about marriage. . . . That doesn't mean that I don't value it; in fact I guess I value my relationship with Rennie more than anything else in the world. All it means is that once you admit it's no absolute, you have to decide for yourself the conditions under which marriage is important to you.[13]

[For Joe, the conditions are extreme but rational: that he and Rennie "respect each other in every way," "take each other seriously," and "that means not making a lot of kinds of allowances" (pp. 41–42). On every subject, no matter how trivial, they compare and examine ideas as deeply as they can. Every phrase, every sentence must be articulated clearly, must be as thoughtful and considered as possible] Every interest must be shared and every goal must somehow relate to furthering the respect between them.[It is an absurdly taxing program, stringently demanding,]and Rennie is not always as strong at it as Joe. So Joe has to "straighten Rennie out now and then, or tell her that some statement of hers is stupid as hell, or even slug her"—because he respects her, he says (p. 42). Only under these conditions is his marriage important to him, and he will take drastic action to preserve them, like offering Rennie a pistol with which to shoot herself if that is what she wants. In *The Floating Opera,* Todd Andrews was so intensely rational that he attributed "to abstract ideas a life-or-death significance" (p. 241). Now in *The End of the Road,* Joe Morgan works out of the same rationalist philosophy, attaching the same kind of significance to his ideas. "Philosophizing was no game to Mr. Morgan; . . . he lived his conclusions down to the fine print" (p. 44). "This is a life-and-death business with him" (p. 120).

Directly opposite to Joe is the book's main character and its first-person teller, Jacob Horner. "In a sense, I am Jacob Horner," he begins. ("The hero of *The End of the Road,* Jacob Horner, is supposed to remind you first of all of Little Jack Horner, who also sits in a corner and rationalizes," Barth has said.

Then a Horner is somebody who puts horns on, who cuckolds, and this is what Jacob Horner does. But a student told me that I had in mind a character in Wycherley's play *The Country Wife,* which I read last month when the student pointed it out to me. This eighteenth-century Horner does exactly the same thing as mine, it turns out, but Wycherley did it first and I didn't know it.[14])

In a sense, too, he is *not* Jacob Horner: he is anyone he wants to be.

It was never very much of a chore for me, at various times, to maintain with perfectly equal unenthusiasm contradictory, or at least polarized, opinions at once on a given subject. . . . Jacob Horner—owl, peacock, chameleon, donkey, and popinjay, fugitive from a medieval bestiary—was at the same time giant and dwarf, plenum and vacuum, and admirable and contemptible. (P. 114)

Unable to be like Joe Morgan and choose a relative value and act according to it, Jake Horner sees all values as equally attractive, though none of them significant, and chooses one and then another and another as his whims require.

When one is faced with such a multitude of desirable choices, no one choice seems satisfactory for very long by comparison with the aggregate desirability of all the rest, though compared to any *one* of the others it would not be found inferior. (P. 2)

In psychology, this state of mind is known as an approach-approach conflict, and minor examples of it are not rare. Barth himself once offered a personal example to a student who was interviewing him.

The great difficulty of making choices if you have any imagination . . . is a kind of autobiographical element in [my] books. I've often found simple choices terribly difficult. I think I mentioned somewhere the relative ease of buying a book . . . if you're in a store where there are only a few books, and the terrible job of deciding on a book if you're in a store where there are a great many. That's the story of my life. You imagine so many alternatives to each position that it makes you dissatisfied with any.[15]

Normally, of course, a selection is soon made anyway, but Horner is not normal. If possible, he would choose all the books, but if not possible, he would be caught in the tug and pull of opposing forces, in a short time paralyzed. Horner does not call his state of mind an approach-approach conflict, however; he supplies a more thematically meaningful name—"*cosmopsis,* the cosmic view" (p. 69). He is first afflicted by it on the day after his twenty-eighth birthday when he finds he no longer has convincing reasons to continue attending graduate school or doing anything else he has been committed to. He goes to a railroad station and asks the ticket agent what places he can ride to for twenty dollars, all the money he has to spare, and as he considers the list of cities given to him, cosmopsis strikes.

> I left the ticket window and took a seat on one of the benches in the middle of the concourse to make up my mind. And it was there that I simply ran out of motives, as a car runs out of gas. There was no reason to go to Cincinnati, Ohio. There was no reason to go to Crestline, Ohio. Or Dayton, Ohio; or Lima, Ohio. There was no reason, either, to go back to the apartment hotel, or for that matter to go anywhere. There was no reason to do anything. (Pp. 68–69)

This, then, is the contest that Barth has arranged: Jacob Horner who has no values, against Joe Morgan who has the relative values of his marriage and the rationalist principles governing it. Once the two men are polarized like this, *The End of the Road* seems even more related to *The Floating Opera* than was at first evident, for nihilistic thinking is what leads Todd Andrews to attempt suicide and the discovery that there are relative values is what makes him decide to go on living. What Barth has done is to seize Todd's philosophic position before the suicide attempt and assign it to Jake; likewise he assigns Todd's position after the attempt to Joe. Instead of having nihilism develop into relativism as he did in *The Floating Opera,* Barth now has isolated the two and let them clash head on. Todd Andrews is thus still alive, though not very well—extreme, miserable, fragmented in *The End of the Road.* The number of traits that Joe and Jake have in common with Todd is in fact so many that a complete list cannot be provided here—it is a study in itself. A few should nonetheless be noted. Just as Joe, to be true to his ideas, is willing to let his wife blow her brains out with a Colt .45, if that is how she wants to be taken seriously, so Todd is prepared to act out his ideas by blowing up 699 people aboard a showboat. But like Jake (and this correspondence is perhaps the most impressive),

Todd sometimes is not convinced of the value of any idea and rests immobilized. "There was no reason to open my mouth, as there was no reason to do anything," Todd says,

> and I will say that the realization of this worked upon me involuntarily. This is important: it was not that I decided not to speak, but that, aware in every part of me of the unjustifiable nature of action, and completely subject as I was then to the operation of my reasoning, I simply could not open my mouth; my arms and legs would not move. An amazing helplessness. . . . I was simply paralyzed. (P. 264)

The malady cosmopsis has struck again.

But Barth is writing fiction, not debate, and that requires setting up a dramatically convincing reason for Jake and Joe to clash: their respective attitudes toward Rennie. Barth analyzes the plot dynamics this way:

> A probable reason for the recurrence in my stories of the triangle, that takes the form of one woman and two men instead of the other way around, is that if you have for thematic reasons a character who represents single-mindedly some position, then the dictates of drama suggest that you're likely to have another character who's his antithesis—these are likely to be male characters if they're embodiments of ideas—then you need a woman between to be the catalyst for the reaction between the two males so that you can work out your dialectic. This is the case of Mack and Todd Andrews with the woman Jane, in the first novel; Jacob Horner and Joe Morgan and the catalyst Rennie in the second novel.[16]

She is the catalyst on account of Joe, who recognizes that she is not as sure of the principles governing their marriage as he is, and who consequently forces her into contact with Jake and his radically different ideas, to test her. It is like God and Satan vying for a soul, she feels (p. 63), and eventually Jake's fundamental lack of seriousness so confuses her that she commits adultery with him. To a certain extent, Joe has unwittingly invited that adultery by using Horner to test her, but no matter, his life style now is in jeopardy and he has to find out, man of reason and motives that he is, why such an apparently solid marriage relationship has broken.

And so the inquisition begins. Why did you do it? he asks Horner. But Horner does not know why; he just felt like it. Then why did Horner feel like it? He does not know that either. The answer is especially unacceptable to Joe because he is convinced that people do not act without reason, that every action has a motive for it, hence that Horner either is being evasive or else is not yet sure what his motive was. In any case, they will have to adulterate again, Joe demands absurdly, and this time they had better be conscious of their motives and able to explain them. And to ensure that they obey his orders, Joe starts brandishing his Colt .45.

As it turns out, one extra session is not enough, Jake and Rennie are still not sure what their initial motives were, and so more sessions are demanded until finally Rennie becomes pregnant and neither man is positive who is the sire. Rennie is positive about this much, however: she is not going to carry the child, she wants an abortion, she will shoot herself if an abortion is not arranged. The threat of suicide prompts Horner to accept the responsibility for his actions, to accept it perhaps for the first time in his life. He determines to arrange the abortion, and after much frantic searching, he locates a doctor who will operate on her. But Horner's desperate play for responsibility is too late, Rennie dies on the operating table, and Joe calls Horner to ask in an unconscious parody of his rationalist pose, "Well, what's on your mind, Jake? What do you think about things?" "God, Joe—I don't know where to start or what to do!" "What?" "*I said I don't know what to do.*" "Oh." A long pause. Joe hangs up (p. 188). Non-mystical value-thinking has been carried to the end of the road: you cannot impose rational values on irrational human behavior, and if you persist in trying, if you are stubbornly prepared to apply your values to the limit no matter what the results, then this novel provides a fair instance of what those results can be.

But while Joe Morgan learns that painful lesson (he is too bright not to have learned, though he gives no indication he is aware of the lesson), Jacob Horner learns something else.

> I wanted the adventure to teach me this about myself: that regardless of what shifting opinions I held about ethical matters in the abstract, I was not so consistently the same person . . . that I could involve myself seriously in the lives of others without doing damage all around, not least to my own tranquility; that my irrational flashes of conscience and cruelty, of compassion and cynicism—in short, my inability to play the same role long enough—could give me as well

> as others pain. . . . I didn't consistently need or want friends, but
> it was clear (this too I wanted to learn) that, given my own special
> kind of integrity, if I was to have them at all I must remain unin-
> volved—I must leave them alone. (P. 176)

Actions have consequences, and to avoid pain the consequences
should be weighed before taking action. Morgan, too thoughtful;
Horner, too thoughtless. As the Doctor says, "This thing was everybody's fault, Horner. Let it be everybody's lesson" (p. 183).

The Doctor? He is the fourth and last major character in the
book. He is also a Negro and Horner's analyst and Rennie's abor-
tionist, and his ideas suggest one method of living in the complex,
illogical, absurd world that Barth posits. When Horner is sitting
paralyzed on the bench in the train station, the Doctor literally snaps
him out of the trance and, after informing Horner of his interest in
paralytics, takes him for treatment to the Remobilization Farm he
presides over somewhere on the Eastern Shore of Maryland. The
treatment he prescribes for Horner is in two phases, the first of
which is designed to keep Horner simply in motion.

> Don't let yourself get stuck between alternatives, or you're lost.
> You're not that strong. If the alternatives are side by side, choose the
> one on the left; if they're consecutive in time, choose the earlier. If
> neither of these applies, choose the alternative whose name begins
> with the earlier letter of the alphabet. These are the principles of
> Sinistrality, Antecedence, and Alphabetical Priority—there are others,
> and they're arbitrary, but useful. (Pp. 79–80)

Obviously such principles apply only to the more practical choices
in life: what to eat, when to eat, where to eat. But they are no help
when it comes to behaving in society; for that, a second phase of
treatment is required—Mythotherapy.

> Mythotherapy is based on two assumptions: that human existence
> precedes human essence, if either of the two terms really signifies
> anything; and that a man is free not only to choose his own essence
> but to change it at will. (P. 82)

He calls them good existential principles, and what they amount to
is that Horner should choose a role appropriate to each situation in
which he is placed and that as soon as the situation changes he
should stop playing that role and choose another one. Above all, the
role he chooses should be of a kind that he is capable of acting out;

thus in many cases, the simpler the role is, the better. "It's extremely important that you learn to assume these masks whole-heartedly," the Doctor points out.

> Don't think there's anything behind them: *ego* means *I*, and *I* means *ego*, and the ego by definition is a mask. Where there's no ego—this is you on the bench—there's no *I*. If you sometimes have the feeling that your mask is *insincere*—impossible word!—it's only because one of your masks is incompatible with another. You mustn't put on two at a time. There's a source of conflict, and conflict between masks, like absence of masks, is a source of immobility. (Pp. 84–85)

Although the Doctor prescribes this form of existentialism for Horner, he himself is not an existentialist. He is instead what Horner describes him as: a super-pragmatist (p. 79). Whether his principles are true or false is of no concern to him; he is interested only in their utility. Everything to him is either therapeutic, anti-therapeutic, or irrelevant, and for each patient, for each special paralysis, he has different theories, different treatments—Nutritional Therapy, Medicinal Therapy, Informational Therapy, Sexual Therapy, Theotherapy and Atheotherapy, Scriptotherapy, and dozens of others, each of value only as long as it serves its purpose. Horner's case happened to require Mythotherapy, and the treatment might have been successful if he had obeyed instructions and not had a love affair (pp. 79, 171). But once he involved himself emotionally in Rennie's problems, the affair became too complex for him to choose the proper role to play. The Doctor is furious when he discovers that Horner had ignored his instructions.

> It would serve you right if the husband shot you. Mythotherapy— Mythotherapy would have kept you out of any involvement, if you'd practiced it assiduously the whole time. Actually you did practice it, but like a ninny you gave yourself the wrong part. Even the villain's role would have been all right, if you'd been an out-and-out villain with no regrets! But you've made yourself a penitent when it's too late to repent, and that's the best role I can think of to immobilize you. (P. 172)

The Doctor is being pragmatic once again—the practical role is the one with the least amount of disastrous consequences, and Horner's fault is not only that he has failed to foresee consequences, but also that he has accepted responsibility for the consequences after it is impossible for him to make amends.

One critic, Jean Kennard, has provided extraordinary insight into the Doctor and his function in the novel.

> The Doctor realizes that there is no such thing as truth, that the world is arbitrary, is "everything that is the case, and what the case is is not a matter of logic." In this world, the Doctor claims, like Sartre, that human beings have only a chosen identity. . . . The Doctor is the one character who survives in the novel, but this is not because he avows Existentialist principles but because he recognizes the dangers inherent in any generalizations, even Existentialist ones. . . . What the Doctor does in fact is to apply the Existentialist premise that there are no absolutes to Existentialist premises themselves. Joe Morgan's life is destroyed because he fails to do this.[17]

Thus pragmatism and a suspicion of all abstractions that cannot be usefully, beneficially applied to specific actions is the philosophy which the book seems to advocate. But the reader is not allowed to remain secure with this knowledge of how to live; the nature of the world forbids him to. Things break down and fall apart, and just when a person is almost free of trouble, the unpredictable occurs— vomit, strangulation, burial; and all philosophy, pragmatic or any other kind, is foolish mouthing.

So now Jacob Horner has retreated to the Doctor's newly re-located farm (this time it is in Pennsylvania), where he is writing his story "at 7:55 in the evening of Tuesday, October 4, 1955, upstairs in the dormitory" (p. 2). The Doctor is quite likely waiting for the manuscript: with Horner too far gone for Mythotherapy to be of help, Scriptotherapy has evidently been required. And since Horner started his relationship with Joe and Rennie by taking a job as prescriptive grammar teacher at Wicomico State Teachers College where Joe taught, it is appropriate that his newest therapy have to do with words and grammar.*

---

* Barth has incorporated another piece of autobiography into his fiction. Earlier, Todd Andrews began his *Floating Opera* in 1954 about a showboat he had visited in 1937; so too Barth got the idea for *The Floating Opera* in 1954 when he was reminded of a showboat he himself had visited in 1937. Now in *The End of the Road* there is a similar pattern. Jake begins his narrative in October 1955—that is when Barth began *The End of the Road.* Jake is writing about the fall of 1953 when he was a prescriptive grammar teacher at a state teachers college—Barth went to Penn State in the fall of 1953 and for a time he too was a grammar teacher.

In one part, he writes in the present tense and appears to be demonstrating to the Doctor that he does understand the principles of Mythotherapy. The passage has an essay-answer quality, as though the Doctor had instructed him to explain Mythotherapy in 100 words or less.

> We are all casting directors a great deal of the time, if not always, and he is wise who realizes that his role-assigning is at best an arbitrary distortion of the actors' personalities; but he is even wiser who sees in addition that this arbitrariness is probably inevitable, and at any rate is apparently necessary if one would reach the ends he desires. (Pp. 25–26)

In another part, Horner links Mythotherapy with verbalization.

> Assigning names to things is like assigning roles to people: it is necessarily a distortion, but it is a necessary distortion if one would get on with the plot. (P. 135)

And then, in one other part, he writes of articulation alone.

> It is the only thing I can think of about which I ever had, with any frequency at all, the feelings one usually has for one's absolutes. To turn experience into speech—that is, to classify, to categorize, to conceptualize, to grammarize, to syntactify it—is always a betrayal of experience, a falsification of it; but only so betrayed can it be dealt with at all, and only in so dealing with it did I ever feel a man, alive and kicking. (Pp. 112–113)

He seems no longer a nihilist; he has found a more or less imperfect value, but a value nevertheless, and it may indicate the first stage of remobilization, of dealing practically with the world. But then again it may indicate none of this. With Jacob Horner you are never sure of anything. Only in a sense is he Jacob Horner, and typically he closes his section on the value of articulation: "In other senses, of course, I don't believe this at all."

Horner's contradictions are naturally not very pleasing philosophically, however true to the book's nihilistic theme they may be. One wants some answers to the problem of how to live in Horner's world, and none are forthcoming. Even pragmatism is not always of use; it makes no allowance for disastrous accident. But aesthetically, the way in which Horner's contradictions and his nihilistic attitude are treated is a joy. His distortion of the world in order to describe it, his distortion of people's characters in order to keep from being paralyzed among them—these betrayals of experience, these falsifications of it mirror each other. Writing has become an image of living, and living an image of writing.

This trick of matching a book's method and its message Barth had already performed in *The Floating Opera,* where the title is an image of the novel and of life. There too the world is sometimes hard to explain and words not always adequate to explain it, but at least Todd Andrews has a few relative values which enable him to live and write with a certain amount of gusto and confidence. In *The End of the Road,* however, Jake Horner has no values to believe in wholeheartedly; action is difficult for him, and accurate writing almost impossible.

> The apparent ambivalence of Rennie's feelings about me . . . was only a pseudo-ambivalence whose source was in the language, not in the concepts symbolized by the language. . . . What Rennie felt was actually neither ambivalent nor even complex; it was both single and simple, like all feelings, but like all feelings it was also completely particular and individual, and so the trouble started only when she attempted to label it with a common noun such as *love* or *abhorrence.* . . . Rennie loved me, then, and hated me as well! Let us say she x-ed me. (P. 135)

The next step is to use x or y or z for various common nouns—that is, lapse into nonsense—and the step after that is to lapse into silence. For Barth to continue his series about nihilism in this direction, he would have had to cease writing. He had demonstrated that words and things did not exist in a one-to-one relationship, that words were a simplification of things, a distortion of them, hence that realism, which is based on the theory that words can transpose the world onto paper, is not a "truthful" literary technique. His alternative to carrying language to the end of this road was to set out in a different direction and on a different road, to imitate not the world directly, but the world as it has already been distorted in the eighteenth-century novel, to embrace distortion and use it as a "true representation of the distortion we all make of life."[18] And in his next book, *The Sot-Weed Factor,* he tried just that.

3

Ebenezer Cooke, Sot-Weed Factor Redivivus

I found colonial history so fantastic that the work of the imagination consisted mainly of toning things down so they'd be believable in a farcical novel. In fact, most of the truly preposterous incidents in *The Sot-Weed Factor* are based on fact. . . . There was a marvelous case, for example, which I can't remember whether I used in the novel or not: the first murder in the Province of Maryland. They arrested the man and found they had no court to try him in—they'd just gotten off the boats— so they convened the Governor's Council. By a rap of the gavel they turned the Governor's Council into an inquest, decided there was a True Bill, rapped the gavel and became a court, tried the case, convicted the man, found that they had no law to sentence him under—murder wasn't against the law yet—so they reconvened themselves into a legislature, passed a law against murder, punishable by death, convened themselves back into a court, condemned the man to death—and suspended the sentence lest justice be miscarried. That story would sound outrageous even in a farcical novel; nobody would believe it.

(John Barth in conversation)[1]

Perhaps Barth could not remember whether he used that incident in *The Sot-Weed Factor*, but he did use it: Lord Baltimore, telling Ebenezer Cooke about seventeenth-century Maryland, recounts a version of it. As interesting as the story is by itself, Barth's reference to it here makes it doubly interesting and indeed quite another story, no longer about the first murder trial in Maryland, instead about

27

Barth's composition of *The Sot-Weed Factor*. And that story in fuller detail is worth going into.

By the end of 1955, Barth had two novels in his announced series of nihilism already complete, and with the start of the new year he was decided that his next book would be the third and last in that series. Earlier he had thought that he invented nihilism, "and when I found out I hadn't," he said, "I lost interest."[2] Having written the first two in three months each, he hoped to do the same again and write the third in the early months of 1956—at the very most he figured to be finished by his twenty-sixth birthday on May 27—but he took a little longer than that and did not finish until three years later, shortly before he turned twenty-nine. The delay was caused in part by the scope and volume of the book: it spanned the Old World and the New, and its 806 pages made it almost four times as large as either of his earlier novels. Another and more significant reason for the delay was that while he prepared to write the book his ideas about the nature of fiction changed drastically.

So far in his fiction he had portrayed contemporary incidents and characters, had made the action and locale appear believable, had provided dialogue sounding more or less the way people talk— had, that is, relied on the techniques of realism. In some passages (like Todd Andrews's bayoneting a German soldier in *The Floating Opera* and Rennie Morgan's abortion table death in *The End of the Road*), he achieved so great a sense of immediacy that this reader, for one, has the feel of witnessing the events rather than of reading about them. And although in other passages (like Jake's lengthy talks with Rennie) there is not as much vividness, the reader still is able to accept the events as lifelike and credible. That is not to imply that these books are realistic in any conventional manner. After all, *The Floating Opera* is somewhat a rarity, a novelistic minstrel show, floating on a tide of vagrant prose. *The End of the Road* is no less a rarity, told by a manic-depressive Jacob Horner, and striking the reader as a wide-awake nightmare. Also unconventional are a very few passages which push realism and the reader's suspension of disbelief to their limits—the 129 jars of human excrement in *The Floating Opera*, for example, and the Negro doctor in *The End of the Road* who with his multi-personalities, his Homosexual Therapy, and his Remobilization Farm seems a fugitive from another dimension. Both are possible: one encounters similar bizarre items every day in the newspaper. Yet both are fantastic too, and as such they indicate the direction Barth was to take in his next fiction; for although he had been writing in the realistic mode, he had more and more found it a hamper to his imagination.

The signs of his dissatisfaction with realism are unmistakable in *The End of the Road.* Twice—when Joe explains his value system to Jake, and again when Rennie explains to Jake how she and Joe came to be married—the speakers relate their stories in huge chunks, and Jake, the narrator, adds that no such long, coherent speeches were actually made, that he has combined various short statements and ordered them for the sake of convenience. Clearly, if these sections had been absolutely realistic with numerous reactions, diversions, and asides, the result would have been as tedious as a transcription of everyday conversation so often is. Barth, via Jake, understood that in order to write dramatically interesting fiction a novelist must avoid duplicating the exact manner of ordinary speech. Instead he has to imitate that manner (something quite different from duplicating it); he has to distort, intensify, and arrange it so that his dialogue can have the length and pace and aesthetic effect he requires.

But realism was for Barth more than just dramatically uninteresting; it was, he had come to feel, philosophically untenable. "To turn experience into speech," he had Jake note, "that is, to classify, to categorize, to conceptualize, to grammarize, to syntactify it—is always a betrayal of experience, a falsification of it" (pp. 112–113). Grammar imposes an order on things that is not there of itself. Abstract words like "good" interpret things rather than describe them. Concrete words like "apple" simplify things that are enormously complex amalgams of other things like "seeds" and "skin" and "juice," and those words simplify things that are themselves enormously complex amalgams of other things. But if the fundamental discrepancy between words and what they refer to makes realism invalid and inaccurate as a means of communicating the truth of things, Barth would not only have to find a different, more "honest" basis for his fiction; he would also have to stop writing about Reality, in the sense of Life As It Is and Things As They Are, for only by words could he understand Reality. But words distort, hence his understanding would always be imperfect and the sole Reality open to him would be his version of it. "One ought to know a lot about Reality before one writes realistic novels," he eventually summed up in an interview. "Since I don't know much about Reality, it will have to be abolished. What the hell, Reality is a nice place to visit but you wouldn't want to live there, and literature never did, very long."³

Once Barth had discounted Reality as a proper subject for his fiction, however, what else was there for him to write about? Fortunately he had already solved that problem in *The End of the Road*. There the Doctor instructs Jake that each person tends to see others as minor characters in a life story whose major character is himself, and that such a view of life is a distortion of it because objectively speaking "in life there are no essentially major or minor characters. To that extent, all fiction and biography, and most historiography, are a lie." But in a different way, the Doctor goes on, fiction is not a lie at all. Since it reflects how people characterize themselves and others, it is "a true representation of the distortion that everyone makes of life" (p. 83). Given these premises, then, Barth had ready his new subject for imitation; not Reality itself but what we make— or what people have made—of Reality. And in one interview given sometime after this crisis in his career, he spoke at length about his new subject, using words very close to those he had attributed to the Doctor in *The End of the Road*. One way to come to terms with the difference between art and life, he said,

> is to define fiction as a kind of true representation of the distortion we all make of life. In other words, it's a representation of a distortion; not a representation of life itself, but a representation of a representation of life. If you acknowledge that premise to begin with, there's no reason in the world why you can't do all sorts of things that otherwise could be objected to on philosophical or other grounds. Like an old-fashioned characterization, for example. If you acknowledge that you're doing it as an imitation of the way we in fact characterize each other in life, then you're not pretending to an illegitimate omniscience—you're not pretending that the novel is something it isn't. Art *is* artificial, after all.⁴

The idea of art-as-artifice could be applied variously, he told the interviewer. By working, say, with fantasy and nontemporal settings as in Barth's own fourth novel, *Giles Goat-Boy*, a writer could remove his book from the literal contemporary and therefore escape the trap of realism. Back in 1956, however, Barth was interested in another application of the art-as-artifice idea, and that was to write a comic, half-farcical novel that made use of historical documents and imitated the conventions of the eighteenth-century novel.[5] It all had to do with an early American poet named Ebenezer Cooke, one of whose poems, *The Sot-Weed Factor,* an awkward, vicious satire on Maryland and its tobacco merchants, had been published in 1708.

At the start Barth did not know very much about Cooke, or Cook as the name sometimes appears in early records. The poet had owned an estate called Malden, located on Cooke's Point at the mouth of the Choptank River in Maryland, and on the title page of several of his poems he had claimed to be the poet laureate of Maryland. Barth himself was born and brought up in Cambridge, Maryland, about fifteen miles up the Choptank River from Cooke's Point, and he had often heard Cooke mentioned. But he had never read *The Sot-Weed Factor* ("Nobody knew the poem—except PhD candidates in American literature. Ebenezer Cooke is a terrible poet.") nor had he visited the Malden estate until after he finished his master's education in the fall of 1952 and was doing some research for the story-cycle, *Dorchester Tales,* that he was writing about Maryland's tidewater area, the inland shores. That project he did not complete, but while reading Cooke's poem, he did see the possibility of another project—the retelling in prose of the poem's action complete with Cooke's voyage to Maryland and his bitter disappointment with the land and its inhabitants. That notion had been left alone for almost four years until now in 1956 Barth began toying with it again.[6]

It seemed obvious to him that the title of his novel would have to be the same as the title of Cooke's poem. Cooke's title is, after all, a striking one, and for Barth to use it would be an indication that he was acting on his new theory of imitating the way people distort the world, in this instance Cooke's dismal view of Maryland. But the imitation would be no superficial one of Cooke's moral indignation only. It would involve, as near as Barth could re-create, the very cosmic assumptions that Cooke supposedly would have had, living at the turn of the seventeenth century. No Marx, no Freud, no Declaration of Independence. Just (just!) Galileo, Newton, Henry More, and such. Aside from the authentic tone Barth would thus give to his book and the fun he would have imagining what it was like to think back then, he would also be implicitly contrasting the world view of the seventeenth century with that of the twentieth century and getting much thematic mileage out of the contrast. (One difference between then and now, for example, is between the sun as the center of man's universe and the atom as the center. There are other differences too, but what they are exactly does not matter so much as the fact of the difference. People in that age had certain premises which they thought represented the nature of the world, and so do we; their premises turned out to be inadequate and misleading, and so will ours.) Barth also wanted to use Cooke's title because he wanted to take advantage of its puns. "Factor" means a merchant, a businessman, and in the poem that is what Eben Cooke is while in the novel that is what his father orders him to be. "Factor" means as well a maker, an author, and that is what the historic and the imaginary Eben Cookes fancy themselves. That is what Barth is: the factor of *The Sot-Weed Factor.* "Factor" can also mean an element, circumstance, or influence that contributes to produce a result—thus the novel's title refers to that circumstance which produces the condition of being sotted and out of joint, a circumstance which in the novel ends up being innocence, but more about that later. For, once Barth had his title and once he had chosen the world view of the seventeenth century as the one he was going to imitate, he had several matters yet to consider before actually working out his theme.

In particular, he needed fictional techniques appropriate to the world view he was presenting, and these techniques were available in the form of the eighteenth-century novel, early samples of which were already being written when Cooke came to America in the late 1600s. Barth's novel would by necessity, then, have to be extremely long; nearly all the eighteenth-century novel masterpieces were several volumes. And all the conventions of those masterpieces would have to be incorporated: a hero on a journey with a nit-wit servant for his companion, a search for one's father and one's long-lost beloved, stories told along the road, tests of virtue and manliness, encounters with bandits, bawds, noblemen, and bullies, unbelievable coincidences, abundant fornication and adultery, possible incest, and more, all woven into a plot whose complications seem designed to set the reader's head aspin. The enterprise sounded marvelous, and after the strictures of realism, Barth was overjoyed to make it all up, to reinvent the eighteenth-century novel as it were. "When I started on *The Sot-Weed Factor,* . . . I had two intentions," he said later.

> One was to write a large book, something that the publisher could print the title on across the spine, and I did, and then the publisher put the title on up-and-down anyhow. The other was to see if I couldn't make up a plot that was fancier than *Tom Jones.*[7]

He was thus not only writing an imitation of Cooke's poem, but also of Fielding's novel, and he was not unaware of the aesthetic advantages.

> The idea of writing a novel which imitates the form of the Novel, or which imitates some other form of document, is not so decadent as it sounds at first blush. In fact, that's where the genre began— with Cervantes pretending that he's Homete Benengeli, Alonzo Quijano pretending that he's Don Quixote; Fielding parodying Richardson, Richardson imitating letters, and so forth. The novel seems to have its origins in documental imitation, really.

So when someone writes a novel in imitation of one kind of novel or even of another genre like poetry, "one feels simply that the novel is coming to a full circle."[8]

But full circle in only a manner of speaking. History does not repeat itself, nor does anything else, exactly. Barth, avoiding realism by returning to the origin of the novel, was parodoxically not going backward at all; he was in effect moving beyond realism a large step forward, coming upon new uses for some of those conventions of the novel lately judged obsolete. For example, the fashion these days is to consider life hardly ordered enough to be represented by a plot that begins by setting the scene and introducing the characters, that later establishes a conflict, adds complications, builds to a climax, and finally resolves itself neatly. Barth's point, though, was that regardless of life's disorder we tend to think of it as ordered; consequently he could use the traditional balanced, unified plot structure as an imitation of that tendency of ours. Moreover, the fashion these days is to consider authorial selection and arrangement of detail, and consistent character development, as misrepresentations of the world's chaos. Nevertheless, most of us do simplify life by attending only to some of its details, by thinking of people as consistent; and Barth's purpose was to represent that simplification. But because these conventions were being used for a new purpose, they stopped being obsolete and overly familiar. They now came across so valid and fresh that it seemed Barth was, far from re-discovering them, actually discovering them for the first time.

Next, after Barth had settled upon the subject of his imitation and the techniques he would employ, he wanted to do a great deal of research in order that he be accurate in his portrayal of Cooke and of seventeenth-century Maryland. His initial source was Lawrence Wroth's biography of Cooke, the only one then available, and although Wroth had been limited by the scarcity of Cooke documents, he nevertheless supplied Barth with at least a few key details for his novel.[9] (Wroth's study was published in 1934. Much later, in 1968, an enterprising critic, Philip Diser, summarized on one page almost all that Wroth had discovered about Cooke, and that summary is here reproduced to show in convenient form the kind of information Barth first had at his disposal.)

1661. An Andrew Cooke served on a jury in St. Mary's City, Maryland; received a license to trade in Maryland.

1662, 64, 68. Andrew Cooke mentioned in land records in Kent and Dorchester Counties, Maryland. One tract of land he bought, located at the mouth of the Choptank River, called "Malden" and then later, "Cooke's Point."

1664. Andrew Cooke applied to the Proprietary of Maryland for 200 acres of land for transporting four people, including a person named Andrew Cooke, from England to America.

Aug. 1, 1665. In England, Andrew Cooke, "merchant and bachelor of the parish of St. Michael, Bassingshawe, London," married Anne Bowyer.

1694. Ebenezer Cooke, a freeman of St. Mary's City, signed a petition against the moving of the capital of Maryland from St. Mary's City to Annapolis.

1708. *The Sot-Weed Factor*, signed "Eben. Cook, Gent." published in London.

Dec. 31, 1711. The will of "Andrew Cooke of the parish of St. Giles in the Fields in the Country of Middlesex Gentleman" filed. The will, probated on Jan. 2, 1711/12 in London, bequeathed to Ebenezer and Anna Cooke "Cooke poynt" and two houses in London.

1717. Ebenezer sold his share of Cooke's Point to Edward Cooke and Anna sold hers to Captain Henry Trippe.

1720, 21, 22. Ebenezer a deputy receiver-general under Henry Lowe, Jr., his successor, Bennet Lowe, and others.

1728. Ebenezer admitted to the practice of law in Prince George's County.
Dec. 17–24, 1728. An elegy, signed "E. Cooke. Laureat.," on the death
   of Nicholas Lowe published in the Maryland Gazette.
1729. Ebenezer Cooke a witness in a trial in Provincial Prerogative Court.
1730. *Sotweed Redivivus*, signed "E. C. Gent.," published in Annapolis.
1731. *The Maryland Muse*, signed "E. Cooke, Gent.," published in
   Annapolis.
1732. An elegy, signed "Ebenezer Cook, Poet Laureat," written on the
   death of William Locke in May, 1732.[10]

Barth, of course, did not have the advantage of Diser's summary;
he had to condense Wroth's essay for himself, and on almost every
page he read he came upon Wroth's proper warning that perhaps
more than one Ebenezer Cooke lived in Maryland around 1700, and
that any reconstruction of Cooke's life must be at best tentative
because the early records might refer to more than one man with
the same name. The several versions of Cooke's name (Eben. Cook,
E. Cooke, and E.C.) lend considerable support to this possibility.
For purposes of his novel, however, Barth was prepared to assume
that both Cooke and Cook were one and the same man. Wroth, for
his own purposes, had made that assumption as well, and the life
history he had then worked out for Cooke was essentially the one
Barth took for his novel. Andrew Cooke, it seems, was a tradesman
in Maryland during the mid-1600s, probably the same Andrew Cooke
who served on a jury in St. Mary's City, Maryland, in 1661. He had a
son, also named Andrew Cooke and also a tradesman, who was
transported to Maryland in 1664, though the son may have traveled
to Maryland several times before then. Together or singly, father and
son bought considerable tracts of land in Maryland from 1662 to
1668; one of these tracts was the Cooke's Point estate of Malden at
the mouth of the Choptank River. Midway between those years,
while Andrew Cooke II was on a visit to England, he married Anne
Bowyer on August 1, 1665, and from that marriage two children
resulted—Ebenezer and Anna Cooke. The children are mentioned
in Andrew Cooke's will of 1711 as well as in the record of their sale
of Cooke's Point during 1717, but aside from these two instances,
there is no other reference to Anna. As for Ebenezer, a signature on
a 1694 petition in Maryland shows that by then he was in the
province. In 1708 his poem *The Sot-Weed Factor* was published in
London, and in 1711 he himself was in London to help probate his
father's will. By 1717 he had returned to Maryland to sell his share

of Cooke's Point along with Anna's; from 1720 to 1722 he worked for the provincial government as a Deputy Receiver-General; and in 1728 he became a lawyer. In the following years, he wrote more verse and saw several of his poems published at Annapolis, Maryland, until in 1732 his last work appeared, and no further record of his affairs has since been found.[11] This life and Barth's rendering of it are quite close, although there are minor differences. Barth combined the two Andrew Cookes into one, for example, and as Philip Diser points out, "while Wroth suggests Ebenezer returned to England before the publication of *The Sot-Weed Factor* in 1708 and returned to Maryland after 1711 and before 1717, Barth has Cooke remain in Maryland the whole period except for a short time spent in London in 1711 after his father's death."

The sketchiness of Cooke's biography no doubt would have discouraged any novelist intending to write an accurate and factual account of Cooke's life. But Barth was delighted: the little that is known for certain about Cooke only gave him a chance to play loose with history and imagine as fantastic a version of Cooke's life as he wished. "If you are a novelist of a certain type of temperament, then what you really want to do is re-invent the world," he once said, describing some of the motives he had for writing *The Sot-Weed Factor*. And he continued:

> God wasn't too bad a novelist, except he was a Realist. . . . But a certain kind of sensibility can be made very uncomfortable by the recognition of the *arbitrariness* of physical facts and the inability to accept their *finality*. Take France, for example: France is shaped like a tea pot, and Italy is shaped like a boot. Well, okay. But the idea that that's the only way it's ever going to be, that they'll never be shaped like anything else—that can get to you after a while. . . . This impulse to imagine alternatives to the world can become a driving impulse for writers. I confess that it is for me. So that really what you want to do is re-invent philosophy and the rest—make up your own whole history of the world.[12]

The substance of this quotation recurs frequently in Barth's work. The Doctor in *The End of the Road*, for example, informs Jake that part of the reason for his paralysis is that he knows very little about the world as it exists. "There's no reason in the long run why Italy shouldn't be shaped like a sausage instead of a boot, but that doesn't happen to be the case. *The world is everything that is the case*"

(p. 76). And the sooner Jake learns more about the world, the Doctor feels, the sooner he will be able to cope with it. *The Sot-Weed Factor* provides a similar example. As a child, Ebenezer Cooke is taught to have a "great imagination and enthusiasm for the world," but although these

> led him to a great sense of the arbitrariness of the particular real world, they did not endow him with a corresponding realization of its finality. He very well knew, for instance, that "France is shaped like a teapot," but he could scarcely accept the fact that there was actually in existence *at that instant* such a place as France. . . , and that despite the virtual infinitude of imaginable shapes, this France would have to go on resembling a teapot forever. (P. 8)

These notions are characteristic of someone who is innocent, a quality which Barth elsewhere defines as "the sort of ingenuous fancy that reimagines history and creation, sees the arbitrariness of the universe but shies away from its finality."[13]

In this case, he was making up his own history of Ebenezer Cooke and by extension his own history of early Maryland. Since no certificate of Cooke's birth had then (and still has not) been located, Barth could imagine that Cooke was born in America: the pattern of his life was then circular, the hero leaving America to go to England and be educated, and later coming back to America where he is more profoundly educated. In need of a date for Cooke's birth, he assigned it to June of 1666, perhaps because that was well over nine months after Andrew Cooke married Anne Bowyer. And in need of a date for Cooke's death, he assigned it to 1732, the last year Cooke's name appears in any document. Cooke's poem *The Sot-Weed Factor* has a line about "Mother Cambridge," so Barth invented some experience for him at that school. And on the basis of the 1694 petition Cooke signed in Maryland, Barth chose that year as the one in which the poet commenced his adult residence there. In addition he supposed that Cooke knew B. Bragg (the man who printed the first edition of *The Sot-Weed Factor*) and then developed a character for Bragg and devised a wild meeting between him and Cooke.

These details, of course, could all be logically inferred from Wroth's biography of Cooke, but other details had little, often no, connection with it. Barth had Cooke's mother die shortly after she gave birth to him; made Cooke and his sister, Anna, twins; provided them with a chameleon tutor, Henry Burlingame; arranged for Cooke to have a long conference with Lord Baltimore, the former governor of Maryland, during which Baltimore commissions him laureate of the province. And so on.

Barth also relied on Cooke's poem *The Sot-Weed Factor* to give him some of the poet's adventures in Maryland and at times he even lifted passages from the poem with little change except in meter and arrangement, the vocabulary in particular remaining almost the same. One instance among many: in the novel, a planter invites Cooke to dine with him.

> Being very hungry, Ebenezer fell to at once and stuffed himself with pone, milk, hominy, and cider-pap flavored with bacon fat and dulcified with molasses, washing down the whole with hard cider from the cask that stood at hand. (P. 314)

In the poem, a planter also invites Cooke to dine with him, and the menu is alike:

> A Cask of Sider on the Fret:
> . . . .
> . . . Pone, with Milk and Mush well stor'd,
> . . . .
> With Hominy and Sider-Pap,
> . . . .
> Well stuff'd with Fat from Bacon fry'd,
> And with Melasses dulcify'd.
> (LL. 117–129)

Not only did Barth insert phrases from Cooke's poetry in his prose, but on occasion he quoted from the poems directly. Indeed all of the poetry in the novel is by Cooke, except for the concluding verses on his grave stone. But at other times Barth invented accounts very different from those in the poem. Thus Barth's version of how Cooke arrives in Maryland in 1694 is that he wades onto a barren coast after pirates have forced him to walk the plank into the Chesapeake Bay. In the poem, however, Cooke arrives by ship at a harbor cove and there goes ashore to open a business. A similar difference between the novel and the poem has to do with a night Cooke spends at a planter's house shortly after arriving in Maryland. In the novel, he slips outside to seduce a female servant, does not find her, is attacked by farm animals and shinnies up a tree where he remains a long while, particularly since he thinks he hears a rattlesnake and is afraid to come down. In the poem, though, no mention is made of a lecherous intent. The animals attack him while he is trying to sleep in his room; he repairs to the orchard seeking peace and quiet, there hears the rattlesnake and shinnies up a tree (not the other way around as in the novel). There are many other differences between the novel and the poem, and Barth justified them by insisting that Cooke wrote the poem not as a biography but as a fiction. "I shall make the piece a fiction!" his character says at the start of writing the poem.

> I'll be a tradesman, say—nay, a factor that comes to Maryland on's business, with every good opinion of the country, and is swindled of his goods and property. All my trials I'll reconceive to suit the plot and alter just enough to pass the printer![14]

Likewise, Barth looked upon history as itself a kind of fiction and felt at ease to treat it as he had treated Cooke's poem, that is, to imagine that actual past events were different from historical accounts of them. Thus, in life, a 1694 Maryland petition was apparently signed by Ebenezer Cooke, but in the novel it is not Cooke, rather his friend, Burlingame, who signs the petition, forging Cooke's signature in order to confuse the poet's enemies and lead them toward a part of the country where he no longer is (p. 332). Also, in life, Isaac Newton and Henry More were at Cambridge in 1670 and carried on a long and bitter debate about the nature of the universe. But in the novel Barth postulates that their arguments were kept alive in part because they were both rivals for the love of a young man, and that their enmity resolved itself when they put away the boy and took to loving one another. "When I read biographies and papers of both men, it semed to me that just on philosophical grounds there should have been a love affair," Barth said.[15] And his urge to imagine that what actually happened in the past was different from historical reports of it even led him to reinterpret the overall pattern of early Maryland politics: "I studied a year or so, very carefully, what they call *The Archives of Maryland.* This is a series of bound volumes, the records of the colonial Assembly and the Governor's Council from the time the Province was chartered until it became a state in 1776."[16] He learned that the compilers of the Archives were as one in believing Lord Baltimore an extreme good man and John Coode an extreme villain. He found evidence in the Archives, however, that Baltimore may have been a very oppressive governor and that Coode may have plotted against him for just reasons. Accordingly, when he wrote his novel, he had Cooke accept first one view and then the other of Baltimore and Coode, and finally throw up his hands, unable to decide which man is good and which is bad, unable to decide whether the two even exist or not, so confusing does the matter seem.[17] We have already noted Barth's statement that he recast historical incidents because he was disturbed by the idea that things are and were only one way and never any other. But he seems to have had another reason as well, and that was to demonstrate how little we can be certain of what actually happened in history.

Just as a person who describes an event he has experienced must inevitably distort it, so too a person who describes an event he has not experienced and who gathers his information about it from past accounts must also distort that event, and worse: the description is now two degrees away from reality. In addition, there is always the chance that the documents he uses to reconstruct the past are fraught with omissions and mistakes of the pen. A fascinating and relevant example of the distortion people make of the past has to do with the textual history of Cooke's poem *The Sot-Weed Factor*. "A satyr . . . in burlesque verse" on the evils of Maryland, it was first published by B. Bragg in London in 1708. But English readers did not accept it as an attack on Maryland's decadence; they were so amused that instead they felt the poem was ironic, a demonstration of the wit and culture in that province. To these views of Maryland as vice-ridden and as cultured, there was next added a third in the form of a sequel to *The Sot-Weed Factor* titled *Sotweed Redivivus*, published in Maryland in 1730. It ignored vices and concentrated on the hard physical and economic lot of the tobacco planter, and it was followed the next year by a revised text of *The Sot-Weed Factor* in which the original savage attack on Maryland was so modified that some good traits of the people there were highlighted and the province became a "Land where Hospitality / Is every Planter's darling Quality." With so many various and at times contradictory opinions of Maryland, one hesitates to trust any of them as a guide to what Maryland was like. Even if they were not various and contradictory, they still are not absolutely to be trusted. In 1865, when *The Sot-Weed Factor* was long out of print and not readily at hand, a literary historian, Brantz Mayer, decided to reissue the poem in its original 1708 text. He composed a scholarly introduction to it, saw it cast in type again, and took particular care that the first edition title page was reproduced exactly.[18] A photocopy of that duplicate title page is here provided. It includes the poem's complete subtitle, which could very well serve as the subtitle for Barth's novel; it also includes an error. B. Bragg has been changed to D. Bragg, and that difference is enough to invite the suspicion that other documents relating to Cooke are themselves in error. Maybe the 1694 petition that Cooke signed is indeed the forgery Barth pretends it is. Maybe Cooke's name on the poems was only somebody's literary persona and the name on the legal documents only an identity someone had assumed to circumvent a law. The idea is hardly farfetched. Even Wroth, in his biography of Cooke, admits that there may never have been anyone like the Ebenezer Cooke whose life he has examined. In the novel, Barth develops this possibility to a kind of ultimate when Cooke, heartsick and confused, tries to resolve his conflicting attitudes toward Baltimore and Coode; never having seen them, he wonders if they exist; and at last he doubts that he himself exists (pp. 513–515). And Barth's invention of history is but another illustration of this doubt and confusion: nothing is what it seems, both present and past—things could have happened any number of ways, if indeed they happened at all.

A final (and delightful) case in point concerns Captain John Smith's famous story of how the Indian maiden Pocahontas saved his life by throwing herself between him and a band of club-wielding warriors. According to Barth, that story may not be the true one. He imagines that Smith had a companion, Sir Henry Burlingame I, who in his *Privie Journall* told another version of the Smith-Pocahontas affair—and affair it was: Pocahontas had an impregnable virgin's membrane, and the Indian emperor, Powhatan, decreed that Smith's life depended on his splitting that membrane, a superhuman feat he managed only through the mystical rites of the Sacred Eggplant and a staggering vegetable addition to his physiognomy. Smith "made so bold," Sir Henry complained,

THE

𝕾𝖔𝖙-𝖜𝖊𝖊𝖉 𝕱𝖆𝖈𝖙𝖔𝖗:

Or, a Voyage to

MARYLAND.
A
SATYR.

In which is defcrib'd

The Laws, Government, Courts and Conftitutions of the Country, and alfo the Buildings, Feafts, Frolicks, Entertainments and Drunken Humours of the Inhabitants of that Part of *America*.

In Burlefque Verfe.

By *Eben. Cook*, Gent.

LONDON:

Printed and Sold by *D. Bragg*, at the *Raven* in *Pater-Nofter-Row*. 1708. (Price 6d.)

Figure 2. Brantz Mayer's 1865 facsimile of the 1708 title page for *The Sot-Weed Factor*.

as to shew me a written account of his salvation by Pocahontas, the
wch he meant to include in his lying *Historie:* this version made no
mention whatever of his scurrilous deflowering of the Princesse, but
merelie imply'd, she was overcome by his manlie bearing & comelie
face! It was this farce and travestie, then, wherein I was oblig'd to
feign belief, and wch hath mov'd me, in hopes of pacifying my
anguish'd conscience, to committ this true accounting to my Journall-
booke. (P. 734)

But while Sir Henry charges that Smith is a liar, Smith charges that
Sir Henry is a jealous troublemaker and that his portrait of Smith as
a lascivious deviate is highly biased. What he says about Sir Henry's
character is a part of his *Secret Historie of the Voiage Up the Bay
of Chesapeake,* which Barth invents for the occasion, and these contrary documents and opinions are akin to the contrary versions of
Maryland in Cooke's *The Sot-Weed Factor,* the sequel to it, and the
radical interpretations that readers in England gave to it. Burlingame's *Privie Journall* and Smith's *Secret Historie* are also akin to
the various forms of the Pocahontas story that have actually been
passed down to us. Philip Young has carried on an intensive study of
this matter and points out that Pocahontas may never have saved
Smith in the innocent fashion Smith would have us believe. For one
thing, Smith was addicted to stories about how he was "offered
rescue and protection in my greatest dangers" by various "honorable
and vertuous Ladies." For another, and perhaps most suspect, Smith
wrote about his escape from these Indians four times, but only in
the third did he refer (and then very briefly) to Pocahontas—"God
made Pocahontas the King's daughter the means to deliver me."—
and only in the fourth did he get around to the tale of how she saved
him. "The obvious inference here," Young writes, "is that if the
rescue was actually performed Smith would have said so in the first
place or, if he had not, would have told the story to others who
would have repeated it." Moreover, Smith's "*Historie* is boastful;
it is hard to know how much of it he made up or borrowed from
other travelers of the period."[19] Young's essay was published in 1962,
but he had been working on it during the late 1950s at the time
Barth was writing his novel and at a time when he and Barth were
colleagues in the English Department of The Pennsylvania State
University. Barth read as much of the essay as Young had then
finished, wanting to see how his own treatment of the Pocahontas

story compared with how it was treated in the historical sources, and he was pleased that Smith's *Historie* may have been as much a lie in life as it is in the novel. "Lest it be objected by a certain stodgy variety of squint-minded antiquarians," Barth concluded in the book,

> that he has in this lengthy history played more fast and loose with Clio, the chronicler's muse, than ever Captain John Smith dared, the Author here posits in advance . . . that we all invent our pasts, more or less, as we go along, at the dictates of Whim and Interest; the happenings of former times are a clay in the present moment that will-we, nill-we, the lot of us must sculpt. (P. 743)

This discussion of how Barth used history has necessarily involved some of the themes in his novel—the topics are much related. But having gone this far into literary matters, we must now stop short and return to biographical ones, for while the book on its own will be examined in the following chapter, it is the purpose of this chapter to illustrate how Barth composed the book, and that particular history is not yet complete. For the record, Barth has generally been reluctant to talk about how he puts his fiction together. Once, asked "Do you outline your novels before writing?" he answered, "That is the kind of question the answer to which is not going to do anybody any good. What difference does it make to anybody whether I outline my novels before writing?"[20] His own question he did not answer, but one possible reply is that from a pure aesthetic point of view it makes no difference whether he outlines his novels, but that from the point of view of interest it makes a great deal of difference, and in *The Sot-Weed Factor* he allowed that much. There Burlingame hears Cooke recite an original poem, and the two men debate how to judge it. Burlingame says that our response to a work of literature often depends on our knowledge of who wrote it. Cooke, however, disagrees. " 'Tis the present poem alone, methinks, that matters, not its origins, and it must stand or fall on's own merits, apart from maker and age." To which Burlingame counters and wins the argument:

> No doubt, no doubt, . . . though this word *merit*'s total mystery to me. What I spoke of was *interest*, and whether 'tis good or bad in itself, certain your *Hymn to Innocence* is of greater interest to one who knows the history of its author than to one who knows not a bean of the circumstances that gave it birth. (P. 122)

Hence the concluding section of this chapter.

Barth did outline *The Sot-Weed Factor*, very thoroughly. "I don't see how anybody starts a novel without knowing how it's going to end. I usually make detailed outlines: how many chapters it will be and so forth."[21] He also summarized his research and his characters on 150 library punch cards to help him keep his memory clear, and as with his earlier two books, the actual writing was done in longhand. "I . . . find it makes a difference in style. I don't write in a short abbreviated style—my sentences tend to go on a little way before they stop. When I compose in long hand I get a more eloquent line than when I try to write on a typewriter."[22] Frequently the cadence and rhyme of his imitation eighteenth-century English style became so infectious that his letters and conversations became filled with them.

> Once you get in the spirit of writing in Hudibrastic couplets, say, then you start to think in Hudibrastic couplets and talk on the telephone in Hudibrastic couplets. Sometimes when I read and talk to people and fall into this vein, they begin to answer my letters in the same way. It's like syphilis.[23]

By April 12, 1958, he had 1000 manuscript pages, roughly half of the first draft, completed, and was hoping to finish all of the first draft by the end of 1958 and then to prepare a final draft during 1959. Two things were holding him back, though. He wanted to do more historical research and he wanted to have the manuscript professionally typed, so he applied to the Liberal Arts Research Office at The Pennsylvania State University for money to cover his expenses. On his request form, he explained some of his financial difficulties as a writer, how he could not depend on future royalties to finance the work he had in progress because he was not a commercial writer and had no guarantee that *The Sot-Weed Factor* would even be published. After all, he explained further, each of his preceding novels had been published by a different company and neither seemed like it was going to earn its sponsor, let alone himself, a penny. He was granted the $250 he requested, and with it he went to Maryland to look at such unpublished documents as deeds and wills on file at the Clerk's Office in Cambridge and at the Land Office in Annapolis. He also passed a few days in the Baltimore County Land Records Office, as well as in the Maryland Historical Society Library and the Enoch Pratt Free Library, and found among other items a transcript of the will of Edward Cooke, the man to whom Ebenezer Cooke had sold his share of Malden. All this accomplished, he came back to Penn State, saying in his report to the Liberal Arts Research Office that however many other grounds the critics would have for attacking his novel they could not in justice charge that it was biographically inaccurate in those places where he was not actually inventing. (What is more, although he did not say this, he could also be confident that the novel was geographically accurate. The adventures he imagined for Ebenezer Cooke in Maryland were all plotted on a map, and within the novel he provided very specific compass directions for anyone who cared to chart Cooke's journey. A random sample is on page 292: "The four moved stealthily through a final grove of trees to where the forest ended at a riverbank on the north and a roadway paved with bare logs on the west." See figure 6 in chapter 8 for his map of Cooke's adventures.)

With Barth's research at an end, he recommenced writing the book, finishing the first draft, moving on to the final draft, until finally on May 21, 1959, six days before his twenty-ninth birthday and three years after the May 1956 deadline he had long ago set himself, he was able to report to the Liberal Arts Research Office that his book was complete. In his 1958 application for a grant, he had called *The Sot-Weed Factor* a "philosophical-picaresque extravaganza"; now he called it an "ideological farce," and his immediate hopes were, he said, to see the book published before he was thirty.

That was almost a year away, and he perhaps allowed so long a time because he recalled the trouble he had gone through with Appleton-Century-Crofts, the publisher of his first novel. Any fears he may have had were justified. Doubleday had published his second novel, happy to do it, so the new book was sent to them. But their initial reactions were not entirely favorable. They did not mind putting out short novels of quality like *The End of the Road* and losing money on the venture, but they were not very eager to finance the publication of such a huge book as *The Sot-Weed Factor*: it would be extremely expensive to print and perhaps would not sell any more copies than Barth's other novels. Thanks to Timothy Seldes, however, they accepted it. Seldes was at that time Barth's editor at Doubleday, and he was convinced that *The Sot-Weed Factor* was a work of genius, well worth any money his firm would lose on it. His argument was persuasive enough that the publishers agreed to compromise. They would print the book if Barth shortened it and, in particular, cut some of the "extraneous" scenes. Barth, in turn, asked what scenes could possibly be taken out, and when the publishers tried to find some, they discovered that, unlike the usual picaresque novel, *The Sot-Weed Factor* was so carefully and integrally plotted that no part could be eliminated without damage to the whole.[24] So they published it anyway and with no cuts, although they did not bring it out within the time Barth had hoped. The release date was August 19, 1960, long after May 27 and his thirtieth birthday.

Then came the reviews. So far Barth had been treated pleasantly in book reviews; there had been isolated attacks but mostly compliments. These compliments, though, had all been to a degree founded on Barth's youth and comparative inexperience, on his being a new author who looked as though he would someday be great. But now that he had written this long, complex, and ambitious novel, reviewers were no longer content to think of him as an author full of promise. He had been given sufficient time to mature, they seemed to feel, and off went their reviewing kid gloves. Terry Southern thought the book was *not* one to be recommended.

> Readers familiar with the extraordinary art of Mr. Barth's earlier novel, *The End of the Road*, will probably find *The Sot-Weed Factor* prolix and overwhelmingly tedious. This is, of course, an integral part of the book's destructive function, as is its prohibitive price ($7.50) and its grotesque length—sections of which seem designed, specifically, to *bore one to tears*. . . . *The Sot-Weed Factor* is perhaps more a literary event than a book, and it should be approached warily.[25]

Helen Arthur's comments were equally devastating. She was confused by the book's plot and theme and concluded that

> Mr. Barth's objectives are, perhaps, not fully clear to himself, in which case the reader's failure to receive a clear impression may be forgiven. This reader finds Mr. Barth and *The Sot-Weed Factor* talented but unco-ordinated, precious, repetitive, and (I am certainly being repetitive myself) too long, too long, too long.[26]

There were others more favorable. *Time,* echoing its description of *The End of the Road* as "that rarity of U.S. letters—a true novel of ideas," now described *The Sot-Weed Factor* as "that rare literary creation—a genuinely serious comedy."[27] And *Newsweek*, which up to now had been silent about Barth, maintained that he had written "a very solid book which has, for all its sophistication, the same kind of captivating quality that one remembers from the storybooks of one's childhood."[28]

Taking into account these diverse reviews and the novel's uncommon length, it is understandable that *The Sot-Weed Factor* sold about as poorly (5000 copies) as Barth's other novels.[29] (All the same, its poor sales may come as a surprise to some students of Barth's work. Because *The Sot-Weed Factor* was Barth's first major piece of fiction, they have erroneously assumed that it was also Barth's first financial success. He was to be successful that way all right, but not until six years later and *Giles Goat-Boy*.) Most people who did buy the book, however, liked it exceedingly, and *The Sot-Weed Factor* went underground, much talked about, much borrowed. When in 1964 it was issued in paperback, considerably reduced in price from $7.50 to $2.95, it had a more respectable turnover—within two years over 20,000 copies had been sold. That *Book Week*'s 1965 poll rated *The Sot-Weed Factor* among the twenty best American novels since 1945 no doubt helped to create some of this new interest, enough so that in 1967 a second hardback edition was published, revised by Barth, nearly fifty pages shorter though not substantially different. Initial sales amounted to 4000. A paperback of this revised text followed in 1969, and the novel has remained in fairly constant demand. For a time, there was even a chance that it would be metamorphosed into a musical comedy. We can only speculate how Ebenezer Cooke would react in his grave to knowing that his attack on Maryland might finally have got him impersonated in dance and song on a Broadway stage. Not that anyone knows where he is buried. At the very end of the novel, Barth refers to his headstone, but that is Barth's invention. "Because I wanted to write his epitaph," Barth said.[30]

4

Ebenezer Cooke, Virgin, Poet, and Laureate of Maryland

The fall of virgins always is
instructive, nor doth the world
e'er weary of the tale.
(Burlingame to Eben Cooke, p. 155)

In 1958 Barth had called *The Sot-Weed Factor* "a philosophical-picaresque extravaganza," and in 1959 an "ideological farce." But a few years later he furnished one more description of the book: "a moral allegory cloaked in terms of colonial history." And that description Barth eventually regretted: "I mentioned the word *allegory* to somebody off the cuff, and then they cheated and put it on the cover of the book, which embarrassed me. Maybe *allegory*'s not the word I should have used."[1] The word does mislead; *The Sot-Weed Factor* is no allegory in any strict sense: its characters are not personified ideas. To some degree the novel is even an anti-allegory: Ebenezer Cooke *tries* to personify Innocence, and all he gains for his effort is great trouble. Nevertheless, our understanding of the book is helped considerably if we view it as something *like* an allegory. Eben's journey from London to Cooke's Point is, after all, more than physical. It is a moral, political, and philosophical progress as well. But whereas in an allegory our concern is for the extra-literal dimensions and how they control the action, here our concern is for the action and only then for what it signifies. The book is not so much allegoric, then, as symbolic.

Specifically, Eben's journey is symbolic of his passage from innocence to experience. The theme appears remarkably traditional for such an innovative book, but actually it is not traditional at all. Barth does not prefer innocence over experience, which many writers

49

like Blake, say, have done; nor does he regret the loss of innocence. Rather he treats it as a crime and holds that most of our troubles come from not knowing enough, not having experienced enough. His development of that theme, however, takes up nearly 800 pages of extremely complex narrative. A summary of the main action will, then, be provided—both to refresh the reader's memory and to show how various incidents relate to the novel's theme.

Barth begins with a situation much like the one in *The End of the Road*. Eben is taught by Henry Burlingame to be fascinated by the multiplicity of the universe, and he comes to have so wide an imagination that he cannot choose a career. All the possibilities are equally attractive but none finally inviting. Soon he is incapable of simpler choices. He languishes in his room, smoking and reading, then no longer smoking and reading; prowling restlessly, then no longer prowling. Eventually, neither dressing nor eating, he stares immobile out his window and cannot choose even to relieve his swelling bladder. The symptoms are unmistakable: Eben has turned into a seventeenth-century Jacob Horner, he too suffering from the dreaded malady Cosmopsis, the cosmic view. It is a disease of too much imagination and too little will, and so afflicted is he that we are told he would have mossed over where he sat had not Burlingame happened on him shortly. "My dear fellow," Burlingame advises him,

> we sit here on a blind rock careening through space; we are all of
> us rushing headlong to the grave. Think you the worms will care,
> when anon they make a meal of you, whether you spent your moment
> sighing wigless in your chamber, or sacked the golden towns of
> Montezuma? . . . We are dying men, Ebenezer: i'faith, there's time
> for naught but bold resolves! (P. 25)

With Eben a kind of Jacob Horner, Burlingame has become a sort of Negro Doctor, exhorting his patient to act.

And for a time Eben does. He decides to go to Maryland and oversee his father's tobacco plantation. The idyllic, gentlemanly life he imagines for himself there is strong in its appeal. But when he tries to learn the tobacco business from a London merchant, his overly developed imagination ill equips him to add up dull figures on account ledgers. Gradually again losing his will to act, he languishes in coffeehouses with third-rate poets for companions, and at this point in his life, at an age of almost twenty-eight, his story properly begins.

Just as earlier his Cosmopsis prevented him from choosing a career, so now it keeps him from choosing a consistent personality. Hence he remains a virgin.

> He was no person at all: he could picture any kind of man taking a woman—the bold as well as the bashful, the clean green boy and the dottering gray lecher—and work out in his mind the speeches appropriate to each under any of several sorts of circumstances. But because he felt himself no more one of these than another and admired all, when a situation presented itself he could never choose one role to play over all the rest he knew, and so always ended up either turning down the chance or, what was more usually the case, retreating gracelessly and in confusion, if not always embarrassment. (P. 45)

One night a whore, Joan Toast, propositions him, and when he beats his customary retreat, she follows him to his room. It is the closest he has ever come to intimacy with a woman. He is so moved that he thinks he loves her, and though he claims he would gladly make love to her, he refuses to cheapen his emotion and herself by paying for the privilege. His attitude is far too unbusinesslike; she leaves in a rage. But Eben is delighted: while penning a song of chaste love to her, he discovers a consistent role to play.

> Faith, 'tis a rare wise man knows who he is: had I not stood firm with Joan Toast, I might well ne'er have discovered that knowledge! . . . What am I? *Virgin*, sir! *Poet*, sir! I am a virgin and a poet; less than mortal and more; not a man, but Mankind! I shall regard my innocence as badge of my strength and proof of my calling: let her who's worthy of it take it from me! (Pp. 59–60)

He is no longer Jacob Horner, instead a kind of Joe Morgan who selects one role appropriate to him and attempts to act in total accord with it. And from here on, the novel is about what happens to this ideal Ebenezer devotes himself to, the badge of his strength, his innocence. (About this shift in emphasis, Barth has said, "In my first three novels, it was my intention to speak about nihilism, which innocently I felt to be my own discovery; I ended by speaking instead of innocence, which had discovered me.")[2] Soon it will be tattered and abused. Eben himself will undergo a second education with Burlingame again as his tutor. He will learn that Maryland, and by extension the world, are not as idyllic as he imagined. He will one day recognize the truth of what Joan Toast's pimp tells him.

> 'Tis not simply love ye know naught of, 'tis the *entire great real world!* Your senses fail ye; your busy fancy plays ye false and fills your head with foolish pictures. Things are not as ye see 'em, friend— the world's a tangled skein, and all is knottier than ye take it for. You understand naught o' life. (P. 62)

But for Eben, the alternatives are either the role of Virgin and Poet or else the lack of any role and the immobility of Cosmopsis. Recalling Burlingame's advice that "there's time for naught but bold resolves," he arranges for an audience with Lord Baltimore, asks to be made the poet-laureate of Maryland, and much to his surprise is commissioned.

Thus ends part one of the novel. Part two depicts his voyage to Maryland, his journey to Malden, and his mishaps along the way. Preparing to board ship, he is enmeshed in political intrigue; the conspirator, John Coode, fears him a threat to his scheme for revolt in Maryland and sends his agents to capture Eben. In his flight, he is forced to exchange identities with his servant, and he never fully regains his identity until the book is almost finished. Aboard a ship on the Atlantic, he is sexually abused by the crew and nearly sodomized, is captured by pirates, has his first sight of death and is stunned by it, watches the pirates attack a whore ship and rape more than one hundred women, and himself comes close to raping a woman who looks somewhat like Joan Toast. (In fact, she *is* Joan Toast, but he does not discover that until months later.) Only by accident does he fail to rape her, and the incident causes him much anguish in trying to justify his eagerness to give up his virginity. Next, having seen this much violence and death, he learns a little about what it is like to die when he and his servant come close to drowning after they have been made to walk the plank.

They are saved only by the nearness of an unfamiliar shore, which turns out to be the western shore of Maryland, and his adventures there illustrate the further loss of his innocence. Maryland is not at all the idyllic spot he imagined it would be: there are slaves and rude planters and opium and the pox. He himself is not as chaste as he wants to be: his attempt to rape the swine-maid,

Susan Warren, is as difficult for him to justify as his attempt on the woman aboard the whore ship. (Susan Warren is Joan Toast yet again, but this too he does not find out until much later.)

A literal high-point in his education comes when he and Burlingame are riding horseback and Burlingame describes man's lot.

> He is by mindless lust engendered and by mindless wrench expelled, from the Eden of the womb to the motley, mindless world. He is Chance's fool, the toy of aimless Nature—a mayfly flitting down the winds of Chaos! (P. 344)

And if a man should ever see what the universe truly is, the sight would drive him mad. It is night, and Burlingame tells Eben to look at the sky but to forget the flatness the word "sky" connotes. Eben looks up, blinks, and sees what is above for what it is: points of light, big and small, near and far, heading off into the length and breadth of infinity.

> Ebenezer's stomach churned; he swayed in the saddle and covered his eyes. For a swooning moment before he turned away it seemed that he was heels over head on the bottom of the planet, looking *down* on the stars instead of up, and that only by dint of clutching his legs about the roan mare's girth and holding fast to the saddle-bow with both his hands did he keep from dropping headlong into those vasty reaches! (Pp. 346–347)

Chaos, Burlingame concludes. Humankind cannot bear very much reality.

Another major lesson for Ebenezer comes after he brags about his innocence to Burlingame, and Burlingame argues that innocence is nothing but pride and ignorance. This Eben stubbornly denies, and to prove the value of his virtue he interferes with a court. He feels that justice is not being done, that he alone can set matters right. But all he accomplishes is to sign away unwittingly his father's ownership of Malden. So much for the advantages of innocence.

Yet he still has much to learn and much to suffer before he recognizes the falsity of his role. By the end of part two, he is indentured as a servant to the new master of Cooke's Point; watches helplessly as the place is converted into a den of opium and whores; is tricked into marrying the bepoxed Joan Toast; rejects the idea he once had of writing a poem in honor of Maryland and Lord Baltimore; instead writes a scathing satire, *The Sot-Weed Factor,* on the viciousness of the colonies; sends his wife to earn their passage to England by prostituting herself to the Indians; and while she is hard at her work, deserts her, fleeing from Malden into the winter's night.

In part three, he regains his father's estate, not easily. What makes him fit for the job is the responsibility he accepts for his deeds and their effect upon others. Jacob Horner tried to be responsible as well, but unlike Eben he was too late to do any good. Having fled from Cooke's Point, Eben finds out that his sister, Anna, lately arrived in Maryland, may have gone there in search of him. Afraid of the revenge certain people at Cooke's Point may wreak on her because he has escaped them, he determines to go back and save her. And that bid for responsibility is the cause of other bids. On his way by boat to Malden, a storm drives the craft off course and leads to his capture by Indians. Both his servant and the captain of the boat he chartered are prisoners with him, and during their captivity he has plenty of time to realize that he is as responsible for their plight as he is for the danger to his sister, for the grief he has given his father by signing away Malden, and for the wretched condition in which he has left Joan Toast. The burden of this newfound responsibility lends him a resolve and a mobility he has never before known. First, he makes a deal with the Indians whereby his companions will be allowed to live, provided that he find and bring back one of the Chief's long-lost sons—he has reason to believe that the son is none other than his friend Henry Burlingame. Second, he sets off to save Maryland from an Indian uprising and warns the proper authorities in time. Finally, in exchange for certain documents that regain him ownership of Malden, he gives up the last of his innocence by consummating his marriage with the poxed whore, Joan Toast. "I little care now for my legacy, save that I must earn it," he says. " 'Tis *atonement* I crave: redemption for my sins." But "what sins?" Anna protests; "thou'rt the very spirit of Innocence." And he replies:

> That is the crime I stand indicted for . . . : the crime of innocence, whereof the Knowledged must bear the burthen. There's the true Original Sin our souls are born in: not that Adam *learned,* but that he *had* to learn—in short, that he was innocent. (P. 739)

Innocence has now shifted its meaning, not moral as much as intellectual: the condition of being fascinated by the world, aware of its arbitrariness, but unable to accept its finality; the condition that Eben has been in almost from the start of the book (p. 8). Now in giving up his moral innocence to Joan Toast, he also gives up his intellectual innocence because the responsibility he feels for what he has done to her is partially why he consummates his marriage with her. No matter how arbitrary the world is, he has discovered, one nevertheless is a part of it and must accept the consequences of what one does in it.

His self-admitted crime of innocence is representative of a larger crime: that of remaining obstinately constant in a changing world. Early in the novel the bookseller Ben Bragg had asked him to choose from a dizzying variety of notebooks, and Eben had not been able to choose any one that would suit his poet's task exactly. At last he had snatched a book at random, determined to make it do for all his writing needs, certain that "the fault is not in the nature of the world, but in Bragg's categories" (p. 114). He did not see the point of that adventure then, but presumably he now does. No one categorization of the world, no one stance toward it, will enable him to get along in it very well. He has to be like that notebook, ready to meet any demand required of it, ready to take up any stance required of him. Having changed his value from innocence to responsibility, having accepted the finality of the world, he has in effect met the world on its terms rather than his own. Says Burlingame to Eben, "A man *must* alter willy-nilly in's flight to the grave; he is a river running seawards, that is ne'er the same from hour to hour . . . : the very universe is naught but change and motion" (pp. 125–126).

Burlingame is a prime example of his own teaching, impersonator and shape-change that he is. Indeed the number of impersonations by him and Ebenezer and other is amazing. Burlingame assumes the identity of Peter Sayer, John Coode, Timothy Mitchell, Lord Baltimore, Monsieur Casteene, Nicholas Lowe, Bertrand Burton, Ebenezer Cooke, and (for half a day, he claims on p. 705) Governor Nicholson. Ebenezer pretends that he is John Coode's servant, his own servant, Bertrand Burton, Sir Benjamin Oliver, and Edward Cooke. But Eben is on those occasions still innocent and reluctant to change into someone else. He has still a great deal to go through and learn before he will change wholeheartedly. He in turn is eagerly impersonated by others who are more worldly-wise, Henry Burlingame, Bertrand Burton, and John McEvoy. We never see but are told that John Coode "hath been Catholic priest, Church-of-England minister, sheriff, captain, colonel, general, and Heav'n alone knows what else" (p. 487). To a lesser extent, Joan Toast pretends that she is Susan Warren, while Eben's sister, Anna, is Miss Meg Bromly and Mrs. Billy Rumbly. So many shifting characters does Eben meet, he comes to suspect that Coode and Baltimore do not exist, that they are Burlingame's invention, that he himself exists only in a dream.

The suspicion is correct. He is in a dream that Barth has called *The Sot-Weed Factor,* and the dream is as shifting as any of the characters in it. There are twenty-five separate stories within the body of the novel, each self-contained yet with direct relation to the book's main action. There are a six-page swearing contest in French and English, a fifteen-page summation of Maryland's early history, a rhyming contest in which Barth repeats couplets from Cooke's *The Sot-Weed Factor* and *Bacon's Rebellion,* a dream of Parnassus and one of Hell, two sections from two diaries, a discourse on twins, a debate each on the meaning of innocence, justice, history and civilization, a recipe for the mystical rites of the Sacred Eggplant, a lengthy inventory of foods consumed in an eating contest, a liberal peppering of proverbs, some delightful descriptive chapter headings ("The Laureate Is Exposed to Two Assassinations of Character, a Piracy, a Near-Deflowering, a Near-Mutiny, a Murder, and an Appalling Colloquy Between Captains of the Sea, All Within the Space of a Few Pages"), an author's apology, and one of the best and best-controlled first sentences in memory, too long to quote but well worth looking up. One is reminded of *The Floating Opera* and its multitude of narrative devices. And as in *The Floating Opera,* these formal ingenuities are not mere tricks; they are a reflection and an embodiment of the novel's world.

Not only of its world but also of its myth. At the start, so the ancient story has come down to us, the universe was whole and simple, but then it split asunder, fragmented outward in every direction, hurtled farther and farther away from the core and wider and wider apart. The account has many versions, and Burlingame explains a few to Eben. "In every land and time," he says,

folk have maintained that what we see as *two* are the fallen halves
of some ancient *one*—that night and day, Heaven and Earth, or man
and woman were long since severed by their sinful natures, and that
not till Kingdom Come will the fallen twain be a blessed one. 'Tis
this lies 'neath the tale of Eve and Adam, and Plato's fable, and the
fall of Lucifer, and Heav'n knows how many other lovely lies. . . .
Thus all men reverence the act of fornication as portraying the fruitful union of opposites: the Heavenly Twins embraced; the Two as
One! (Pp. 493–494)

Thus, too, Eben has incestuous desire for his twin sister, Anna, and
she for him, and Burlingame dreams fondly of one day catching them
in union and joining with them. "I am Suitor of Totality," he an-
nounces to Eben,

Embracer of Contradictories, Husband to all Creation, the Cosmic
Lover! . . . I have known my great Bride part by splendrous part,
and have made love to her *disjecta membra*, her sundry brilliant
pieces; but I crave the Whole—the tenon in the mortise, the jointure
of polarities, the seamless universe—whereof you twain are token,
in coito! (P. 497)

But the world is too fragmented for it ever to come back fully together. There are man-made laws to prevent it, like the taboo of
incest. And there are tricks of nature, like Burlingame's congenital
dwarved member. And self-restrictions, like Eben's refusal for a
time to join with anyone, even though he has not the physical
limitation that Burlingame does. Plenty of copulations there are, of
course, but plenty of pox and perversion as well. And much beshit-
ting, belching and breaking of wind: people have as much trouble
holding themselves together as they do getting together fruitfully
with someone else. There are related instances of this fragmented
condition: Eben's paralysis in the face of infinite choice, Burlingame's multiple shapes, the book's various plots that converge and
diverge and never finally combine until the climactic courtroom
sequence. After that, however, the author makes his apology. The
demands of form require, he says, a neat tying together of the
story, but the demands of history require a detailing of what
happened to everyone following the trial. And what happened is
that the knot of resolution was in life untied and everyone threaded
his separate way. In this sense, the novel's fragmented form, its
stories and lists and dreams and debates, is one more illustration of

the novel's fragmented world. Yet just as Ebenezer does achieve a slight measure of atonement for his sins and of at-one-ness with himself, so too the book comes across as unified and whole.

Writing an afterword to Smollett's *Roderick Random,* Barth concluded that "adventure and adversity—hazarding forth and overcoming—are what the enduring attractiveness of *Roderick Random* comes to. Those ancient, most profoundly lifelike human sports, the obstacle race and the scavenger hunt, are also the oldest, appealingest matter for the storyteller."[3] His conclusion serves very well to lead into a conclusion of this discussion of *The Sot-Weed Factor.* Adventure and adversity, these may turn out to be the enduring attractions in this novel as well. True, we are fascinated by the ideas in the book and the mental gymnastics its characters perform. But we are fascinated as well by Eben's obstacle race to earn his estate and Burlingame's scavenger hunt to learn the identity of his father. The diaries in the book, the stories, the incredible plots, we remember them and fondly, long after the ideas behind them have fuzzed in our minds and disappeared. "No pleasure pleasures me as doth a well-spun tale, be't sad or merry, shallow or deep!" an old trapper rhapsodizes—and it seems Barth speaking for himself.

> If the subject's privy business, or unpleasant, who cares a fig? The road to Heaven's beset with thistles, and methinks there's many a cow-pat on't. As for length, fie, fie! . . . A bad tale's long though it want but an eyeblink for the telling, and a good tale short though it take from St. Swithin's to Michaelmas to have done with't. Ha! And the plot is tangled, d'ye say? Is't more knotful or bewildered than the skein o' life, that a good tale tangles the better to unsnarl? . . . Spin and tangle till the Dog-star sets i' the Bay; a tale well wrought is the gossip o' the gods, that see the heart and point o' life on earth; the web o' the world; the Warp and the Woof. . . I'Christ, I do love a story, sirs! (Pp. 588–589)

5

The Revised
New Syllabus of
Giles the Goat-Boy

> What I really wanted to write after *The Sot-
> Weed Factor* was a new Old Testament, a comic
> Old Testament. I guess that's what this new
> novel *Giles Goat-Boy* is going to be. A souped-up
> Bible. Its subtitle would be *The Revised New
> Syllabus of George Giles Our Grand Tutor.*
> (John Barth in conversation)[1]

In 1964, four years after the publication of *The Sot-Weed Factor,*
Barth wrote that "Afterword" to the Signet edition of Smollett's
Roderick Random. We have already seen how part of the piece has
bearing on *The Sot-Weed Factor,* but another part deserves notice
too, and for a reason that will shortly be evident. Barth spoke of the
adventure and adversity in *Roderick Random*—not the painful
searching and futile running around we are accustomed to in much
recent fiction, but the kind of heroic enterprise in which obstacles
can be overcome and quests can indeed be accomplished. Proper
adventure and adversity, he said, "imply a racer, a hunter—that is,
a hero, scapegrace or otherwise, not an antihero; and heroes . . .
are hard come by in the age of antimatter and the antinovel." He
regretted this absence of a hero in our fiction, and thus he was all
too happy to detect some signs of change: what he called

> evidence, in some *really* recent novels, . . . of the possibility of a
> post-naturalistic, post-existentialist, post-psychological, post-antinovel
> novel in which the astonishing, the extravagant ("out-wandering"),
> the heroical—in sum, the adventurous—will come again and wel-
> comely into its own.[2]

He ought to have known. One of the *really* recent novels he must
have been thinking of was so recent that it had not yet been fully

written. It was in fact the novel he was working on at the time, *Giles Goat-Boy,* and this part of the "Afterword" to *Roderick Random* gives the impression that Barth was not so much commenting on Smollett's novel as drumming up business for his own. Such a novel of adventure and heroism "can't happen too soon" is how he finished the essay, and considering that by then Barth had already spent nearly four years on *Giles Goat-Boy,* that he still had almost two more years to put in, we can sympathize with his impatience.

There is a sense, of course, in which the word "hero" can apply to the main character of any story and "adventure" can mean any sequence of exciting action. But Barth was using these words in a less popular, more technical sense. Shortly after *The Sot-Weed Factor* had appeared, a colleague of his at Penn State, Philip Young, noticed that Ebenezer Cooke had much in common with the wandering heroes of several ancient myths. As Young remembers it, he assumed that Barth had intended the parallel and that his source of information had been Lord Raglan's famous treatise, *The Hero:* in that book, various forms of the wandering hero myth are synthesized into a basic twenty-two–stage pattern. But when Young mentioned *The Hero,* Barth did not know anything about it. His interest was sufficiently provoked, however, for him to take the book out of the Penn State library and read it—and he discovered that not only Ebenezer Cooke but also Henry Burlingame correspond with some of Raglan's pattern. More, if taken together, they match nearly all of Raglan's twenty-two stages. So also do characters by many other writers, he learned: Odysseus, Aeneas, Dante in *The Divine Comedy,* Alice in her wonderland, Leopold Bloom, to name a few at random. And as he became more interested and did more research (Otto Rank's *The Myth of the Birth of the Hero,* Joseph Campbell's *The Hero with a Thousand Faces*), it seemed to him close to impossible to write a story about a wandering hero that does not have affinities with hero myths. After all, there are only a limited number of variations a writer can make on the theme of the wanderer, and these variations have been used so often that a writer is hard-pressed not to repeat them, consciously or otherwise. Moreover, many psychologists, Jung among them, have maintained that there are certain basic universal structures in our lives and personalities which have analogies outside ourself and which we find inherently intriguing. These structures Jung called *archetypes:* the growth of our minds,

for example, or our passage from birth through age to death represented metaphorically, say, by the passage of the sun and moon,
the progress of the seasons, or in terms of narrative, a hero's journey.
In this sense, it is no wonder that so many ancient heroes (many
modern ones as well) have much in common. Their stories are essentially the same. In performing their adventures they are working
out symbolically the adventure of the individual and species. Many
critics, Leslie Fiedler and Philip Young among them, have picked
up on Jung, using his ideas as the rationale for a new kind of
criticism, loosely called mythic, which employs psychological principles to account for the power certain types of literary incident
have for readers when that power seems out of all proportion to the
words used to describe them, and Barth, for his part, wanted to
employ some aspects of the mythic hero's journey to gain a similar
kind of resonance and power, finally becoming so interested in the
concept that he decided Raglan's twenty-two stages would be a
good general outline for a large comic novel he had in mind.[3]

  This novel would be another attempt to avoid the techniques of
realism. That is why he wanted it comic: to free him to be outrageous and extravagant. His subject matter would also be non-
realistic, a fantasy about a world constructed along the lines of a
modern university ("a university that *is* the world—not one that is
just *like* the world") in which a young man who has been raised as
a goat sets out to discover the ultimate truth of life.[4] And Raglan's
twenty-two stages in the hero's life Barth employed in this way.

1. The hero's mother is a royal virgin.	Giles the goat-boy's mother is Virginia Hector, who, as her first name suggests, is a virgin. She is royal, the daughter of the former Chancellor of New Tammany College.
2. His father is a king.	His father is the computer WESCAC, virtual ruler of the University.
3. His father is often a near relative of his mother.	It is falsely rumored that his father was his mother's uncle.
4. The circumstances of his conception are unusual.	His mother is seduced one night by the computer.

5. He is reputed to be the son of a god.

His father, the computer, is so powerful that it is in effect a god.

6. At birth an attempt is made, usually by his father or his maternal grandfather, to kill him.

His maternal grandfather, concerned that his daughter's reputation be ruined if it were known that she had a child out of wedlock, arranges for the infant to be sent into the belly of the computer where he will almost certainly be destroyed. Thus both his father and his grandfather are involved in the plot to kill him, although the computer is not a willing accomplice.

7. He is spirited away.

A Negro by the name of George Herrold hears Giles crying in the computer and pulls him out. The computer's defense mechanism has not harmed Giles but does render George insane. George takes the child to Max Spielman, a former professor who has been disgraced, in part because Virginia Hector falsely accused him of being the father of Giles, and who has been demoted to the position of Goat Herder.

8. He is reared by foster parents in a far country.

Giles is reared in the goatbarns far out of New Tammany College. Max Spielman is his mentor and foster father, and Giles believes that one of the goats is his mother.

9. We are told nothing of his childhood.

He spends his childhood in obscurity, himself not able to recall most of his youth. The record of his life commences in full just before he comes of age.

10. On reaching manhood he returns or goes to his future kingdom.

He feels instinctively that he is a kind of hero and messiah, a Grand Tutor. When he comes of age, he sets off toward New Tammany College, the place from which he came, to achieve his vaguely understood destiny.

11. He has a victory over the king and/or a giant, dragon, or wild beast.

He overcomes such metaphoric monsters as a broken motorcycle and a brute named Croaker. He re-enters the belly of the computer and victoriously unplugs it. He drives the false Grand Tutor, Harold Bray, out of the College.

12. He marries a princess, often the daughter of his predecessor.

He marries Anastasia, a kind of Earth Mother Goddess, who is the stepdaughter of his mother and who, he suspects, is another child of his father, the computer. For a time he even suspects that she is his twin sister and that they have committed incest.

13. He becomes king.

Having passed all the tests for Grand Tutorhood, he is accepted by some students as their messiah.

14. For a time he reigns uneventfully.

Not enough people accept him as their leader for him to have any sweeping influence. His reign is thus uneventful, inconsequential.

15. He prescribes laws.

He gives people certain rules to live by. Among other things, he counsels them to love.

16. Later he loses favor with the gods and/or his subjects.

His major truths are too complex for him to express them lucidly. Soon he is barely heeded by his few followers. "Gilesianism" splits into factions, each with its own leader, and he himself is periodically thrown in jail.

17. He is driven from the throne and city.

He has a vision of the crowd thrusting him upon a rusty bicycle and literally driving him out of the College.

18. He meets with a mysterious death.

He foresees that he will die by three flashes of lightning some evening at quarter after seven.

19. He dies at the top of a hill.

He predicts that his death will be far off on top of the sacred Founder's Hill.

20. His children, if any, do not succeed him.

He is disillusioned with his son, Giles Stoker, and has no confidence that the boy will carry on his father's work. (To an extent he is mistaken. Giles Stoker brings his father's book to John Barth for publication and claims to be acting in his father's interest.)

21. His body is not buried.

What happens to his body is not certain. Perhaps it disappears. Perhaps it is cremated in the lightning. Perhaps it sinks into a cleft in the hill.

22. He has one or more holy sepulchres.[5]

Founder's Hill is his sepulchre. He is revered by some few devotees after his death, but his legend has not yet reached the point where his body is said to be resting in various other holy places.

As this outline shows, Barth did not attend to Raglan's stages in a very literal respect, nor did he put equal emphasis on every stage. And these things because he did not want *Giles Goat-Boy* to be a mindless exercise whereby he contrived his plot to fit Raglan's outline merely for the sake of fitting the outline. Then too he did not want to be self-conscious about the writing of his novel—aware of what he was doing, yes, but not cripplingly self-conscious[6]—and so, after he had learned a considerable amount about the ancient wandering heroes, he forced himself to stop before he learned too much. "It was necessary . . . to turn my back on knowledge lest it paralyze action," he told an audience at Geneseo, New York (December 10, 1964).

> The storyteller's stock-in-trade, after all, is lies, not facts, and though he may require a few seeds of truth from which to sprout his fabrications, there's nothing in his contract obliging him to spill those beans, and too many of them will only clutter up his plot.

Barth had commenced research on *Giles Goat-Boy* in June of 1960. Prior to then he had been working on a novel begun shortly after

The Sot-Weed Factor was completed in March of 1959. This was *The Seeker;* its alternate title was *The Amateur,* and in his prefatory note to *Giles Goat-Boy,* Barth described it.

> My hero . . . was to be a Cosmic Amateur; a man enchanted with history, geography, nature, the people around him—everything that *is the case*—because he saw its arbitrariness but couldn't understand or accept its finality.[7]

Such enchantment Barth called Innocent Imagination; it is a quality that Ebenezer Cooke has in *The Sot-Weed Factor.* But whereas Cooke wanders around Maryland getting into trouble because of his innocence, this character passes all his time at the top of a tower looking at the men and women outside through all sorts of microscopes and telescopes, through a "huge *camera obscura* into which images of life outside were projected, ten times more luminous and interesting than the real thing." He is determined to be utterly detached from what he sees, but eventually he does get involved with what goes on outside and does accept the universe as it is and at last aspires "to a kind of honorary membership in the human fraternity" —much as Eben Cooke shucks the last of his innocence, tries to be responsible for his deeds, and in so doing ends up a man. Barth labored on this book for almost fifteen months, managed to fill over 150 hand-written pages, and then in June of 1960 abandoned the whole thing as uninspired. "I knew what novels were," he remarked in the introduction to *Giles Goat-Boy: "The Seeker* wasn't one" (p. xx).*

---

* In that introduction to *Giles Goat-Boy,* he also described how a young man, faintly goatlike, came to his office one gusty autumn evening in 1960 and gave him the typescript for a long book, *The Revised New Syllabus of George Giles Our Grand Tutor.* Giles, it seems, had dictated his teachings to the computer Wescac which in turn had collated those teachings, edited them, and recomposed them into a first-person narrative told by Giles. And Barth's goatlike visitor, the son of Giles, had in turn edited the computer's narrative before bringing it to Barth in hopes that Barth would have it published. On his own, Barth claims, he himself then edited the book to make it more dramatically effective, and sent it to his publisher who also edited the book, altering "certain passages clearly libelous, obscene, discrepant, or false" (p. xvi). With so many stages between us and the original, we have little idea what on earth Giles actually dictated to the computer, and we recognize a familiar theme of Barth:

He moved directly to the goat-boy project, making lengthy notes about mythic wanderers and re-reading such stories about them as the *Odyssey*, the *Aeneid*, and the Gospels. Writing began in January of 1962, was left off for the first six months of 1963 while he was on sabbatical in Spain and elsewhere, then restarted in July of 1963 and continued until the end of 1965. In its final form, the book was so long (741 pages when Doubleday set it in type) that proofreading it took him the first three months of 1966.[8]

Not counting his six-month sabbatical, then, Barth worked for five years and three months on *Giles Goat-Boy*, roughly twice as long as he had worked on *The Sot-Weed Factor*, a book of com-

---

that reality comes to us filtered and truth distorted. Similarly, at the end of the book a posttape is appended to the narrative: it is supposed to have been dictated to the computer by Giles, but in a postscript to the posttape Barth argues that it is neither thematically nor stylistically in keeping with what came before. Then in a footnote to the postscript to the posttape, Barth's editor argues that Barth may not himself have written the postscript refuting the posttape. For one thing, the editor points out, the typewriter used for "Barth's" postscript is not the same as that used for his introduction. The series of documents is all complex and confusing, and sufficiently suspect that we do not know which, if any, of Giles's teachings to place faith in. That same uncertainty again.

On July 13, 1965, Barth read the introduction he had written for *Giles* to the Penn State English faculty, prefacing it with some explanations of why he had written it at all. "A few years ago I had the experience called writer's block," he told them. "I'd begun the novel which was to follow *The Sot-Weed Factor*, and found that I couldn't write it, or anything else. After the first hysteria came the black peace that astronauts must know: the booster was gone; the next stage might or might not fire, and there was absolutely nothing one could do about it—the button was not one's own to press. In this instance, the issue was happy—the goat-boy appeared and drove out his false rival. But it could quite as easily not have happened, and may well not next time, or time after that: the pitcher that goes always to the well is one day broken. Anyhow, looking back on that dark interval a few hundred pages later, it occurred to me that fictional use might be made of it in several ways at once."

The university of *Giles Goat-Boy* is, after all, unlike any in our experience, and a false preface, involving an imaginary Author who disavows ownership of the story, might serve he thought to mediate between Giles's campus and the reader's, between himself and the first-person narrator. Furthermore, it would give him a chance to work with what he called "a quaint sub-genre of literature—the Author's Preface, bonafide or fictitious—and a couple of novelistic standbys, such as the cliché that inspiration is a love-affair with the Muse, and the Authorial pretense that his manuscript is a factual chronicle inadvertently happened upon—not a very bad metaphor for the truth, in *Giles*'s case."

parable size. "The reason it took so long," he said, "was that, while the matter of *The Sot-Weed Factor* was more complicated, the manner of *Giles* was more difficult. But once the narrator's voice was worked out, the writing came swiftly."[9] There was, for example, the problem of diction. Giles the Grand Tutor narrates his own story, but how does a Grand Tutor speak? There ought to be something sacred and mythic about his voice, Barth decided, and he achieved that effect by occasionally accenting final *ed* syllables, by making his sentences heavily rhythmic, by carefully balancing his sentences, by introducing archaic-sounding words and arrangements of words. The first paragraph of his story is as good an instance of this technique as any.

> George is my name; my deeds have been heard of in Tower Hall,
> and my childhood has been chronicled in the *Journal of Experimental
> Psychology*. I am he that was called in those days Billy Bocksfuss—
> cruel misnomer. For had I indeed a cloven foot I'd not now hobble
> upon a stick or need ride pick-a-back to class in humid weather.
> Aye, it was just for want of a proper hoof that in my fourteenth
> year I was the kicked instead of the kicker; that I lay crippled on
> the reeking peat and saw my first love tupped by a brute Angora. . . .
> This bare brow, shame of my kidship, he crowned with the shame
> of men: I bade farewell to my hornless goathood and struck out, a
> hornèd human student, for Commencement Gate. (P. 5)

Obviously the words draw attention to themselves, and this too, like Barth's use of comedy and fantasy, is a reaction against realism. A novelist of realism must always limit his power of language; his words must not distract from the action; they must be invisible, like windows through which the action is seen. But since Barth was being nonrealistic, he could have as much fun with his style as with his action, and the reader could delight in both.

Many readers did hope to delight in the book. Upon its release in August of 1966, *Giles* turned up on the best seller charts and was an alternate selection of the Literary Guild. This success was well-earned and long overdue, yet it is at first puzzling. The book is full of ideas that are difficult to understand; often the action stops and characters engage in lengthy, heady philosophical debate. The book is just not what one expects to find on a best seller chart. Hence one is especially interested in Anne Freedgood's explanation of the book's success. She was Doubleday's editor for *Giles,* and she wrote to this writer:

> The biggest thing working for . . . GILES GOAT-BOY was the under-
> ground reputation Mr. Barth had built up by the time it was pub-
> lished, the constant references to him when leading American
> novelists were being discussed, the fact that the *Book Week* poll
> [26 September 1965] called THE SOT-WEED FACTOR one of the best
> American novels since 1945, and the feeling in every department of
> Doubleday, and perhaps especially among the sales force, that Barth
> was one of the leading American writers and should be presented as
> such. I think it is also correct, however, to say that the critics were
> ready and waiting for GILES when it appeared.[10]

She later added that three months before *Giles's* publication Doubleday had asked the *New York Times Book Review* to do a retro-
spective piece on Barth, assessing the worth of his novels to date
and, without saying so, preparing readers for this new one. The
Times agreed, selecting critic Robert Scholes to do it, and Scholes
himself would later say that his strong favorable response to Barth
might inadvertently have caused other reviewers in reaction to take
a different stand,[11] for the critics were ready and waiting all right, a
good many, with clubs in their hands.

Never before had the press been so disinclined toward Barth.
Webster Schott, reviewing for *Life,* attacked the novel as

> a gluey mass of serio-comic belligerence that hardens into epoxy.
> Long, boring, frustrating, *Giles Goat-Boy* cultivates tedium. . . .
> [Barth] develops no characters. He creates no drama. He finds no
> emotional ranges and searches no human depths.[12]

The critic for *The New Yorker* was even more enraged.

> It is an allegory whose symbolism is embarrassingly transparent and
> heavyhanded. Its characters, all of them parodies of the famous and
> the infamous, of the living and the dead, have no breath and spirit of
> their own. . . . It is written in an arch, belaboring prose full of
> *accents graves* and Latinisms. It is a picaresque novel without sur-
> prise, suspense, or variety.[13]

Perhaps most vehement was Robert Garis, who maintained in *Commentary* that

The Sot-Weed Factor and *Giles Goat-Boy* are about as bad as novels can be. They are, to begin with, appallingly tedious, and what is worse, their tediousness seems to be almost deliberate. . . . Barth's episodic structure has the effect of casting a merciless spotlight on the puerility of his thinking.

In particular, Garis was put off by what he claimed was "the failure of Barth's Swiftian allegory." He confided that he himself was not the world's greatest admirer of Books I and II of *Gulliver's Travels*, nevertheless that he did see value in "Swift's invention of little and big men" because it offered "a strange and special perspective on human affairs." But Garis felt that

Barth's version of Swiftian methods . . . , his elaborate translation of our world into a university is precisely *not* a new perspective. We learn nothing new about the way our world works simply by having it called a university; Barth, in fact, hardly ever actually *describes* the world in terms of a university, and even when he does, there is no meaningful counterpart in our world to what happens in Barth's university. It is all on the surface, all a matter of substituting one term for another. . . . It is as if Barth had written a 710-page imitation of Swift just to demonstrate as convincingly as possible that he does not, in the most basic sense, understand how Swift's methods operate.[14]

The article by Garis was long and all of a piece. It is here given space as a fair representation of the opposition *Giles Goat-Boy* was up against.

Still, the book was not without its champions. Richard Poirier led off his *Book Week* review: "With this fourth novel, John Barth at 36 increases the likelihood that the years since World War II are among the most rewarding in the history of American fiction."[15] *Newsweek* delivered the impressive comment that "Barth could have cut [*Giles Goat-Boy*] by a third (though one would hate to see a line of it go) and made the reputation of a dozen novelists by distributing the pieces among them."[16] But it was Robert Scholes, reviewing again for the *New York Times* book section, who came up with the outstanding compliment.

Giles Goat-Boy is a great novel. Its greatness is most readily apparent in its striking originality of structure and language, an originality that depends upon a superb command of literary and linguistic tradition. . . . This is not an experiment but a solution—an achievement which . . . in my opinion stamps Barth as the best writer of fiction we have at present, and one of the best we have ever had.[17]

With critical opinion so sharply divided, one hesitates to agree with Anne Freedgood that the reviews were a major reason for the financial success of *Giles Goat-Boy:* there were so many bad reviews that in the normal course of events readers would have been driven away from the book. Yet these adverse reviews did have an immense positive effect on how well *Giles* sold. The dissenting critics, by concentrating on the most obvious allegory in the book, convinced many book buyers that *Giles Goat-Boy* was almost purely a *roman à clef,* a novel in which real persons and actual events figure under disguise; a who's who contest. East Campus and West Campus are pretty obviously Russia and the United States. Siegfrieder College is Germany. The Bonifascists are the Nazis, and the Student-Unionists are the Communists. Campus Riots One and Two are the World Wars. The computer WESCAC with its devastating EAT-rays is the atomic bomb. All that is easy to identify. But what about the novel's characters? Are there real-life counterparts to them as well? A search in that direction is fascinating. Thinly disguised are Dwight and Milton Eisenhower, Krushchev and his son-in-law, the Kennedys (Joe, John, Robert, and Jacqueline), J. Edgar Hoover, Bernard Baruch, Oppenheimer and Einstein, Joe McCarthy, Leslie Fiedler, the Dalai Lama, and lord knows who else. Anyone who prefers to run the guessing game on a more literary level can go through the book finding the originals for the first two students in the Botanical Garden, Remus College (Rome), Lykeion (Greece), Moishe (Moses) and the Promised Quad, Maios (Socrates), Enos Enoch (Jesus Christ) and the Twelve Trustees, the *Campus Cantos* (*The Divine Comedy*), *The Encyclopedia Tammanica,* and hundreds more. Partly on this basis, *Giles* attracted customers, just as novels by commercial writers like Harold Robbins are in demand partly because their main characters are admittedly based on such public figures as Howard Hughes, Frank Sinatra, former television mogul James Aubrey, and the like.* The rich seasoning of sex definitely

---

* Readers from Penn State had one other extra-literary reason to be intrigued by *Giles Goat-Boy.* Nearly all of it was written while Barth was

helped also to promote the book. But readers who bought the book
for these reasons very soon learned that the identification game and
the sex were only incidental to what *Giles* was about and lost interest. Other, more serious readers found the pattern of the book and
its ideas hard to follow, and many of them gave the book up as
well. It seems the least read of Barth's work.

Understandably. Barth was trying something new here, not
just re-telling in a comic fashion the myth of the wandering hero.
He was attempting to combine tragedy and mysticism and satire
and allegory smoothly into one integrated book, and the result is so
unusual that some of its readers do best to approach it prepared by
an introduction.

Barth learned from Raglan, Rank, Campbell, and others that as
children many heroes are associated with animals. He did not care
to scavenge further through these sources to find out what kind of
animal is most often mentioned; he already knew the kind of animal
he needed to use: a goat. "I'm delighted by the old spurious etymol-
ogy of the words *tragedy* and *satire*," he told an interviewer,

> both of which have been traced back to the root word for goat.
> Because what I was after in [*Giles Goat Boy*], as in most of my
> work, is a way to get at some of the passion and power of the tragic
> view of life, which I share, through the medium of farce and
> satire. To fuse those elements has been an inspiration of mine from
> the beginning.[18]

Leaving aside for now the matter of how *Giles Goat-Boy* is a
tragedy, it is worth understanding why Barth wanted to make the

---

teaching English there (he moved to teach English at The State University of
New York at Buffalo in the fall of 1965), and he used the Penn State campus
as the source for his book's geography: East and West Campus, the bell tower,
the infirmary, the prominent mall, the goatbarns far off from the center of
campus, the motto inscribed in the stone front of the library "A True University
Is a Collection of Books," the elevator in the core of the library, the immense
confusing registration, the omnipresent computer. Barth lived near the man in
charge of Penn State's goatbarns. He remembered that Milton Eisenhower was
President of Penn State while his brother Dwight was President of the United
States, and he combined them into the character of Reginald Hector, former
Chancellor of New Tammany College.

tragedy a satire. One reason we have already touched on lightly: the comedy of a satire was a chance for him to be outrageous and thus not realistic. Another reason is that he felt it pointless to write a straight tragedy, something that other writers had done plenty of before him and that would be redundant if tried again. "The cathedral at Chartres is a remarkable piece of architecture," he explained to another interviewer, "but if it were built today, it would be embarrassing—unless it were done tongue-in-cheek, deliberately, as an ironic comment."[19] But by treating the subject of tragedy in a comic, satiric way, he would be fairly innovative, especially if the comedy did not detract from, but instead enhanced, the powerful cathartic effect of the tragedy. At times, Giles appears no more than a rustic blockhead (he thinks he's part goat and gimps around half-naked, bleating advice that nearly destroys the world), a stone-faced slapstick figure out of a Buster Keaton movie who in spite of himself somehow does a couple of things right in the end. At other times, he appears the sacred, heroic Grand Tutor he imagines himself to be, his mirrored stick and woolly wrapper faintly Biblical, his language prophetlike, his simplicity the clear-headedness of a saint. Then toward the finish the two kinds of Giles merge into one complex character. His downfall and periodic imprisonments, his foresight that the mob will one day thrust him upon a rusty bicycle and drive him out of the college, that he will coast to Founder's Hill where three strokes of lightning will destroy him—these add up to one among the best of tragically moving conclusions. The details of the comedy remain, like the rusty bicycle, but they no longer amuse.

Yet while Barth's intention was to fuse the elements of tragedy and satire, it was also to fuse to them a third: mysticism, what Barth calls mystery. In December of 1964, he gave a talk at Geneseo, New York, on the subject of "Mystery and Tragedy: The Two Motions of Ritual Heroism" and how these two could be combined in one novel. And what he said has unmistakable application to *Giles Goat-Boy*, even though he never referred to the book by name. Especially applicable was a diagram (Figure 3) that he had sketched to show to his audience, a diagram that was based on a similar one by Campbell,[20] with ideas from himself and Raglan and Jung thrown in.

The first quadrant of the circle (working counter-clockwise) relates to the early parts of the novel, up to page 112. Like any good

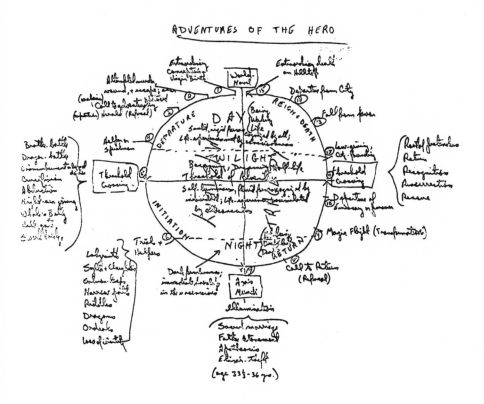

Figure 3. Barth's diagram of the hero's adventures (reproduced with
Barth's permission). For a slightly different version, see *Chimera* (New
York: Random House, 1972), p. 261.

storyteller, though, Barth has made a puzzle out of Giles's birth and his attempted murder, arousing the curiosity of the reader and not satisfying it until more than halfway through the book where Virginia Hector explains her seduction by the computer and her father's subsequent plot against Giles (pp. 490–495). The rest of the details on the chart are chronologically the same in the novel. Giles is literally called to adventure by a herald, in this case a Negro by the name of G. Herrold who one night blows a horn three times and wakens Giles to begin his adventure. Herrold blows the horn on the advice of Max Spielman, the helper or spielman of stage four on the chart, who is the goat-boy's loquacious mentor. Then they set out from the goatbarns toward New Tammany College.

The threshold crossing is a kind of night-sea journey: they cross a wide river under cover of dark. On the other side, Giles does battle with the brute Croaker and comes up against Maurice Stoker, a form of devil, who takes him to the Power House, which is a type of hell-gate. The plot of the novel could here be matched entirely with Barth's diagram, but that would be tedious, and once the reader is in the spirit of the diagram perhaps the matching should be left to him. Enough to say that the second quadrant of the circle —the initiation—corresponds to just about the whole of *Giles Goat-Boy*, and that in it Giles works to find the meaning of life, finding inadvertently that the College is a mental and physical labyrinth, a maze of riddles and ordeals.

Once again, as in *The Sot-Weed Factor*, the hero is engaged in an obstacle race and a scavenger hunt. He passes through the Turnstile and the Scrapegoat Grate. They are tests to determine if he is a possible Grand Tutor, and after he comes through them, the computer, WESCAC, prints out his Assignment Sheet. On one side of it is the circular device PASS ALL FAIL ALL, and on the other side of it are his instructions.

ASSIGNMENT

To Be Done At Once, In No Time

1) Fix the Clock
2) End the Boundary Dispute
3) Overcome Your Infirmity
4) See Through Your Ladyship
5) Re-place the Founder's Scroll

6) Pass the Finals
7) Present Your ID-card, Appropriately
    Signed, to the Proper Authority. (P. 383)

The pursuit of these objectives takes him on a round of visits through the College: to the scientist Eblis Eierkopf in the Clockworks, to Chancellor Lucius (Lucky) Rexford at his home in the Light House, to Dr. Kennard Sear at the College Infirmary, to his mother in the Library, to WESCAC's belly, to ex-Chancellor Reginald Hector in his mansion. These and other people he encounters hold as a group almost every possible religious, social, political, and philosophical position. The positions conflict with each other and cancel each other, and in their place he formulates his own truth, which he hopes has a twofold advantage: it will help him to fulfill his seven curious assignments; it will enable mankind to live better. The truth is based on the circle of PASS ALL FAIL ALL, and it is that passing and failing must be carefully distinguished. The first is not the second, they are opposites, and all of mankind's troubles come from a lack of differentiation between unlike concepts. Accordingly, to give an example of how he applies this apparent truth, he decides that his assignment to "end the boundary dispute" can be accomplished by counseling the politicians to separate the boundaries between East and West Campus as far as possible. Instead of ending the boundary dispute, however, his advice causes further East and West misunderstanding and almost results in a major inter-campus riot. His misadvice also gets him thrown in jail and nearly lynched.

While in jail, he tries to understand why his truth did not succeed and finally concludes that he misinterpreted the circle of PASS ALL FAIL ALL. They are round and interconnected, not different at all but one and the same, and all of mankind's troubles come from insisting too much on the difference between things. Convinced of this new truth, he makes a second round of visits to inform people that all categories are meaningless and ought to be denied. Accordingly, to use again the example of the boundary dispute, Chancellor Rexford moves the western border close to the eastern in an attempt to deny the difference between the two campuses, and again a misunderstanding almost causes an inter-campus riot. Once more Giles is almost lynched, saved only when again he is arrested.

He has yet another round of visits to make. Thinking through the error of his unsuccessful truths, he trembles and sweats and agonizes.

> That circular device on my Assignment–sheet—beginningless, endless, infinite equivalence ["PASS ALL FAIL ALL"]—constricted my reason like a torture-tool from the Age of Faith. Passage *was* Failure, and Failure Passage; yet Passage was Passage, Failure Failure! Equally true, none was the Answer; the two were not different, neither were they the same; and *true* and *false,* and *same* and *different*—Unspeakable! Unnamable! Unimaginable! Surely my mind must crack!

"Don't try to get loose!" he hears someone say about another topic, and he applies the words to himself.

> I gave myself up utterly to that which bound, possessed, and bore me. I let go, I let all go; relief went through me like a purge. And as if in signal of my freedom, over the reaches of the campus the bells of Tower Clock suddenly rang out. (P. 650)

The bells ascend the scale from *sol* to *la* to *ti*, and then climactically unbinding and releasing him, to *do* (the top of the scale), do (the exhortation to act). He and his mistress, Anastasia, descend into the belly of the computer—the third time he has been there, not counting his near-murder as a child. They go down in a small elevator, the lift he had been put in as a child, and they can only fit if their bodies are interlocked "knees to chin and arsy-turvy" like the Eastern symbol for oneness and eternity. They enter the computer's belly, unite, and in that instant, only for an instant, lovingly transported, the truth is given to him that he sought but could not find because he was not until now ready to receive it.

> There was no East, no West, but an entire, single, seamless campus: Turnstile, Scrapegoat Grate, the Mall, the barns, the awful fires of the Powerhouse, the balmy heights of Founder's Hill—I saw them all; rank jungles of Frumentius, Nikolay's cold fastness, teeming T'ang—all one, and one with me. *Here* lay with *there, tick* clipped *tock, all* serviced *nothing;* I and My Ladyship, all, were one. (Pp. 672–673)

It is tantamount to a mystical experience, the transcension of the categories that he previously affirmed and later denied, the arrival at the state of total being, an arrival that is not in mind but in emotion, the miracle of Love, what he had to become a man to know.*

But male and female having merged, they cannot forever hold. Being must become has been. That is the first pain of the experience: it has to end. The second pain is almost as bad: the experience is ineffable.

> . . . Words strain,
> Crack and sometimes break, under the burden,
> Under the tension, slip, slide, perish,
> Decay with imprecision, will not stay in place,
> Will not stay still.
>
> ("Burnt Norton," 11. 150–154)

---

* The business of a novel is to dramatize, not philosophize. That is why Barth did not provide a direct, overt, intrusive explanation of what Giles learned at the moment of his union with Anastasia in the computer's belly. Nevertheless, early in his writing of *Giles,* Barth did work out such an explanation. It was a part of a very informal essay he prepared to help himself better understand the meaning and the plot of the novel. "What is George's characteristic manner of encountering and passing his obstacles?" he asked himself. What is the issue of the book? What is graduation? In terms of the goat-boy's university-universe, what is salvation? "Solve this and the plot should write itself."

That particular essay—"The Goat-Boy: Politics and Graduation"—was definitely not written to be published nor to be used by a reader as a gloss to *Giles Goat-Boy.* It took him five days in March of 1962, is ten handwritten pages long and extremely concentrated, and its main interest for us is not what it says but what it is: an example of the kind of research a writer like Barth goes through when trying to figure out a lengthy, complicated novel. The following explanation by Barth of what it means for Giles to be saved is therefore offered with qualification. It is not the author's last word on the meaning of his novel; it is his first word, and it puts us in the confines of literary history, not fictional analysis.

"*Salvation* in the individual," Barth wrote, "consists of the realization (brought about usually after a period of suffering, anxiety, and despair) of a transcendent reality beyond the particular visible world; union with it, release from conflicts of reason vs. passion; good vs. evil. Affirmation of wholeness of psyche and body; loving affirmation of unreason, passions, appetite, corporeity; freedom from vanity and selfishness; spiritual energy and 'lyric enchantment' with reality; a *joie de vivre* that accepts and exults in its suffering or whatever else comes; that discharges the force of its personality in love (compassion and charity); which may include lustful appetite out of joy but will involve no cruelty or destructiveness" (on file at the Library of Congress, Manuscript Division).

So T.S. Eliot concluded, trying to write his *Four Quartets* about the mystical experience. So too with *Giles*. Having gone all the way, he has the Answer, but by its very personal and profound nature, it is not communicable.

> For me, Sense and Nonsense lost their meaning on a night twelve years four months ago, in WESCAC's Belly—as did every such distinction, including that between Same and Different. Thus it is . . . I have lingered on the campus these dozen years, in the humblest capacity, advising one at a time undergraduates to whom my words convey nothing. (P. 699)

Having passed, he is doomed to fail. And this too is a kind of ultimate knowledge. As Barth told his audience at Geneseo,

> The mystic One can't be described, because language is analytical, or drawn, because it has no attribute; Very Beauty is not like any beautiful thing. So they all come back and do their best, but their best can never quite work out perfectly: a pox will come upon Thebes; the disciples will misconstrue the master's gospel; even the model republic, Plato acknowledges, must ultimately degenerate and fall.

"What does Giles learn in his heroic quest?" Barth said another time. "That the tragedy is you can't transmit wisdom and insight."[21]

Tragedy. At the moment of mystical illumination is when the tragedy begins, at the Axis Mundi, in the belly of the computer where he was conceived, at the center of all earthly power. All else is anticlimax: the call from his mother to return from the computer, the flight to the goatbarn and his further return now cleansed with goatdip to the College, the execution of his mentor, Max, the rout of his opponent, the false tutor, Harold Bray. He crosses the threshold into the fourth quadrant of his adventure during that execution and the rout, in the frightening smoke and ashes that appear and the panic they bring to the crowd come to see Max die. There follow his brief period as partially accepted Grand Tutor, his fall from favor, his expulsion from the College, his extraordinary death. His life, like each day, season, and year, like cities and civilizations, like universities and universes, turns and rolls round to a close. That too is his lesson. Ontogeny recapitulates cosmogeny, his Max used to tell him as a child. Wheels are within wheels and cycles within cycles, and all unwinding, slowing down to stop. That is what Max used to tell him, but it took him nearly thirty-three years to get the point.

Tragic heroes have tragic flaws, and his is a trait of character we have seen before in Barth's fiction: the passionate urge to know. It gives to Giles his chance for glory and also brings about his downfall, because, although the unexamined life is for him not worth living, his examined life is not capable of being lived. And thus to date this book is Barth's most optimistic, and *that* because it is mystical or perhaps "optimystic": a person with the proper attributes can, if he tries desperately hard, achieve ultimate knowledge. Thus too the book is pessimistic, though it does not approach the pessimism of an earlier book like *The End of the Road*, or even *The Sot-Weed Factor*. Ebenezer Cooke learns something of what Giles learns, that he is doomed to fail, that things never work out as hoped, that the best he can do is try to atone for his past mistakes. But Eben never has any compensation for his knowledge, no joy to offset his pain and sorrow. Giles does. That instant of illumination in the belly of the computer seems worth all that comes after. Hence the reader feels both elated and depressed by Giles's extra-brilliant rhetoric as he foresees his destruction in the lightning on the hilltop —which is how the reader ought to feel at the consummation of a tragedy. Yet the reader is elated and depressed in no common wise. His emotions are caused not only by sympathy for Giles but as well because the reader has seen how high a person can go and because he knows the odds are he himself will never get that high. In respect to the tragedy, that critic for *Life* magazine was correct when he said that Barth "has brought black humor to a dead end. It may get funnier, but not blacker."[22] In other respects, the critic was dead wrong.

6

Ambrose is Lost
in the Funhouse

"We cried 'Help!' all together as loudly
as we could so many times my throat almost
broke."

> (A fourteen-year-old sailor
> rescued from Ambrose Channel
> after a tanker sank a
> fishing boat)[1]

The experience of writing two novels so long as *The Sot-Weed Factor* and *Giles Goat-Boy* had been a great strain on Barth. Together they accounted for almost nine years of his life. *Giles* alone had taken him more than five, and after that effort, he told an interviewer, he was "not interested in writing another very long book, at least for a while." Instead he wanted to try something quite different, he explained: to compose several small pieces, what he called "fictions." They would have to be arranged in a volume because they would take resonance from each other. But for full effect—and this is what would set them apart from anything else he had written—many would have to be performed on a stage or else recorded on a tape, rather than printed on a page.[2]

The idea had been with him ever since *The Sot-Weed Factor* was published in 1960. Although not a financial success, that novel *had* attracted much favorable attention on college campuses, and as a result he had received frequent invitations to read his work at various schools. Sometimes he read sections from the novels he had already published; other times he tested the reception of excerpts from the as-yet-unpublished *Giles*. But that fiction had been designed to appear in a book, and the more he read in public, the more he considered writing something especially for a voice and an audience. The project was a logical outcome of the determination he had shown in *The Sot-Weed Factor* to take up old narrative forms and rejuvenate them. After all, the oldest kind of storytelling is oral, and Barth found the virtues of such a medium rare, hence appealing, in an age of print: the dramatic quality of the human voice, plus the intimacy between the storyteller and his audience.[3]

His interest in oral fiction was stimulated when he left Penn State in the fall of 1965 and went to teach at The State University of New York in Buffalo. The English department there had rented the music department's electronic laboratory, and in early 1966, once Barth had finished correcting the proof sheets for *Giles*, he took advantage of the laboratory to experiment with fiction recorded on tape. The device was ideal for his purposes; it offered a chance to overcome certain limitations of the oral medium as it existed before the twentieth century. For one thing, a tape recorder removed the necessity of having an actual storyteller in the room every time the story is told. For another, it enabled the listener to stop the story at any moment and play back whatever passages he felt like.[4]

To an extent, Barth's goal from the outset of his career had been to concentrate on the sound of his prose. In 1953, when he applied for a position in the English department at Penn State, he summed up his fictional aims: "My object has been to explore sounds, rhythms and ideas more thoroughly, and to develop more rigorously disciplined eyes, ears and attitudes." And years later, speaking of *The Sot-Weed Factor* and *Giles Goat-Boy,* he remarked to an interviewer, "I think I can be allowed the statement that whatever the faults of my writing, it usually reads pretty well out loud, to the ear."[5] All this was appropriate to a writer who had considered a career in music (playing drums and orchestrating) before he decided to be a teacher and a writer.

But what he had in mind now was not just fiction that sounds "pretty well" when read out loud, but fiction that works best when read out loud, that gains part of its drama from being read out loud. For example, he conceived of a story called "Autobiography: A Self-Recorded Fiction," in which the main character and first-person narrator is a story that speaks from a tape machine and talks about itself.

> Mother was a mere passing fancy who didn't pass quickly enough; there's evidence also that she was a mere novel device, just in style, soon to become a commonplace, to which Dad resorted one day when he found himself by himself with pointless pen.[6]

Dad, of course, is Barth, and Mother the tape machine (as Barth himself makes clear in a prefatory author's note). And when he presents the story in public, he is on stage in the guise of Dad and author, smoking, drinking coffee, and listening to the story in the machine complain to him about its hard lot. "I don't recall asking to be conceived!" it says. "I see no point in going further. . . . I'll turn myself off if I can this instant" (pp. 35, 38). But it cannot, so it implores Barth to end it. But Barth does not; instead he walks disgustedly off the stage, leaving the story to ramble on about itself until at last its tape flaps abruptly off the reel. The story's life is analogous to one possible view of our own: we did not ask to be born, our existence seems pointless, it goes on too long, we wish to kill ourselves but do not have the means (or if we do, we cannot overcome our instinct to remain alive), thus we drag on, lapsing into nonsense, finally silence. And completing the analogy, Barth, who ignores the plea of his story to end it, is like one fashionable view of God, who having created us has abandoned us, helpless and hopeless, to misery.

Barth underscores the failed nature of this story and its life by noting a partial resemblance between it and ancient heroes. Its conception was unnatural, it says. Its father tried to kill it young, but it survived, and now thinking of itself as blind and crippled, it would like vengeance on the father. "One [parent] hoped I'd be astonishing, forceful, triumphant—heroical in other words" (p. 37), but as the story admits, it turned out merely conventional. Even *it* "aspired to immortality" (p. 38), but instead of being a "crippled hero" it became a "heroic cripple," not the same thing at all. And that is another point of the story's story, of everyone's story. Our struggle almost makes us heroical, but almost is not good enough. We aspire, but we do not achieve what we intend. We start out hoping, as do our parents generally hope, that we are special, and end up realizing that we are pathetically ordinary. "A change for the better still isn't unthinkable; miracles can be cited. But the odds . . . aren't encouraging" (p. 38). "The story of our life," a character in a later story says (p. 107).

Another fiction of this type Barth called "Echo." It too has a voice out of a machine, although this time Barth is not on stage with it. The plot of the story is similar to the myth of its namesake; Barth took most of the incidents from a well-known two-volume survey, *The Greek Myths*, compiled by Robert Graves.[7] "In the myth, you remember," Barth told an audience at Harvard University on August 13, 1967,

> the nymph Echo is raped by Pan and later becomes a master
> storyteller. Zeus employs her to entertain his wife with her fictions
> while he slips out and makes free with certain mountain-nymphs.
> When Hera [Zeus's wife] realizes she's been tricked, she punishes
> Echo (who hadn't known Zeus was using her) by depriving her of
> the ability to speak for herself; she can only repeat others' words,
> though the voice is still her own. Later on she falls in love with
> Narcissus, the son of Leirope and a minor river-god, and when he
> rebuffs her she grieves away until nothing's left of her but her
> voice: pure medium without substance or original content. Narcissus
> himself, of course, tries to embrace his reflected image and then
> also pines away for frustration until he becomes a blooming narcotic.
> Somewhat later the blind prophet Tiresias, who'd foreseen all these
> events from the beginning and had warned Narcissus's mother
> that her boy would lead a long happy life if he never came to know
> himself, meets his own death beside the same spring where
> Narcissus blossoms and Echo laments. To the myth I've added
> one refinement: in her final state Echo loses her individual voice as
> well, and repeats the words of others in their own voices.

The solitary voice from the machine is, then, a perfect representation of Echo's bodiless condition. But since Barth presents her in her "final state" where she can speak only the words of others in their own voices, the audience cannot be certain whose words and voice are on the tape, those of Tiresias, Narcissus, or, at the extreme, Barth. Accordingly the story is extra-rich, able to be approached and appreciated from several equally valid points of view. If Echo is arranging the words and voice of another in order to tell her own story, then the tale is about love and its disastrous consequences. If she is repeating the words and voice of Narcissus, then the tale is about self-love and its disasters. If she is repeating the words and voice of Tiresias, then the tale is about cruel knowledge and the burdensome foresight that everything will turn out badly for everyone in the end. Finally, if Echo is repeating the words and voice of

Barth, then the viewpoints of Echo, Narcissus, and Tiresias are headspinningly co-existent.

Barth wrote "Autobiography" and "Echo" exclusively for monophonic tape, but the electronics laboratory at Buffalo also gave him the opportunity to work with multitrack tape, and the principal result of this medium was the story "Title." It is about an imaginary writer debating with himself, and in Barth's favorite performance of the story, the debate is carried on by recorded stereo voices. The narrator says something to himself through a speaker on one side of the stage, then answers himself from the speaker on the other side, and all the while Barth himself stands between the two speakers, listening to what the voices say to each other. As for the debate, it "has to do with three things simultaneously," Barth told that Harvard audience on August 13, 1967:

> the narrator's difficulties with his lady-friend; his difficulties with the story he's trying to compose; and the difficult situation he feels his art-form and his civilization to be in too. The question is raised whether one might "go on," at least provisionally—in a love affair, say, or an art-form, or a society—by making the difficulty one's subject. The answer is equivocal.

The difficulties of the imaginary author are the result of his failure to find meaning in his love affair, his art, his civilization. Yet he recognizes that these things are not themselves meaningless, that they only appear that way to *him*, and so he tries to make some sense out of them. "Everything leads to nothing," he says. "The final question is, Can nothing be made meaningful?" (p. 105). At least in terms of the story he's having trouble with, he comes up with an answer: he can write a meaningful story about the impossibility of writing a meaningful story. As it happens, though, he never writes that story; he merely debates with himself about writing it. Even if he did write it, the result would be redundant, for the kind of story he would write is very close to the story in which he is a character: "Title." Barth has managed quite a trick—through the voices of the imaginary author, he has talked about writing a meaningful story about the impossibility of writing a meaningful story, and in the process he has written the story he talked about. "You tell me it's self-defeating to talk about it instead of just up and doing it; but to acknowledge what I'm doing while I'm doing it is exactly the point"

(p. 111). And more, as will be clear in a moment, Barth has matched his technique with his subject matter: he stands on stage between the two voices, looking like some devilish magician, and as the voices debate he interrupts them, censoring their remarks and replacing what he has cut out either with the phrase "fill in the blank" or else with senseless grammatical expressions. "I'll fill in the blank with this noun here in my prepositional object" (p. 105) is one statement when Barth is done censoring it. The technique conforms with the subject matter because it dramatizes the impossibility of saying anything meaningful; an absolute example of that impossibility, of course, would be to write nothing at all, instead to provide blank tape or pages, or better yet, no tape or pages. But that silence would not be fiction, and since Barth is above all a fictionist, he demonstrates the trouble one can have filling the blank of nothingness by acknowledging that he himself cannot do it, by telling his audience to "fill in the blank" for themselves, the blank of this title, "Title," this sentence, this art, this civilization, this life. And paradoxically, by acknowledging that he cannot fill in the blank, by dramatizing that he cannot, he has actually done it, brilliantly.

Yet, however successful Barth was at writing fiction for the recorded voice, he did not restrict himself to that medium very long. "God knows I have the greatest love for the voice," he maintained to an interviewer, but he was, he had to admit, a "print-oriented bastard. . . . I'm thinking more and more about what print can do that nothing else can do,"[8] and by way of illustration he had ready several stories that made as brilliant use of print as "Title" did of voice.

One of them, "Petition," is especially suited for print since it is a letter, something which in its natural state has to be read on a page. As Barth is well aware, the letter format is a traditional way to tell a story.

> The other day a student came to me and said he wasn't going to pretend anything anymore, that henceforth his fiction would deal only in printed documents. But that's precisely how the novel began: Richardson with his letters, saying they were real, not a story.[9]

The epistolary technique is not a frequent one these days, of course, and that would be a reason why Barth chose it: the traditional can become innovative if it is taken up after a comparatively long period of disuse. Another reason why Barth chose it would be the dramatic contrast between the apparent authenticity of the document (it is addressed to Prajadhipok, the King of Siam, who was indeed, as the letter states, at Ophir Hall in White Plains, New York, on April 21, 1931, preparing to undergo an eye operation)[10] and the patently made-up subject matter (a man with his belly attached to the small of his twin brother's back is in love with a female contortionist to whom his brother is consort). The letter-writer describes his situation with his brother:

> I am slight, my brother is gross. He's incoherent but vocal; I'm
> articulate and mute. He's ignorant but full of guile; I think I may
> call myself reasonably educated, and if ingenuous, no more so I
> hope than the run of scholars. My brother is gregarious. . . .
> For my part, I am by nature withdrawn, even solitary. (P. 62)

The differences between them are now so intolerable that the brother in back is writing to the King in hopes "that at your bidding the world's most accomplished surgeons may successfully divide my brother from myself" (p. 71). If his plea is unsuccessful, he determines to kill himself and his brother with him. The relation between these two brothers is analogous to many things; Tony Tanner has suggested that the incoherent brother is, for example,

> like life itself, constantly shrugging off the attempts of language
> to circumscribe it within particular definitions. Language, in the
> form of the articulate brother, would be happy to pursue its
> inclination to ponder its elegant patternings in pure detachment
> from the soiling contacts of reality. But they are brothers, divided
> yet related—neither one nor two.[11]

Perhaps better, the brothers are somewhat like the mind and the body, one pondering while the other eats, humps, defecates. "To be one: paradise! To be two: bliss! But to be both and neither is unspeakable," the narrator concludes (p. 71), describing as it were the condition of a mind living within a body which too has a life of its own, yet a mind that is dependent on a body for its life. It is true that the narrator is not yet within his brother's body; still he senses that this is what is going to happen. He feels his brother straining to suck him in, and he has a fair idea that one day he will be inside like the woman he loves who lives within the body of the woman his brother humps.

Another story that Barth wrote especially for the printed medium is "Lost in the Funhouse." It is about a thirteen-year-old boy, Ambrose, who has gone with his family to enjoy a holiday at the Ocean City amusement park on the Atlantic coast of Maryland. While there, Ambrose gets lost in the funhouse and is some time threading the maze back out, and this incident is explicitly meant to symbolize many things: that Ambrose is becoming aware of himself, his sexuality, his mind, his world, his life, and that he is confused by it all. The problems of a sensitive adolescent are hardly original subject matter; they are indeed, as the narrator goes far to admit, tiresomely familiar (pp. 91–92). But here they have special interest because of the manner in which they are presented. The narrator employs such devices of print as italics, dashes, and plot diagrams to draw attention to his technique. He points out the effectiveness or failure of various descriptions; he digresses to explain the functions of his metaphors; he criticizes the action for its lack of clarity, direction, and pace. The following passage is typical:

> *En route* to Ocean City [Ambrose] sat in the back seat of the family car with his brother Peter, age fifteen, and Magda G————, age fourteen, a pretty girl and exquisite young lady, who lived not far from them on B———— Street in the town of D————, Maryland. Initials, blanks, or both were often substituted for proper names in nineteenth-century fiction to enhance the illusion of reality. It is as if the author felt it necessary to delete the names for reasons of tact or legal liability. Interestingly, as with other aspects of realism, it is an *illusion* that is being enhanced, by purely artificial means. (Pp. 72–73)

The storyteller is trying to present old material in a new way, and he does so by emphasizing the conventions of fiction rather than concealing them. "The technique is advanced, as you see, but the situation . . . is conventionally dramatic" (p. 110) is what the narrator of "Title" says about a story *he* is trying to write, and that remark might just as well have been made by the narrator of this story; it is a close description of what is going on here where technical advancement takes the form of technical—as opposed to philosophical or moralistic—intrusion. Still, as with other stories by Barth, the technique is more than just a presentation of the subject matter; it is a *representation* of that subject matter, for the narrator too, like Ambrose, is lost. His sentences go wrong, he says. His plot "winds upon itself, digresses, retreats, hesitates, sighs, collapses, expires" (p. 96). He is as self-conscious of his style as Ambrose is of growing up, until in his final paragraph what he writes about Ambrose comes to have strong bearing also on himself, his art, and his attitude toward life. And that paragraph, one cannot help feeling, is about the most autobiographical Barth ever wrote.

> He wishes he had never entered the funhouse. But he has. Then he wishes he were dead. But he's not. Therefore he will construct funhouses for others and be their secret operator—though he would rather be among the lovers for whom funhouses are designed. (P. 97)

"Lost in the Funhouse" has interest for us in another way besides the graphic use it makes of print. It is the title piece for the volume in which it and these other short fictions eventually were included. When Barth wrote the story in April of 1967, he once told a friend, he had been working on the book it would be in for over a year but had not yet settled on a title. For a time he considered *Still-Life* in the double sense of *a still form of life* and *still there is life in this writer, in this art, in this civilization*, but soon he rejected the phrase, having seen it too often in print. Then the title of the story "Lost in the Funhouse" struck him with so many implications that he put it on the cover of the book where it now applied less to Ambrose and more to Barth as well as the reader. Both are lost in the labyrinth of the world; to pass the time, the one creates his own more pleasurable labyrinths while the other gets lost in them.

"Lost in the Funhouse" has one more interest for us, and that is the character Ambrose. He occurs in two other *Funhouse* stories, "Ambrose His Mark" and "Water-Message"; he was also the main character in *The Seeker* or *The Amateur*, that novel Barth started between *The Sot-Weed Factor* and *Giles Goat-Boy* and never completed, from which these two stories are salvaged.[12] *The Seeker* (we recall from Barth's introduction to *Giles*) was about a man so detached from life that he stayed in the top room of a high tower, spying down on human affairs through a giant *camera obscura* as well as every kind of telescope and microscope. As the first page of the story's corrected typescript shows, this character's original name was Dan (see Figure 7). But Barth wanted a richer name, one that would connect with *light* and thus relate to the camera in the tower. He asked his Penn State colleague Philip Young for a suggestion, and Young thought of Ambrose, after the famous Ambrose Lightship outside New York harbor.[13] Young was ready to suggest an ancient connotation too, the food the Olympian gods ate to preserve their immortality; but he never got the chance to say that, because as Young remembers it, "Jack just threw up his hands and said 'Ambrose! Ambrosia!' and was off."

That conversation took place in early 1960, although it was not until 1967 when Barth wrote "Lost in the Funhouse" that he worked out a spot for those two connotations of Ambrose, demoting the food of the gods to the rank of dessert:

> In the maze . . . our hero found a name-coin someone else had lost or discarded: AMBROSE, suggestive of the famous lightship and of his late grandfather's favorite dessert, which his mother used to prepare on special occasions out of coconut, oranges, grapes, and what else. (P. 94)

Back in 1960, however, what he did was find another association with Ambrose—the saint of the same name—and used it as the high point in an early chapter he was then writing for *The Seeker*. Soon after, when he gave up on the novel, he saw enough unity of theme and action in the chapter to turn it into a short story, which he called "Ambrose His Mark," letting it stand on its own.

The story has to do with how Ambrose came to be called that. His mother, it seems, never bothered to name him; *Honig* or Honey was the closest she came. One day while she was nursing the child in the backyard, a swarm of bees settled on them, and the family decided that the swarm had been attracted by the bee-shaped birthmark near the child's eyes. Honey was thus an apter nickname than anyone had suspected. But it would not do for a proper name, so Uncle Konrad, who was convinced that the incident with the bees was "as clear a naming-sign as you could ask for" (p. 32), studied the encyclopedias he peddled for a living and learned that bees had swarmed over many famous people: Plato, Sophocles, Xenophon, and Ambrose the saint. Only the last seemed to the family an acceptable name for the boy; they even hoped it was a kind of prediction that the child would grow up to be a famous orator like

Saint Ambrose. Yet whereas the bees had swarmed over the saint's mouth, the bees in this case had swarmed over the child's eyes, so that the family hoped that this modern-day Ambrose might with luck become not only a great speaker but also a clear seer.

Their hope turned out to be more like a curse. In another Ambrose story, "Water-Message," the boy has grown to grade-school age, possessed of a way with words and much awareness. But these gifts only merit him the nickname "Sissy" and the frustration of knowing there is a great deal that he does not know. He is curious about sex and confused by it, a confusion that is represented by a grove of honey locusts, webbed with vines, described as a jungle and a labyrinth, where he likes to play. It is a confusion that will get worse as he grows older, that will be represented in the later story "Lost in the Funhouse" by another labyrinth, also related to sex, the amusement park maze where he gets lost. At the end of this story "Water-Message," however, he has no idea that things will get worse. In the shallows near a beach, he finds a note in a bottle and reads:

TO WHOM IT MAY CONCERN

YOURS TRULY (P. 56)

Like "Title," then, the story involves filling a blank, and Ambrose fills it optimistically, if somewhat obscurely:

> Ambrose's spirit bore new and subtle burdens. He would not tattle
> on Peter for cursing and the rest of it. The thought of his brother's
> sins no longer troubled him or even much moved his curiosity.
> Tonight, tomorrow night, unhurriedly, he would find out from
> Peter just what it was they had discovered. . . , and what-all done:
> the things he'd learn would not surprise now nor distress him, for
> though he was still innocent of that knowledge, he had the feel of
> it in his heart, and of other truth. (P. 56)

The one real truth he does not feel is that the future will always be a blank, that he will never learn the absolute knowledge he expects, that he will forever be as confused and uncertain as now.* In "Lost

---

* "Water-Message" was first published in *Southwest Review* (September 1963): 226–237. For inclusion in *The Funhouse*, Barth revised it ("to make

in the Funhouse" he has some experience with that truth, and although there are only these three Ambrose stories, which never depict him past adolescence, it is not hard to figure that he will continue to be *Lost* in one way or another. He will end up a man very like the rest of the articulate "characters" *in the Funhouse* (the spermatozoon making its "Night-Sea Journey," for example, or the story telling its "Autobiography," or the back-brother submitting his "Petition," or Menelaus composing his "Menelaiad," or the nameless minstrel writing his "Anonymiad"), led on and let down by love, dissatisfied by how he lives and what he writes, eager to come to an end, yet desperate to fill as much time as he can with his words.

Having taken up these Ambrose stories and several others on their own, we then ought also to group them with the rest and consider them all as the whole they make up. That the stories are meant to be considered as parts of a whole is something Barth emphasizes in his introductory "Author's Note."

> This book differs . . . from most volumes of short fiction. . . . It's neither a collection nor a selection, but a series; though several of its items have appeared separately in periodicals, the series will be seen to be have been meant to be received "all at once" and as here arranged. (P. ix)

For instance, the structure of the book is cyclical. The first tale, "Night-Sea Journey," concerns a spermatozoon swimming toward its half-understood destination, all the while brooding about its origins and purpose. The last tale, "Anonymiad," concerns a minstrel from

---

it less sentimental and obvious" he once told a friend), and to a degree he changed the tone of the conclusion. The revised version ends optimistically with Ambrose deciding that his confusion will pass, that he will learn about life soon enough; but the original version ends with Ambrose almost depressed. He does not find the blank letter that is in the revised version. Rather he comes upon the note "It was Bill Bell," and having been very curious about what great truth the message might contain, he is let down by its triviality, its meaninglessness. "The heart of Ambrose Mensch bore a new and subtle burden: neither despair nor yet disappointment, but a sweet melancholy" (*Southwest Review*, p. 237). Now he no longer is anxious to learn about sex and life in general, for he has the feel "of other, yet farther-reaching truth," the presumable "Barthian" truth that whatever he learns will be no more satisfying and meaningful than the water-message "It was Bill Bell."

ancient Greece who has been marooned on a barren island where he
scribbles yarns on goatskin, floating them out to sea in wine jugs.
The spermatozoon's account of its life, the minstrel's version of *his*
life—these things echo each other and to a degree are linked, the
spermatozoon possibly the start from which the minstrel sprang (as
it is possibly the start of *every* main character in the book), its
monologue about its life possibly one of the yarns that the minstrel
wrote down and launched. Barth intended these stories to be
complexly related, and in order that his intentions would be clear,
he prefaced *Lost in the Funhouse* with a device he called a "Frame-
Tale." On one side of a page are the words *Once upon a time there;*
on the other side are the words *was a story that began.* If the reader
follows the instruction Barth provides, if he cuts a strip from the
page and twists it once in the middle and joins the ends, then he
holds what is known as a Moebius strip. It is circular; it is involuted,
somewhat like a three-dimensional figure 8; it is continuous: "Once
upon a time there was a story that began once upon a time there was
a story that began once upon a time there was a story that
began. . . ." The device resembles the way the last story, its yarn
afloat, leads the reader back into the first story, its main character
aswim; it "becomes a metaphor," Barth has said, "for the content of
the book."[14]

In general that content has to do with characters who recognize
the insufferable facts of life (the kind of facts presented in "Two
Meditations" where we are told that things always get worse, that
we help to make them worse, that even when we recognize the
process we can do nothing to prevent it), and who then turn to storytelling to preserve their sanity ("Ill fortune, constraint and terror,
generate guileful art; despair inspires," we are told in "Glossolalia,"
p. 115). In respect to this twofold reaction by the characters, the
book can be more or less divided: up to "Lost in the Funhouse," and
after it. The main characters of "Night-Sea Journey," "Autobiography," and "Petition" bemoan their lot and plead for a change;
alternating with their stories are "Ambrose His Mark" and "Water-
Message," in which Ambrose has not yet realized how insufferable
life can be. But then in "Lost in the Funhouse" he comes to be like
the characters who came before: unable to deal with the facts,
which are in this case represented by the facts of sex. Those other
characters go no further than to complain and beg for help, however,
whereas Ambrose decides on a remedy, and that is to reject the

funhouse of life in favor of constructing funhouses of fiction, and his decision marks the turning point in the book.

Henceforth the main concern will be with moving out of the world into the world of fiction. In the next story, "Echo," for example, the title character "turns from life and learns to tell stories" (p. 100), but she discovers that her storytelling funhouse is as difficult to get around in as the other kind that Ambrose is lost in. For the gods have fixed her so that she can speak only in the words and voices of others, and that means she is doomed to wrestle with the basic narrative problems of viewpoint (the multiple voices she must work with) and time scheme (the past, present, and future that Barth reminds us in note 4 are embodied in one of her voices, Tiresias the prophet). She is doomed as well to wrestle with another problem that all storytellers are faced with: how to say what has already been said (she is an echo, after all) and yet say it in a fresh and new and valid way. After "Echo" there come the "Two Meditations" and the most explicit statement of the facts that *The Funhouse* has to offer: that the world is falling apart and we cannot stop it. And in the next piece, "Title," the main character finds that not only the world is falling apart, but also his personal life and his narrative art. "The worst is to come. Everything leads to nothing. . . . The final question is, Can nothing be made meaningful?" (p. 106). A shift from living to fictioning evidently brings about the same agony of understanding that one had in life. In the next piece, "Glossolalia," six speakers respond to such facts as rape and murder by riddling and hymning and warbling with as much attention to their sound patterns as to their glossed-over sense. But they have not removed the facts, they have only hidden them, and in the next piece, "Life-Story," the two converge, as indeed the title indicates. The main character suspects that he is a fictional character and that the fiction he is in is quite the sort he least prefers (p. 118); he wants to write a story about his condition but he cannot find a way to do it; the problems of his fiction and the problems of the fiction he is in mirror each other and merge. Then in the next-to-last piece, "Menelaiad," the main character more than suspects that he is in a story: he has been changed by a trick of Proteus into his voice telling his story and in short time he will actually be nothing but his story. Still he is not dismayed, he says (p. 167), and he is the sole character so far who is not. His life having become art, he is virtually immortal, what the story in "Autobiography" aspired to be but knew it never *would* be. Finally in "Anonymiad," a nameless minstrel has been forcibly removed from life and marooned on a lonely isle where he lives in the fiction he writes and for a time is content like Menelaus. But then he runs out of goatskin to write upon, and exhausted from his labor he is impatient to return to life and the girl he once knew, whom he wishes were there with him. And that urge brings us full circle, like the Moebius strip, to where the book began with the sperm and the beginning of life and the awful facts. The pattern of the book tells us that if the minstrel ever gets purely to living again he will shortly be put off by the facts of life and take to fictioning again until one day exhausted by his labor he will be impatient to return to life again. And so on. Circles and wheels and the Moebius strip comes round.

The book's shift from living in the world to living in the world of fiction is accomplished by other shifts. The early narrators tend to be young, the later ones old. The early fictional forms tend to be traditional, like an autobiography and a letter; the later ones tend to be innovative, like the story "Title," which deals in part with the death of the short story genre. The early times and settings tend to be contemporary and realistic; the later ones tend to be mythic and fantastic. And these shifts are related: the more the characters mature, the more they leave off the problems of living in favor of the problems of writing, and leave off the present real world in favor of an imaginary, timeless, literary one. In addition, the narrators tend to become more self-conscious as they go along, feeling ever more impotent and frustrated, losing body and mass and turning into the sound of their words.[15]

That is especially evident in the next-to-last story, "Menelaiad." It is about Menelaus and how he ruined his life by examining it too much: not understanding why his wife, Helen, loved him, he asked her over and over why she loved him until he became so great a nuisance that she ran off with Paris and caused the Trojan War. The structure of the story is like a set of Chinese boxes, a tale within a tale within a tale to the seventh degree, for the narrator, Menelaus, tells the reader how one night he told the sons of Nestor and Odysseus how he told Helen how he told Proteus how he told the daughter of Proteus how he rehearsed to Helen how he destroyed their love. Going through this complex story for the first time, the reader is often hard pressed to figure out who is saying what to whom; and the difficulty the reader has keeping hold of all the tales within tales is much like the difficulty Menelaus has had keeping hold of himself. "I'm not the man I used to be" (p. 147), Menelaus says, and he is right. Once, returning home from the Trojan War, he had to grapple with the shape-change Proteus in order to force the god to give him directions, and Proteus tricked him, ending his chain of transformations by turning into Menelaus. Now, with the body of Menelaus long since wormed, Proteus survives in the voice of Menelaus. And when his voice is no longer, we are told, Proteus will yet continue as the story of how Menelaus tried to understand love. And when even the story is no longer, Proteus will still go on in "terrifying last disguise" as the story's bitter theme: "the absurd, unending possibility of love" (p. 167).

Lastly, in "Anonymiad" we read all that is left, to an extent all that ever was, of a nameless joyless minstrel. It gathers various themes of *Lost in the Funhouse*—disastrous innocence, foolish love, paralyzing self-knowledge. It depicts again the terrible loneliness that comes to the writers in this book. And it sums up both Barth's career to date and the attitude he at times has had toward his calling. That is, the minstrel imagines that the *opera* he floated to sea has gone down undiscovered, much as Barth's *Floating Opera* went mostly unread for years. He recalls his works in a series that loosely resembles the order of Barth's own books: his "long prose fictions of the realistical, the romantical, and the fantastical" (p. 194), roughly corresponding with *The Floating Opera* plus *The End of the Road, The Sot-Weed Factor,* and *Giles Goat-Boy;* a long comic history that never survived (*The Seeker*); a major novel in which *tragedy* and *satire* were combined, words which the minstrel claims derive from the root word for *goat* (*Giles Goat-Boy* again). But in his middle years (Barth was thirty-eight when *Lost in the Funhouse* was published), the minstrel senses himself running down.

> I was older and slower, more careful but less concerned; as my craft improved, my interest waned, and my earlier zeal seemed hollow as the jugs it filled. Was there any new thing to say, new way to say the old? The memory of literature, my own included, gave me less and less delight; the "immortality" of even the noblest works I knew seemed a paltry thing. It appeared as fine a lot to me, and as poor, to wallow . . . in the stews as to indite the goldenest verses ever and wallow in the ages' admiration. (Pp. 194–195)

He comes out of his mood to write his "Anonymiad," a work that he hopes will be "neither longfaced nor idiotly grinning, but adventuresome, passionately humored, merry with the pain of insight, wise and smiling in the terror of our life" (p. 198). And he fails: nothing he ever tried quite turned out the way he hoped. So too with Barth and *Lost in the Funhouse,* some critics would say; however good the book is, they seem to feel that it is not as good as Barth wanted. Addressing an audience at the Library of Congress (May 1, 1967), Barth once remarked that if the pieces in *Lost in the Funhouse*

> are to be successful by my personal standards, they have to be more
> than just clever: if my writing was no more than the intellectual
> fun-and-games that *Time* magazine makes it out, I'd take up some
> other line of work. That's why one objects to the word *experiment,*
> I suppose: it suggests cold technique, and technique in art, as we all
> know, has the same sort of value that it has in love: heartless skill
> has its appeal, as does heartfelt ineptitude; but passionate virtuosity's
> what we all wish for, and aspire to. If these pieces aren't also moving,
> then the experiment is unsuccessful.

But for some critics, a few pieces *are* more clever than moving. Those critics are mostly Americans, unused to recent independent developments in European fiction very similar to *The Funhouse*— Italo Calvino's *Cosmicomics* (trans. 1968), for example. And it may be that these critics will warm to *The Funhouse* the more they are acquainted with and used to other books of its type. For now, at least, we can say that a good many of its pieces ("Night-Sea Journey," for example, "Lost in the Funhouse," "Menelaiad," and "Anonymiad") are moving and eloquent far out of proportion to their size. And at least one of these, the title piece, "Lost in the Funhouse," seems in retrospect the most important, progressive, trend-defining American short fiction of its decade.

7

John Barth:
His Fiction, 1968

Language *is* the matter of his books, as
much as anything else, and for that
reason ought to be "splendrously
musicked out."
> ("Publisher's Disclaimer"
> to *Giles Goat-Boy,* p. xiii)

These five books that we have so far examined are apparently
diverse and dissimilar. Their main characters range from a would-be
suicide to a paralytic, from a virgin poet to a randy goat-boy, from
a sperm to a story talking about itself, to a brother attached to the
small of his twin brother's back, to a young boy lost in a funhouse,
to an echo, to an author in debate with himself, to an author who
thinks he may be a character in a story, to Menelaus who has become
the sound of his own voice, to an anonymous minstrel abandoned
on a beach, launching casks full of his fiction. Their tones range from
comic to tragic to mystic, their modes from realistic to fantastic to
what will shortly be termed metaphysic. As Barth says, he does
not want to repeat himself.[1] Nevertheless, when we put these varying
books together we get the definite impression that they are all the
work of one man, that they amount to a corpus and not just a
scattering of members. There is something about them which co-
heres and unifies and stamps them with the trademark *Barth.*

Some critics, in particular Bruce Jay Friedman,[2] believe that this
unifying principle is "Black Humor." Barth does make us laugh,
after all, and what he makes us laugh about is seldom pleasant, often
grotesque, frequently hysterical: the antic postures that precede
mental breakdown. As Barth understands Black Humor, though, he
does not think his books are examples of it.

I beseech the Muse to keep me from ever becoming a Black Humorist. Mind, I don't object to Black Humorists, in their place, but to be numbered with them inspires me to a kind of spiritual White Backlash. For one thing they are in their way *responsible*, like more conventional social satirists: they dramatize—and good for them!—the Madness of Contemporary Society, of Modern Warfare, of Life with the Bomb, of What Have We Nowadays. But I say, Muse spare me (at the desk, I mean) from Social-Historical Responsibility, and in the last analysis from every other kind as well, except Artistic. Your teller of stories will likely be responsive to his time; he needn't be responsible to it.*

Rather than dramatize the madness of contemporary society as the Black Humorists do, Barth's aim has always been to "dramatize alternatives to philosophical positions,"[3] to imagine people with opposing philosophies and then to join them in battle. It is true that sections of Barth's work do have a certain modern relevance: the First World War in *The Floating Opera*, psychiatry in *The End of the Road*, somewhat altered versions of the Second World War, Communism, and the atomic bomb in *Giles Goat-Boy* along with not-so-altered versions of computer technology and today's multiversity. But these are not the main show; they are the backdrop before which the characters elaborate their respective conflicting ideas. The ideas themselves—that self-knowledge is generally bad news, to name one—are at home in any historical circumstance: seventeenth-century England and America in *The Sot-Weed Factor*, for example, and mythical Greece in *Lost in the Funhouse*.

If the term "Black Humor" has no strict application to Barth's work, neither does "literature of the absurd," what critics like Richard Kostelanetz have called it.[4] Barth admits that to the extent literature of the absurd "means a literary conceit that is, say, bizarre, grotesque in some way perhaps, nonrealistic or surrealistic, I suppose some of that could be said about *The Sot-Weed Factor*," *Giles Goat-*

---

* "Muse, Spare Me," *Book Week*, 26 September 1965, p. 28. Asked how he felt about student unrest at the University of Buffalo where he was teaching, he once replied that he was not the sort of person to get involved in such turmoil. "The fact the situation is desperate doesn't make it any more interesting. I'm prepared to be bored by the man who murders me. I'm totally bored by the situation, the critical importance of which I absolutely affirm." ("The Buffalo Strike," *New York Times*, 18 March 1970, p. 30.)

Boy, and parts of *Lost in the Funhouse;* they are not "written in a realistic manner." But literature of the absurd implies a specific world outlook as well as a particular technique of presentation, and Barth does not feel that such a world view is uniformly present in his work.

> To the extent that the term includes some kind of philosophical atitude that's one brand or another of nihilism, this is, in my case, truer of the earlier books which were, however, both done in a manner of conventional realism, than of the later ones where it seems to me the nihilism is not too important in the story.[5]

There is one term, however, that to date suits Barth's fiction almost exactly: *fabulation.* It comes from *The Fabulators* by Robert Scholes,[6] who in turn got it from one of the first books printed in Britain, a collection of Latin fables put into English by Caxton in 1484. As Scholes explains the word, it signifies a narrative in which the author has had great joy arranging words, designing structures, developing ideas. Whether the ideas are optimistic, pessimistic, or whatever, makes no difference; the joy in developing them, a joy that very often displays itself as humor, is the same. Put this way, fabulation is present just about everywhere in Barth, beginning with his first published novel, *The Floating Opera,* and its complex form of interflowing subplots. The book is fraught with formal curiosities. Each of its sentences is full of figures and implications that its narrator loves nothing better than to chase to their dens (p. 2); this love of implication, language, and design is typical of fabulation. The same love of these is present in the other books, with the exception of *The End of the Road* where the narrative structure is very simple and contrasts strikingly with the structures of the longer novels like *The Sot-Weed Factor,* in which Barth intended the plot to be "fancier" than *Tom Jones*[7] (indeed it seems among the most complex plots that one can think of). But although *The End of the Road* is not a full-blown fabulation because of its lack of elaborate design, it is almost one. Its narrator, Jacob Horner, vows that articulation is his absolute, and duels of philosophy his exhilaration (p. 112).

> To turn experience into speech—that is, to classify, to categorize, to conceptualize, to grammarize, to syntactify it—is always a betrayal

of experience, a falsification of it; but only so betrayed can it be dealt with at all, and only in so dealing with it did I ever feel a man, alive and kicking. (Pp. 112–113)

And these are sound fabulative principles. Regardless, *The Road* is more like a novel of ideas than a fabulation, and as such it can help us better understand the nature of fabulation. "[I work out] positions in order to contradict them," Barth has said. "My writing has finally nothing to do with polemics or the propagandizing of some philosophical position of my own, since my values change with the weather."[8] The others are novels of ideas only to a limited extent because for the most part they are much more. They have that extravagant artifice which *The Road* does not have and which makes the rest fabulations. "A more verbal kind of fiction" is what Scholes would say the rest were: "more shapely, more evocative,"[9] less realistic, more fantastic.

For the best writers, of course, technique is never gratuitous. They have something to say, a theme or idea that will control the narrative, give it direction and purpose, unity and coherence; and they need some way to say it, some particular style or manner that not only will feel right to themselves and sound good to their readers, but that also will perfectly represent, enhance, support, and in general be equivalent to their theme. At times they fuse the matter and manner so well that an analytic reader, thinking of a fiction's theme, ends up concentrating on its style—or thinking of its style, ends up concentrating on its theme: what is by now a classic example, Philip Young's analysis of Hemingway's story "Big Two-Hearted River."[10] Young demonstrated that the story's lean style, its short punchy sentences, its repeated words and rhythms, its monosyllabics, its concrete details and virtual absence of both abstraction and grammatical complexity, everything terse and highly controlled, are the exact counterpart of the story's theme which is that Nick Adams is close to a mental breakdown, must hold tight control of himself, must not think, must concentrate solely on things, must keep his life as lean and simple and ordered as he possibly can.

With this example from Hemingway in mind, one is curious to see how style and subject matter operate in Barth, a fictionist very different from Hemingway yet in one respect remarkably like him. Certainly Barth's fabulative style is the opposite of Hemingway's:

his sentences tend to be long, highly complex and easy flowing, his vocabulary extremely varied, polysyllabic, and abstract. Yet the same strict control of language and grammar is present in the styles of both writers, and that control turns out to represent *life* styles that serve the same function—to protect and keep sane, in Hemingway's case by focusing on things as a refuge from thought, in Barth's case by focusing on language as a refuge from the complexity of things.

How the style and subject matter relate in this way, how the style is indeed a part of the subject matter, becomes clearer if we look closely at the plots of these various books, or rather at *the* plot, because at heart they are basically one. The time and place vary from book to book, but the lives of the main characters remain just about the same. Early they are enamored of the world, happy, care-free, curious (the chief exception, Jacob Horner, whose early life is not recorded).

Todd Andrews: "Never have I regarded my boyhood as anything but pleasant." (*The Floating Opera*, p. 66; rev. ed. p. 58)

Ebenezer Cooke: "The twins grew quite enamoured of the world—especially Ebenezer." (*The Sot-Weed Factor*, p. 8)

Giles Goat-Boy: "What a fair and sprightly thing my kidship was!" (P. 8)

Nameless Sperm: "Hundreds of millions have expired since we surged forth, brave in our innocence, upon our dreadful way. 'Love! Love!' we sang then, a quarter-billion strong, and churned the warm sea white with joy of swimming!" ("Night-Sea Journey," *Lost in the Funhouse*, p. 4)

But then something horrid destroys their joyful innocence—they let their curiosity get the better of them, they start thinking about things too much, and before long they are mixed up in such dizzying complexity that they come near to falling into what Hemingway called Black Ass and Ebenezer Cooke calls *the pit*. Todd Andrews broods about his heart disease until he decides to kill himself; Jacob Horner about the lack of reasons for action until he is paralyzed; Ebenezer Cooke about the too-many reasons for action until *he* is paralyzed; Giles Goat-Boy about the meaning of life until he twice almost destroys the University with his counsel, is constricted by paradox and his mind almost cracked; the sperm about the meaning of his night-sea journey until he passes through "wonder, doubt, despair" (p. 4). That sperm is drawn unwillingly onto the Female Shore and transmits his "private legacy" (p. 12) of despair and rejection to the other characters in his book; they seem born old men, feeling as does Ambrose that "everything was wrong from the outset" (p. 88), pondering their place in the world until they end up wandering lost in it. To an audience at the Library of Congress (1 May 1967) Barth summed up his protagonists' dilemma this way:

> An imaginative enough temperament, given a liberal enough education, may find itself bound between two great premises of Western civilization: the lesson of Socrates, that the unexamined life isn't worth living, and the lesson of King Oedipus, that the well-examined life may turn out to be unlivable.

To Jacob Horner in *The End of the Road,* Rennie Morgan puts the matter more simply: "I think all our trouble comes from thinking too much and talking too much" (p. 125).

For the most part, the protagonists manage to survive only by means of a complicated system of role-playing that the Doctor in *The End of the Road* calls Mythotherapy. Its main assumption is clearly existential: that a person is free to choose and change his personality at will.* "We [are] the heroes of our own life stories," the Doctor maintains—

---

* In the sense that Mythotherapy encourages a person to imagine and act out any number of different roles, it is related to *the sense of possibility* that the Austrian novelist Robert Musil discussed in his multi-volume work, *The Man Without Qualities* (1930–1942). "Anyone possessing it does not say, for instance: Here this or that has happened, will happen, must happen. He uses his imagination and says: Here such and such might, should or ought to happen. And if he is told that something *is* the way it is, then he thinks: Well, it could probably just as easily be some other way. So the sense of possibility might be defined outright as the capacity to think how everything could 'just as easily' be, and to attach no more importance to what is than to what is not," trans. Eithne Wilkins and Ernst Kaiser (New York: Capricorn Books, 1965), p. 12. Barth was aware of *The Man Without Qualities* at the time he wrote *The End of the Road,* but he had not read it. When he did, he was fascinated that Musil had worked through the same kind of notions that he himself was working through independently (John Barth to D.M., 4 February 1970). See Tony Tanner's excellent article about the sense of the possible in Barth's *Lost in the Funhouse*: "No Exit," *Partisan Review* 86, no. 2 (1969): 293–295, 297–299.

we're the ones who conceive the story, and give other people the
essences of minor characters. But since no man's life story as a rule
is ever one story with a coherent plot, we're always reconceiving
just the sort of hero we are, and consequently just the sort of minor
roles that other people are supposed to play. (P. 83)

So when Barth's protagonists examine their lives and their world
until everything becomes intolerably complex and overpowering,
they escape by shifting their characters and distorting their situations, by putting on masks to face what they are up against. Thus
Todd Andrews is at times a rake, saint, cynic, and relativist; Jacob
Horner is a nihilist, an "owl, peacock, chameleon, donkey, and
popinjay" (p. 114); Ebenezer Cooke is a gentleman, poet, and virgin; Giles Goat-Boy is a student, hero, and Grand Tutor; Ambrose
Mensch is a storyteller, substituting his own kind of funhouses for
the one he is lost in.

> *Todd Andrews:* "It was to hide my enigmatic heart that I became
> a rake, a saint, and then a cynic. For when one mask no longer served
> its purpose of disguise, another had perforce to take its place."
> (P. 239; rev. ed. p. 223)

> *Jacob Horner:* "Assigning names to things is like assigning roles to
> people: it is necessarily a distortion, but it is a necessary distortion
> if one would get on with the plot." (P. 135)

> *Henry Burlingame to Ebenezer Cooke:* "Did you not by your own
> testimony resolve, not that you *were*, but that you'd *be* virgin and
> poet from that moment hence? Nay, a man *must* alter willy-nilly in's
> flight to the grave; he is a river running seawards, that is ne'er the
> same from hour to hour." (P. 125)

> *Giles Goat-Boy:* "I had lived in goatdom as Billy Bocksfuss the Kid,
> now I meant to live in studentdom as George the Undergraduate;
> surely there would be other roles in other realms, an endless succes-
> sion of names and natures." (P. 81)

> *Ambrose Mensch:* "He wishes he had never entered the funhouse.
> . . . Therefore he will construct funhouses for others and be their
> secret operator—though he would rather be among the lovers for
> whom funhouses are designed." (P. 97)

> *Echo:* "Afflicted with immortality she turns from life and learns to
> tell stories. . . . With her tongue-tried tales she amuses others and
> preserves her reason." (P. 100)

Nameless Minstrel: "If I never took seriously the world and its tire-
some concerns, it's because I was never able to take myself seriously;
and the reason for that, I've known for some while, is the fearsome-
ness of the facts of life . . . ; all this business of seizing life, grab-
bing hold with both hands—it must've scared the daylights out of
me from the first. While other fellows played with their spears, I
learned to play the lyre." (P. 171)

The trouble is that the protagonists are not always able to come
up with viable roles to play, and the drama of their lives, the interest
of their stories, are the consequence. "Many crises in people's lives
occur because the hero role that they've assumed for one situation or
set of situations no longer applies to some new situation," is what
the Doctor says (p. 84). And Todd Andrews says much the same
thing about the crises in *his* life.

My whole life . . . has been directed toward the solution of a
problem, or mastery of a fact [his heart disease]. It is a matter of
attitudes, of stances—of masks, if you wish, though the term has a
pejorativeness that I won't accept. During my life I've assumed four
or five such stances. . . . Each stance, it seemed to me at the time,
represented the answer to my dilemma, the mastery of my fact; but
always something would happen to demonstrate its inadequacy, or
else the stance would simply lose its persuasiveness, imperceptibly,
until suddenly it didn't work . . . and then I had the job to face
again of changing masks: a slow and, for me, painful process.
(Rev. ed. p. 16; orig. ed., somewhat different, p. 22)

His main crisis occurs when the mask of his cynicism no longer hides
his mind from his heart, and he is never all right again until he
assumes the new mask of relativist. Jacob Horner keeps in motion
by practicing a variety of roles until he commits adultery with a
friend's wife, and then he nearly immobilizes himself because, as
the Doctor points out, he gives himself the "wrong part" to play, that
of penitent instead of villain (p. 172). After the wife dies in an
abortion, he heads off with the Doctor and assumes the new role of
autobiographer (Scriptotherapy is the Doctor's name for this treatment), writing down his story in an effort to come to terms with
himself. Ebenezer Cooke's problem is that he adheres too long to his
role of moral innocent, and the crisis comes when he realizes how
much harm he has done himself and others by persisting in that

role.* At last he casts off innocence in favor of the role of penitent that did not sit so well on Jacob Horner. " 'Tis *atonement* I crave: redemption for my sins" (p. 739). In his case, penitence no more undoes or prevents disasters than it did in Jacob Horner's case; the difference is that Eben has enough strength of courage and will to make do with it. Giles Goat-Boy is as persistent as Eben: he chooses the role of Grand Tutor and sticks to it even after twice it almost gets him lynched. The crisis comes when he discovers he has been the wrong kind of Grand Tutor, thinking instead of feeling. The storytellers in *Lost in the Funhouse* stick to their roles as well, the crisis in their lives a continuing one—what and how to keep writing—since to stop would mean getting lost, pining away, or killing themselves in the funhouse of the world. "He reached for the sleeping pills cached conveniently in his writing desk and was restrained from their administration only by his being in the process of completing a sentence" ("Life-Story," p. 124). Barth's brief 1969 fiction, "Help! A Stereophonic Narrative for Authorial Voice,"[11] brings the storyteller to his ultimate crisis, the moment when he has run out of things to say and new ways to say them, when his role is in danger of collapse and he in danger of being crushed by the onrush of the world he has sought to shield himself against. "Help," the author murmurs, states, shouts, in various languages and synonyms, the format of his plea a musical score with time and rhythm notation as well as remarks about which sounds ought to come from which parts of the stage—another version of the disembodied voice. But no use,

---

* Eben's case is especially interesting. All the while he has tried to hang on to his moral innocence, he has been losing another kind of innocence, the kind that involves treating the world as though he is not a part of it. "The poet must engage himself in whate'er world he's born to, but shake free of't ere it shackle him," he resolves innocently. "He is a keen and artful traveller . . . that doth not linger overlong. He may play at love, or learning, or money-getting, or government—aye, even at morals or metaphysic—so long as he recalls 'tis but a game played for the sport of't, and for failure or success alike cares not a fart" (p. 474). Later, in the climactic scene where he gives up his moral innocence by marrying the poxed whore Joan Toast, whom he has greatly wronged, he also gives up his other innocence by understanding that he *is* a part of the world, that he does have to account for his actions, that his marriage to Joan Toast is one way to accept responsibility for the wrong he has done her.

no help comes, and he goes silent for ten seconds at the end, the last
ten seconds, the end of the road. "In some ways, it's a joke," Barth
says.

> Reviewers are fond of saying that some book by a writer is his plea
> for help. So I thought I'd write a piece that was exactly that. The
> idea was that the listener would hear this voice crying for help from
> all sides and speakers, and instead of responding, the listener would
> just sit where he was and be amused.[12]

Barth himself, of course, has not gone silent; he is at work on other
fictions; and each time one is curious what new role or new version
of an old role he is arranging for his characters to rehearse.

In terms of these five books at least, not only the lives of his
protagonists but also the dramatic situations in which they find
themselves have been quite similar. Each book brings its hero in
contact with a mythotherapist *par excellence:* Captain Adam, the
Doctor, Henry Burlingame, Harold Bray, Proteus, each so equipped
with multi-personalities that none is ever caught with a mask down.
They are what Henry Burlingame describes himself: Cosmopholites,
Suitors of Totality, Embracers of Contradictories, Husbands to all
Creation, Cosmic Lovers (*The Sot-Weed Factor,* p. 497); and they
function as foils and sometimes even as advisers to the protagonists
for whom role-changing is not the same easy, painless task. Their
Cosmophilism is at one end of a spectrum, the opposite of which is
Cosmopsis; both are based on a knowledge of the world's complexity,
but mobility is the nature of the first and paralysis of the second,
depending on whether the characters have sufficient strength of will
to dominate the world or sufficient weakness of will to be dominated.
In between, each protagonist vacillates, now paralyzed, now rela-
tively fluid. But whereas each book displays an instance of a hero's
paralysis (Todd Andrews backstage of the 1956 version of *The Floating Opera,* Jacob Horner in the bus terminal, Ebenezer Cooke in
his college quarters, Giles Goat-Boy at the start of his third round of
visits [p. 650], the nameless minstrel on the beach of his despondency
[p. 195]), only one shows a hero achieving any absolute mobility.
Menelaus who wrestles with Proteus and is changed into him, the
possibility of all things. But that is a special circumstance; not
Menelaus but Proteus is in charge; Menelaus is the medium to
Proteus the message, so that he is no more in control of things than

he was before. The reason these protagonists are never able to become fully mobile is related to the nature of those who are. In chapter 2 on *The End of the Road,* it was noted that the Doctor seemed a fugitive from another dimension; so too seem his kind. They do not somehow belong in this world, they are not exactly human. It is as though they are spirits from underground, or messengers from gods, or perhaps like Proteus gods indeed, come to advise mankind on a way to get along. But their advice is not altogether practicable because the talent required is not properly human. So Barth's heroes do their best to continue role-playing in order not to think too seriously about things; but their masks eventually fail, their minds get to probing the complexity that their masks made simple, and unable to bear very much reality they scramble madly for new masks while around and around them dance the cosmic changlings.

Mutability, multiplicity, complication: that is the make-up of the world in Barth's fiction. The world was not always so; as we have seen: in the beginning it was constant, whole, and simple, but then either it broke up on its own, or else the gods played a joke and blew it apart, or else the unity was only in man's mind and once he reached a certain age, he lost his intellectual innocence, ruptured his mind's virginity, and had things split apart for him *that* way. Whatever the cause, this fragmentation is the basis for a myth that goes about as far back as any, and Barth's major explication of the myth is that passage already noted in *The Sot-Weed Factor* where Burlingame lectures Cooke on geminology. "In every land and time folk have maintained that what we see as *two* are the fallen halves of some ancient *one*," he says—

> that night and day, Heaven and Earth, or man and woman were long since severed by their sinful natures, and that not till Kingdom Come will the fallen twain be a blessed one. . . . Thus all men reverence the act of fornication as portraying the fruitful union of opposites.
> (Pp. 493–494)

This passage accounts for the vast amount of fornication in Barth's work. His characters are dissatisfied alone, they feel the urge to become one with another, but the fornications they conduct are not the fruitful unions that Burlingame makes them out to be. At best they bring temporary relief; at worst the pox. The only time fornication ever results in wholeness is when Giles unites with Anastasia in the belly of the computer and he has a vision of the single, seamless universe. But his vision is temporary, things soon fall back apart, and his life thereafter is a depressing anticlimax. Those characters are wise who, like Jacob Horner, expect little from sex and can joke about it. "The whole vaudeville of the world . . . is but a fancy mating dance," he says. And he delights in the idea of telling some extragalactic sightseer,

> On our planet, sir, males and females copulate. Moreover, they enjoy copulating. But for various reasons they cannot do this whenever, wherever, and with whomever they choose. Hence all this running around that you observe. Hence the world. (P. 87)

Coupled with fornication is the number of love triangles in Barth's work—in one of his first published stories, "Lilith and the Lion," and in his unpublished master's project, *Shirt of Nessus* (see the next chapter where both are described), in *The Floating Opera, The End of the Road, The Sot-Weed Factor, Giles Goat-Boy*, "Petition," "Lost in the Funhouse," "Echo," "Menelaiad," and "Anonymiad." To be sure, one attraction that the triangle has for Barth is purely technical: "it has probably more latent dramatic possibility than any other situation between characters that one can dream up," he has said.

> If you have for thematic reasons a character who represents single-mindedly some position, then the dictates of drama suggest that you're likely to have another character who's his antithesis—these are likely to be male characters if they're embodiments of ideas—then you need a woman between to be the catalyst for the reaction between the two males so that you can work out your dialectic.[13]

But the triangle has other attractions besides technical; it is thematic, a further instance of fragmentation. As a rule, it is composed of two sets of opposites: man and woman (physical), man and man (philosophical). And if these sets could ever become fused, as Burlingame dreams will someday happen with himself, Ebenezer and Anna, that would be a unity indeed. " 'Tis not the one nor the other I crave, but the twain as one," Burlingame says to Eben.

Perchance I'll come upon you [and Anna] *sack a sack* as did Catullus
on the lovers, and like that nimble poet pin you to your work—nay,
skewer you both like twin squabs on a spit! (Pp. 490–491)

But that is not physically possible. A substitute harmony is emotional, but it occurs only once in Barth's work, among Todd Andrews,
Jane Mack, and Harrison Mack in *The Floating Opera*. Says Todd:

> She was . . . my mistress, and a fine one. To make the triangle
> equilateral, Harrison Mack was my excellent friend, and I his. Each
> of the three of us loved the other two as thoroughly as each was
> able. (Rev. ed. p. 19; orig. ed., somewhat different, p. 26)

The triangle does not remain equilateral, though; jealousy erupts,
and by the end of the book the geometry is broken. At least it is a
good-natured breakup, the sole example of its kind. In the other
books, the triangles are far from equilateral; the men are at odds
over their woman and their ideas, and what started out as the need
to merge with someone else turns out to accomplish no wholeness
and actually to create dissension.

The triangles in *The Sot-Weed Factor, Giles Goat-Boy,* and
"Petition" are extra-complicated: they include twins, although with
Giles and Anastasia the twinship is not actual, and their relationship
tends to prevent both the union of the two and the consummation of
the triangles they are in. There is something sacred and mystic
about twins, Burlingame is sure, and if they ever come together, he
says, "their union is brilliance, totality, apocalypse—a thing to yearn
and tremble for!" (p. 497). But Eben and Anna recoil because of
the age-old taboo against incest; their minds in short deny the
natural tendency of their bodies to return to the condition of oneness
that they shared in their mother's womb. In *Giles,* the goat-boy does
join with Anastasia, but they are innocent of the knowledge that they
may be twins, and when they learn of the possibility, they decide to
stay apart. Giles's decision too is of mind over body; he is not so
much affected by the "artificial" taboo against incest (pp. 482–483)
as he is by his theory that a Grand Tutor should not "play favorites
among his Tutees." When at least he learns to feel more than think,
he comes together with Anastasia in the belly of the computer and
their union *is* brilliance, totality, apocalypse. They may not be twins,

but they are half-brother, half-sister, and that is the closest fusion Barth has so far allowed, albeit eventually depressing. In "Petition," the twins are unique, a brother attached to the small of his twin brother's back. If they were as alike in mind as in body, they "could make any open-minded woman happy beyond her most amorous reveries—or, lacking women, delight each other" (p. 62). But they are nothing alike. Their relationship prefigured by Dr. Eierkopf riding pick-a-back on Croaker's shoulders in *Giles Goat-Boy,* the brother behind is slight, articulate, educated, and withdrawn; the brother in front is gross, incoherent, ignorant, and gregarious. They did not get along well to begin with; now a woman has come into their lives, and while they both are in love with her, only the brother in front has his way with her. It is the same old story of dissension; their stage act they call *The Eternal Triangle;* in public they are arranged ironically as one, in private they are at odds.

That brother in back is writing about his life, and by now the pattern of that life is familiar to us, so much is it like the lives of Barth's other main characters. He started out innocent and then discovered that things were not as simple as he believed:

> In earliest babyhood I didn't realize I was two; it was the intractability of that creature always before me—going left when I would go right, bawling for food when I would sleep, laughing when I wept—that opened my eyes to the possibility he was other than myself; the teasing of playmates, who mocked our contretemps, verified that suspicion, and I began my painful schooling in detachment. (P. 64)

Detachment is the stance he has assumed to bear his condition:

> I am by nature withdrawn, even solitary: an observer of life, a meditator, a taker of notes, a dreamer if you will. . . . I . . . am stoical, detached as it were—of necessity, or I'd have long since perished of despair. (P. 62)

Still he has not been able to keep up his mask of detachment; he has fallen in love with the woman his brother is going to marry; and this crisis prompts him to act in ways that are typical of Barth's heroes. He distorts the situation by imagining a love affair between himself and a woman who lives within the body of the woman he cannot have. What is more, he writes about his situation, displacing his misery onto paper in an eloquent articulation of his case. His ostensible purpose is to petition the King of Siam for a way of releasing him from his bond. Yet when he says that "the alternative [to writing this petition] is madness" (p. 63), one suspects that he has another reason for writing, that the act is sanative, a preoccupation and diversion.

We know that writing has that effect on Ebenezer Cooke: he composes his poem *The-Sot-Weed Factor* for the ostensible purpose of instructing others how to survive the wickedness of Maryland (p. 458), but in addition he manages to sidetrack his mind from his problems.

> He could scarcely wait to launch into composition: as soon as he was strong enough he left his bed, but only because the writing desk in his chamber was more comfortable to work at; there he spent day after day, and week after week, setting down his long poem. . . . All thoughts of suicide departed from him for the time, as did, on the other hand, all thoughts of regaining his lost estate. He was not disturbed or even curious about the absence of any word from Henry Burlingame. When . . . his legal wife Susan Warren reappeared at Malden, he thanked her brusquely for her aid in nursing him back to health, but although . . . she had become a prostitute exclusively for the Indians, he neither protested her activities . . . on the one hand, nor sought annulment of his marriage on the other. (Pp. 458–459)

And we know that Ambrose and his kind in *The Funhouse* write for the same purpose: the author in "Life-Story" who does not swallow his sleeping pills because he is in the process of composing a sentence; the nameless minstrel in "Anonymiad" who endures his solitary exile because he has "imagination for realm and mistress, and her dower language!" (p. 191). All through Barth's work there have been passages where language itself is center stage, the figures that Todd Andrews loves nothing better than to chase to their dens, the magnificent paragraph-long first sentence of *The Sot-Weed Factor*, the sheer brilliance of vocabulary at the start of the first reel of *Giles Goat-Boy*.

The End of the Road has been taken out of sequence because one section in it is especially illustrative. Close to the beginning, Jacob Horner unwinds a sentence describing how he sits in the Doctor's Progress and Advice Room.

> Arms folded, akimbo, or dangling; hands grasping the seat edges
> or thighs, or clasped behind the head or resting in the lap—these
> (and their numerous degrees and variations) are all in their own
> ways satisfactory positions for the arms and hands, and if I shift
> from one to another, this shifting is really not so much a manifesta-
> tion of embarrassment, or hasn't been since the first half-dozen
> interviews, as a recognition of the fact that when one is faced with
> such a multitude of desirable choices, no one choice seems satis-
> factory for very long by comparison with the aggregate desirability
> of all the rest, though compared to any *one* of the others it would
> not be found inferior.

And he goes on to say that, if the reader should choose

> to consider that final observation as a metaphor, it is the story of my
> life in a sentence—to be precise, in the latter member of a double
> predicate nominative expression in the second independent clause
> of a rather intricate compound sentence. (Pp. 2–3)

That is pure language, devoid of any referent except itself. Later in
Lost in the Funhouse there is another instance of it. Barth edits
certain words out of "Title" (including out of the title) and substi-
tutes their grammatical equivalents.

> Try to fill the blank. Only hope is to fill the blank. Efface what
> can't be faced or else fill the blank. With words or more words,
> otherwise I'll fill in the blank with this noun here in my prepositional
> object. (P. 105)

Barth does this in spite of what the narrator says at the end, that

> literature's not likely ever to manage abstraction successfully, like
> sculpture for example. . . . Because wood and iron have a native
> appeal and first-order reality, whereas words are artificial to begin
> with, invented specifically to represent. . . . Weld iron rods into
> abstract patterns, say, and you've still got real iron, but arrange
> words into abstract patterns and you've got nonsense. (P. 112)

But the story demonstrates that words *can* be arranged in abstract
patterns without being nonsense, provided that there is a reason for
it as here where the narrator of the story feels that he has come to
the end of the road of his civilization, his life, and his storytelling

art: the grammar communicates itself because the author has nothing else to communicate, and paradoxically by communicating nothing he has actually communicated *something*. Jacob Horner's grammar-ful sentence is similar in purpose. He has difficulty making choices and following any course of action through to its consequences. He sees little value in anything—except grammar. It has a logic and a meaning all its own, and it keeps him moving, word after word after word. The narrator of "Help!" has just about run out of words, though. He is reduced to repeating *help* in various tones and synonyms until by the close of the piece the word has been repeated so often that it has lost its significance. It is itself then, a jumble of letters and sounds, and at last it too is lost, refined out of existence into ten seconds worth of silence that speak an infinity of words.

The elaborate structures of Barth's fiction (again, with the exception of *The End of the Road*) tend to have an importance of their own also. No doubt, the interflow of plot in *The Floating Opera* is an image of the way life works, and the enormous plot complications of *The Sot-Weed Factor* that are tied neatly at the end are a representation of the distortion we normally make out of life by taking pains to find a pattern in its disorder. But we also re-ceive a pleasure from recognizing the principles by which the structures have been elaborated. We are impressed by the wheels within wheels of *Giles Goat-Boy*, by the echoes that roll through *Lost in the Funhouse*. The balance and order of these extravagant designs are soothing and resolving; they give a feeling of wholeness, a feeling that one is certain came to the man who arranged them, both the writers within the fictions and the writer *of* the fictions.

That is what fabulation is all about: a delight in putting to-gether and balancing and implicating and designing. The process is at heart a rejection of life and the world in favor of the life and world of art (indeed for Barth and most of his characters, writing seems virtually equatable with living), and the process is demon-strated in the movement of Barth's fiction away from the real world of *The Floating Opera* and *The End of the Road*, through the fantastic world of *The Sot-Weed Factor* and *Giles Goat-Boy* to the universe of language in *Lost in the Funhouse* and "Help!" The tech-nique has become metaphysical, in the sense in which we apply it to certain English poems of the seventeenth century. Puns, par-adoxes, conceits abound everywhere in Barth's work but nowhere as frequently as in *The Funhouse*—and that because they *are* the funhouse.

The reductive nature of that fiction "Help!," however, represents a dead end to abstract language as a value much as *The End of the Road* was itself a dead end, there in terms of realism. Both marked for Barth the need for a new direction in his career, and if the fiction he was now shortly to write would still have some affinity with what had come before, its retelling of myth, for example, as in *Lost in the Funhouse,* or its preponderance of et ceteras, already used in *The Funhouse* too (everything's been said, all more of the same), he would as well try something new, abstraction again but now not so much in terms of language as in structure, in this case a spiral one, and more important (indeed quite unexpected and surprising) a different kind of theme, away from pessimism toward a full-hearted embracement of life, especially love, and a reliance on writing not as an anodyne to painful living but as a metaphor the truth of which is that the joy one can take in words is the same as the joy one can take in everything.

8

John Barth
in Chiaroscuro, 1969

Whether 'tis good or bad in itself, certain your
Hymn to Innocence is of greater interest to one
who knows the history of its author than to one
who knows not a bean of the circumstances that
gave it birth.

> (Burlingame to Eben Cooke,
> *The Sot-Weed Factor,* p. 122)

The Library of Congress stands across the street from the Capitol
Building in downtown Washington. It has a large copper dome and
a fountain at its entrance displaying the Court of Neptune; inside
in a deep, pillared hall, a guard requires all visitors to list any
equipment they are bringing with them, a camera, say, or a tape
recorder. (Later, when they leave, they match their equipment
with the list they gave the guard, and anything more than what is
on the list is suspected stolen.)

The Manuscript Division of the Library of Congress is in an
annex across the street behind the main building. To get there one
goes through the main library building, walks down a tunnel that
leads deep under the back street, and comes up in the annex where
a guard requires him to leave his coat, hat, or anything else un-
necessary for research. The visitor then takes one of many elevators
up to the third floor where the Manuscript Division is located, passes
the guard at the entrance to the manuscript reading room, and
identifies himself to the official in charge, an identification that in
rare cases must include one's passport and/or a letter of endorsement
from those whose manuscripts the visitor has come to see. In the
present case, the donor of the manuscripts has imposed restrictions
as to who can photograph, Xerox, or even look at them, so that it has

been necessary to bring along a letter granting these specific permissions.

The visitor is next required to fill in a registration form. He listens to the official explain the library's rules—no eating in the reading room, no smoking, no use of fountain pens, no writing on the manuscripts, no placing of objects on them, no rearranging them. Last, he is handed a request form on which he writes the name of the collection he wants to see and how much of it. The list given to an attendant, it takes no more than five minutes for the attendant to return, pushing a cart with six manuscript boxes on top, the largest amount a visitor is allowed to have at any time. The boxes are of cardboard, sturdy, narrow, close to fourteen inches high, closed on top by a flap, and it is marked in front that they are a part of the John Barth collection.

If the Manuscript Division allowed the complete collection to be taken from the shelves in the next room and spread out here on one of the large tables, there would be sixteen boxes, containing most of what Barth wrote for his first four novels as well as a small portion of what he wrote for *Lost in the Funhouse*. Each novel is at least represented by a handscript draft, two typescript drafts, and a set of galley proofs. The large novels are represented by a good deal more: two plot outlines for *The Sot-Weed Factor* in company with a calendar of the novel's events, a list of each character's politics, a group of 150 library punch cards on each of which is recorded some character's life history, a map of Eben Cooke's adventures in Maryland. For *Giles Goat-Boy*, there are a long, handwritten essay in which Barth explored the theme of the book before he began to write it, a tightly ordered outline of the plot which he submitted to his publisher very early in composition, some extended notes on what he had learned about the myth of the wandering hero. Apart from all this, the collection has handscript speeches that Barth read at the Library of Congress, the University of Maryland, and Harvard, each one about some stories in *Lost in the Funhouse*. It also has handscript drafts of Barth's two important non-fiction pieces, "Muse, Spare Me" and "The Literature of Exhaustion," and finally it has some remarks about Jorge Luis Borges, John Updike, and Joseph Heller, written to introduce them to an audience at Buffalo.

Sixteen boxes full. They illustrate a good deal of what he once

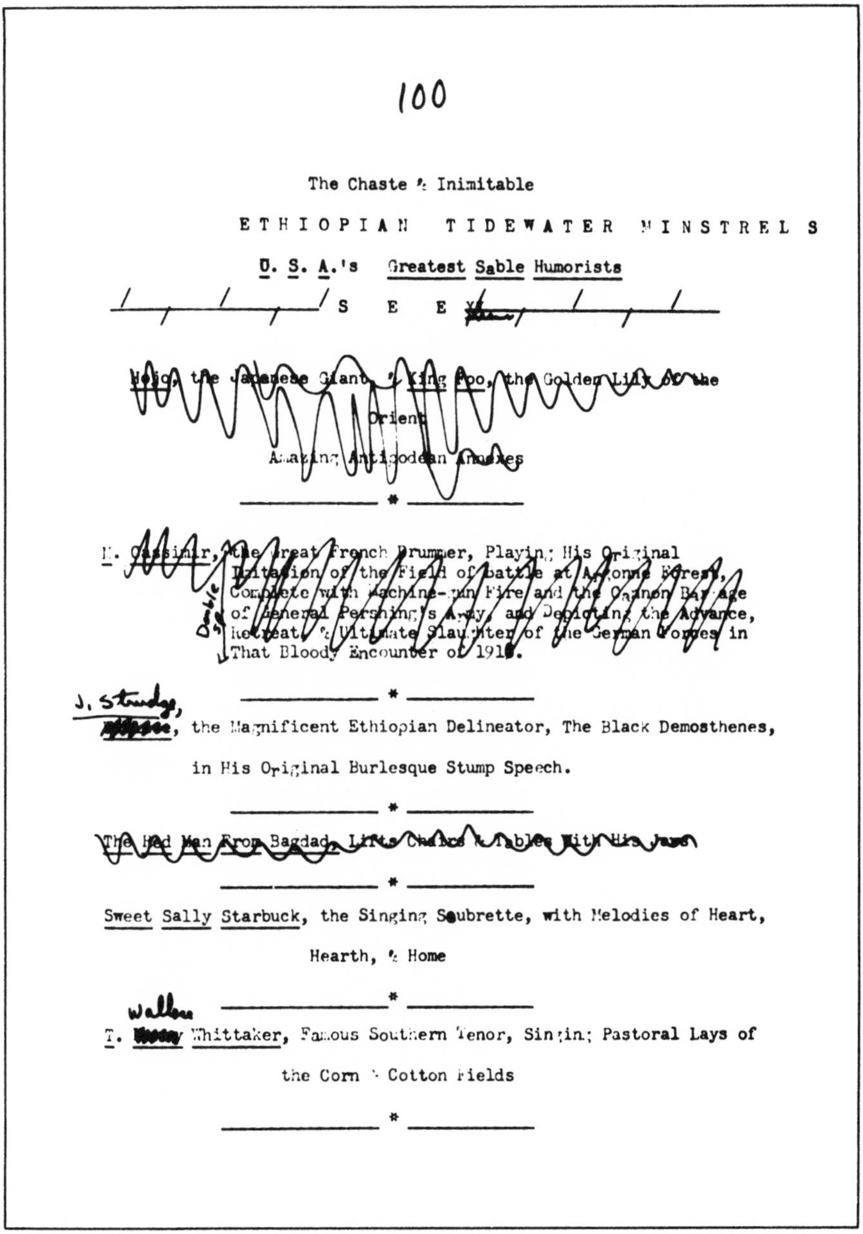

The Chaste & Inimitable

E T H I O P I A N   T I D E W A T E R   M I N S T R E L S

U. S. A.'s   Greatest Sable Humorists

/   /   /   S   E   E   ~~You~~   /   /

~~Hojo the Japanese Giant, King Foo, the Golden Lily of the~~
~~Orient~~

~~Amazing Antipodean Annexes~~

* * *

M. ~~Cassimir, The Great French Drummer, Playing His Original~~
~~Imitation of the Field of battle at Argonne Forest,~~
~~Complete with Machine-gun Fire and the Cannon Barrage~~
~~of General Pershing's Army and Depicting the Advance,~~
~~Retreat & Ultimate Slaughter of the German Forces in~~
~~That Bloody Encounter of 1918.~~

* * *

J. Sturdy,
~~Jubal Jones,~~ the Magnificent Ethiopian Delineator, The Black Demosthenes,

in His Original Burlesque Stump Speech.

* * *

~~The Red Man From Bagdad, Lifts Chairs & Tables With His Jaws~~

* * *

Sweet Sally Starbuck, the Singing Saubrette, with Melodies of Heart,

Hearth, & Home

Wallace
T. ~~Tracy~~ Whittaker, Famous Southern Tenor, Singing Pastoral Lays of

the Corn & Cotton Fields

* * *

Figure 4.   A corrected typescript page from *The Floating Opera,* showing part of an advertisement for a minstrel show (reproduced with Barth's permission).

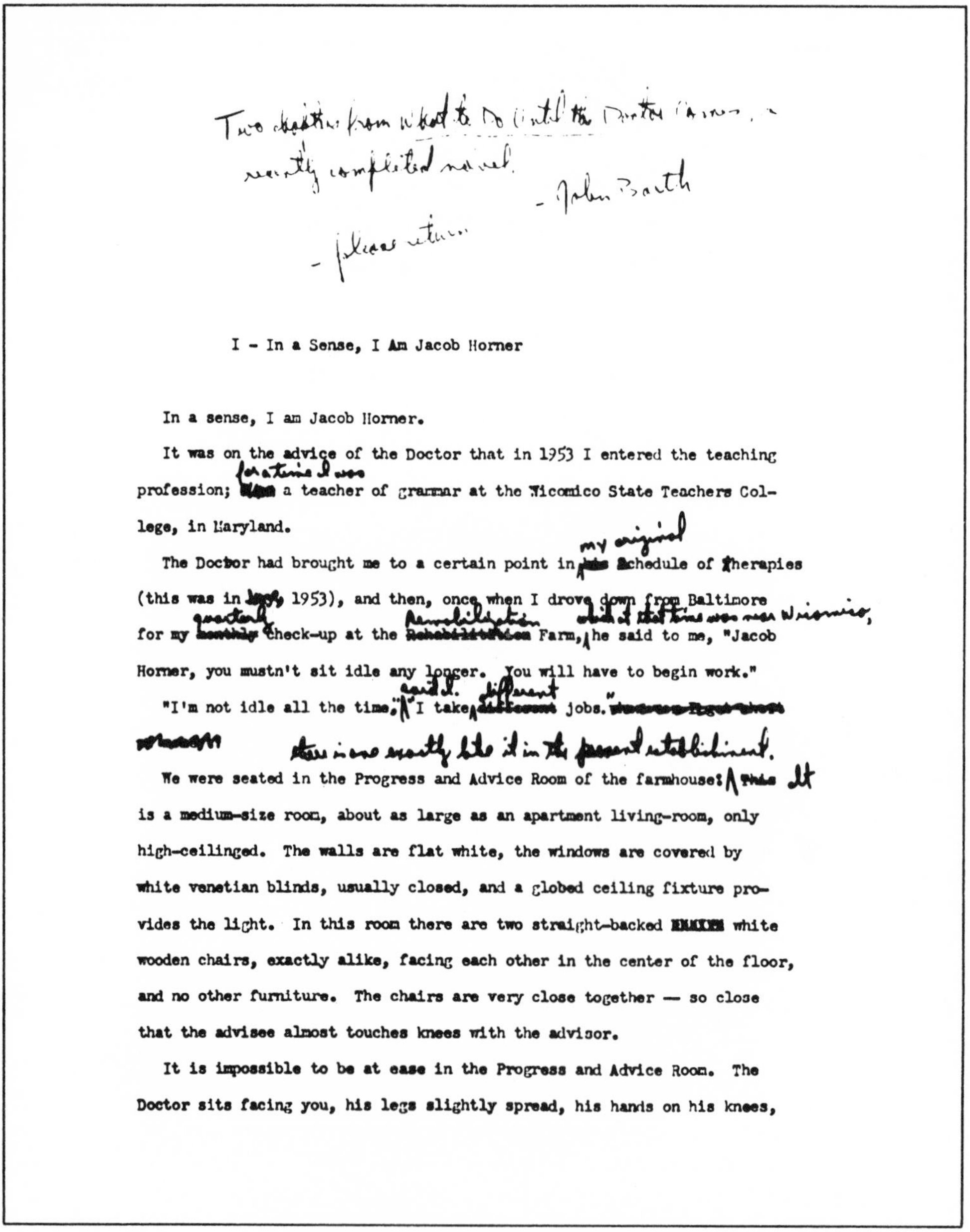

Two chapters from What to Do Until the Doctor Comes, a recently completed novel.

— John Barth

— please return

I - In a Sense, I Am Jacob Horner

In a sense, I am Jacob Horner.

It was on the advice of the Doctor that in 1953 I entered the teaching profession; for a time I was a teacher of grammar at the Wicomico State Teachers College, in Maryland.

The Doctor had brought me to a certain point in my original schedule of therapies (this was in 1953), and then, once when I drove down from Baltimore for my quarterly check-up at the Remobilization Farm, which at that time was near Wicomico, he said to me, "Jacob Horner, you mustn't sit idle any longer. You will have to begin work."

"I'm not idle all the time," I said. "I take different jobs."

there is none exactly like it in the present establishment.

We were seated in the Progress and Advice Room of the farmhouse. It is a medium-size room, about as large as an apartment living-room, only high-ceilinged. The walls are flat white, the windows are covered by white venetian blinds, usually closed, and a globed ceiling fixture provides the light. In this room there are two straight-backed white wooden chairs, exactly alike, facing each other in the center of the floor, and no other furniture. The chairs are very close together — so close that the advisee almost touches knees with the advisor.

It is impossible to be at ease in the Progress and Advice Room. The Doctor sits facing you, his legs slightly spread, his hands on his knees,

Figure 5. The corrected first page of typescript for *The End of the Road* (reproduced with Barth's permission). *What to Do Until the Doctor Comes* was the novel's original title.

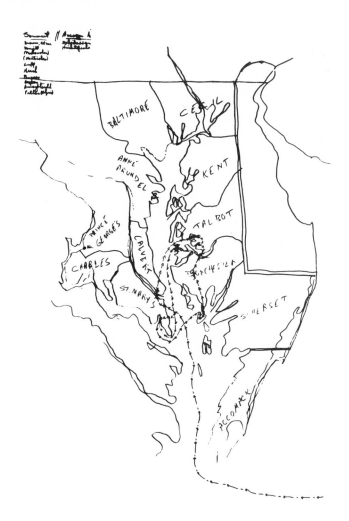

Figure 6. Barth's map of Eben Cooke's adventures in Maryland (reproduced with his permission). Eben sails north up the Chesapeake Bay,
walks the plank, and swims west to St. Mary's County where he travels
north into Calvert County and from there northeast by boat to Oxford
(Ox. on the map). He next heads south to Cambridge (Cam.), west to
Malden (the starred M), far south by boat to St. Mary's City (S.M.C.),
east by boat to Bloodsworth Island, north to the middle of Dorchester
County, and from there the map and the novel differ. Instead of moving
northeast to Cambridge as the map indicates, Eben is captured by pirates
and taken northwest into the Chesapeake Bay where he is forced to jump
ship and swim east to Malden.

119

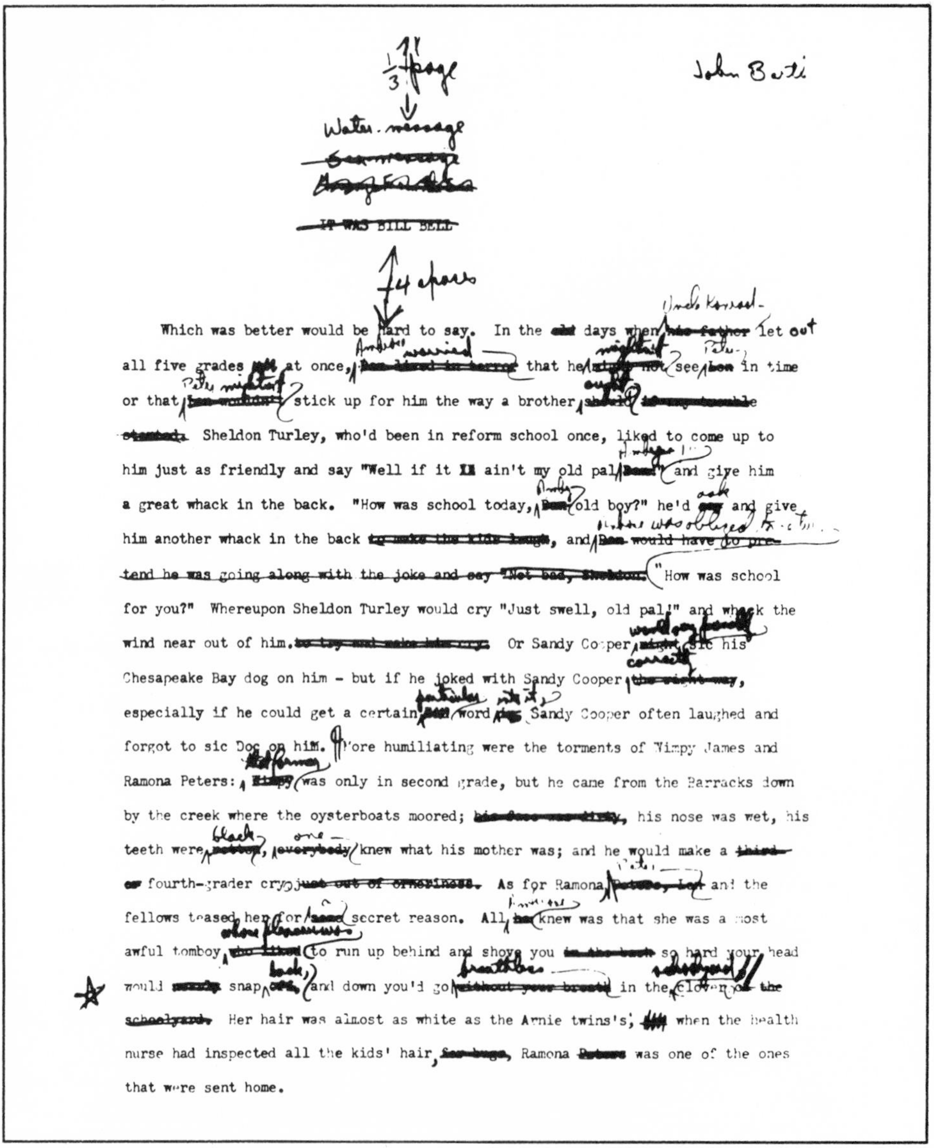

Figure 7. The corrected first page of typescript for "Water-Message," an Ambrose story in *Lost in the Funhouse* (reproduced with Barth's permission). Fairly typical of how meticulously Barth revises, the page is especially interesting because, re-reading it, Barth has chosen the name "Ambrose" and on the second line and elsewhere added it over the character's previous name, "Dan." Note also the several earlier titles: "It Was Bill Bell," "Message From the Sea," and "Sea-Message."

told an interviewer about his working methods. How he outlines and researches a project thoroughly before he begins to dramatize it. How he writes first in longhand:

> I don't type very well or very fast. I also find it makes a difference in style. I don't write in a short, abbreviated style—my sentences tend to go on a little way before they stop. When I compose in long hand I get a more eloquent line than when I try to write on a type-writer. So I compose in this notebook, which must be like the super-stitions athletes have. This is the same [kind of] notebook I had as a student. I usually write until it's full and then transfer it into these 10-cent store binders which I have a great trove of. When it's all done, usually a good-sized novel, one like *The Sot-Weed Factor*, would fill about four of these binders.[1]

How he revises:

> I do most of the rewriting while I'm writing. The first thing I do in the morning is edit and rewrite what I wrote the day before and then go on. I find the resultant manuscript is very sloppy, full of emendations and scratches-over. But then when I have the draft done and go back to revise it not a whole lot has to be done. Usually most of the revision has occurred by that time. The trouble with this system is that no one else can type it except me; no one else can make sense of it. Then I type a draft, revise the typed draft, and if necessary re-type the typed draft, although it's usually not necessary, and then make the final revisions in the galleys.

The manuscripts cannot, of course, tell us about all his working methods; they have no way to show us, for example, how he gets started writing each day.

> I . . . read the last day's work to get in the spirit of the thing again and go on from there. One thing which Hemingway said and that I believe in very firmly and try to do regularly is to stop at a good going place, instead of stopping at the end of a chapter. If you stop in the middle of a sentence, even around 4 o'clock, you can usually pick up in the middle of the sentence once your pen gets going, and get started for the next day.

There are other things they cannot let us know: what sort of man wrote them, why he wrote them, what pressures of experience were behind them, starting on May 27, 1930, when he was born John Simmons Barth, Jr., in the town of Cambridge, Maryland.

Cambridge is a small port up the Choptank River on Maryland's Eastern Shore. It is also the Dorchester County seat and the focus of local crabbing, oystering, fishing, muskrat-trapping, duckhunting, and sailing. The principal attraction is the main street, High Street, near where the town's first two houses were built more than 260 years ago, their slave quarters and porch columns made of ships' masts yet remaining. The street itself Barth accurately described in his first published novel, *The Floating Opera:*

> a wide, flat boulevard . . . gently arched with edge-laid yellow brick. . . . One is tempted to describe it as lined with mansions, until one examines it in winter, when the leaves are down and the trees gaunt as gibbets. Mansions there are—two, three of them—but the majority of the homes are large and inelegant. What makes High Street lovely are the trees and the street itself. The trees are enormous: oaks and cottonwood poplars that rustle loftily above you like pennants atop mighty masts; that when leaved transform the shabbiest houses into mansions; that corrugate the concrete of the wide sidewalks with the idle flexing of their roots. An avenue of edge-laid yellow bricks is the only pavement worthy of such trees, and like them, it dignifies the things around it. Automobiles whisper over this brick like quiet yachts; men walking on the outsized sidewalk under the outsized poplars are dwarfed into dignity. (Rev. ed. pp. 53–54)

Down High Street, past Christ Church and the courthouse, is Long Wharf and the Choptank River; and growing up, Barth sometimes used to see an old, flatbottom showboat, *The Floating Theater,* moored there for an evening performance—years later to remember the boat and its Captain Adam and High Street and use them all in his book *The Floating Opera.* And he sometimes heard, along with his twin sister Jill, how fifteen miles to the west, at the mouth of the Choptank, there was an estate, Malden, that was long ago owned by a fellow, Ebenezer Cooke, who fancied himself the poet-laureate of Maryland—years later to remember that too and use it along with Cambridge and a twin brother and sister in his third published novel, *The Sot-Weed Factor.* Cambridge was also to be a part of his master's project, *Shirt of Nessus,* although in that novel (unpublished) his home town was thinly disguised as the twin towns Hudson and Surrey, disguised along with his father who is yet recognizable because he appears in his actual roles of restaurant owner and chief judge of the local Orphan's Court. Cambridge was to turn up as well in the Ambrose stories of *Lost in the Funhouse*, this time going by the name of East Dorset.

Not that he or anyone else guessed he would grow up to write about these things. The "talent must have come later," his father remembers. "I didn't see it when he was younger. He always liked stories, though—I like to tell stories myself. Funny stories."[2] And his older brother, Bill, agrees: "Looking back I'd never have expected him to be a writer. . . . I will say he always had a vivid, overactive imagination."[3] About the strongest sign of his career to come, not a very strong sign at that, was a column he wrote for his high school newspaper, titled "Ashcan Pete." Says his freshman high school English teacher:

> When he took it over it was gossipy, you know, Bill likes Sue, that sort of thing, but Jack started a new trend and did it in poetry. I thought it was good, but it wasn't very popular. It was too subtle. He had depth of understanding of human nature for someone of that age. His humor was a little sardonic, maybe. I often think when I read his books of his subtle manner in Ashcan Pete. I can see him now as a boy, so serious.[4]

Rather than books and literature, his abiding passion was for music. All through grade school and high school he devoted himself to it, especially jazz and drums, and when he graduated from high school in 1947, he went to New York City as a student of harmony and orchestration at the Juilliard School of Music. His lessons barely lasted a summer, though: Juilliard's tuition was high, as was the cost of living in New York City, and he was forced to leave. In the fall, Johns Hopkins University in Baltimore granted him a scholarship that he had forgotten he had applied for, and so, as he puts it,

> I entered Hopkins reluctantly. . . , tentatively majoring in journalism, although I had no real interest in it. Not until my third year did I decide to write and teach; [this] accounts for the mediocre grades recorded for the first two years and the pretty good ones after that.[5]

By that third year (1949–1950), at the age of nineteen, he had decided that his musical talent was not great enough to sustain a career, and he was becoming interested in literature because of a teacher he had admired in his junior year.

> There was a fine gentleman at Hopkins at that time who is dead now, a Spaniard whom I later learned was a great Spanish poet. He had been run out of Spain by Franco during the civil war and his name was Pedro Salinas. I studied Spanish with him. We were reading *Don Quixote* and he was the first live poet or writer I'd ever met or known. A splendid gentleman and a very inspiring one. It would be foolish to say it was his doing that I ended up writing; nevertheless, when I think about the year I started getting passionately interested in writing and realized that that was what I was going to do for the rest of my life, I always think of him.[6]

Then too he had met some fellow students who already were "passionately interested in writing," and they helped foster *his* interest; but not having written much, he spent his third year doing it "very badly," he says,

> making all the mistakes you have to make at one level before you can begin to make mistakes on the next. I had some good teachers of writing down there: men who were not writers themselves, but who made a great many of us feel as though we were talented and should persist. With their help I began to make a higher class of mistakes after a year or so.[7]

He had not read much either, and he was eager to make up for lost time, "determined to read every short story that had ever been written. I must have read three thousand short stories that year, and that didn't scratch the surface."[8] At least he had a job that gave him an opportunity for all this reading: to pay off his tuition fees, to support his wife, Harriette Anne Strickland (whom he married on January 11, 1950), he worked in the Classics Library at Johns Hopkins, filing books:

> I . . . became absorbed not so much in Western classical literature as in the old Oriental Tale cycles. They fascinated me enormously then; they do yet. The tale-cycle is a notion that haunts me, as it seems to have haunted the narrative imagination historically. Not just Scheherazade's stories, but that huge Sanskrit thing called *The Ocean of Story* which goes on forever; *The Panchatantra,* all the old cycles which involve stories within stories within stories. I read these almost obsessively for a couple of years, and I think I probably absorbed by simple osmosis a good deal of sense about narrative . . . ; certainly it's left me with a great admiration for simple plot, unfashionable as that is nowadays.[9]

He entered his fourth year at Hopkins with two stories—"Fox-Island Incident" and "Parnassus Approached"—in student literary magazines. The first "was a very bad imitation of a war story," he has said, and that is the limit of what he is willing to remember about either of them, happy that the magazines they appeared in are defunct now and copies of the stories unavailable.[10] In that fourth year, another story, "Lilith and the Lion," appeared in a university magazine, *The Hopkins Review*.[11] It is about a Jew who feels guilty because he was partly responsible for the death of his best friend and because he then married his friend's girl, a Gentile. The story opens with the main character, Martin Davis Kahn, lying in bed, staring out a window at a gray sky. He recalls that the sky was also overcast on the days of his Bar Mitzvah and of his friend's death, and after deciding that he has ignored his religion too much, he goes to the synagogue on Rosh Hashana where through intense prayer he expiates his guilt. Coming out of the synagogue, he notices that the sky has cleared. Barth was twenty when the story was published, and his youth is evident in its manner: melodramatic, contrived, full of stream of consciousness and complex word associations that fail to move the reader.

His first *major* effort at writing was far more successful. It came after the spring of 1951 when he received his creative writing B.A. from Johns Hopkins (his average was the highest for any student in the College of Arts and Sciences), after the summer and July 31 when his first child, a daughter Christine, was born, and after the fall when he entered graduate school at Hopkins, remaining in the writing department. It was his master's project, a novel titled *Shirt of Nessus*, about a Maryland father and son who never get along, who take to fighting over a woman and eventually kill each other. The action stretches over a space of twenty-seven years and involves the rape of a woman in the throes of childbirth; bootlegging, wringing the necks of chickens, setting fire to a cat, setting a lunatic free in the center of a town with live firecrackers tied to him; a bottle fight, a knife fight, a gun fight; a man fornicating a woman while she vomits out the back window of a car, a man in orgy with three women ("Three against one! And all four at once!"); a murder and a multilated corpse, among other things. For the most part, the story moves fast and smoothly, is believable and sometimes very moving. Its conflict depends on differing personalities and emotions, not on differing ideas as in Barth's published work, and its manner is starkly realistic, comparable in Barth's published work only to the abortion scene in *The End of the Road.*

Barth finished *Shirt of Nessus* in early 1952 and sent it to a literary agent in New York, Lurton Blassingame, who had helped one of his friends have a work published. Blassingame liked the novel very much, but he could not find a publisher for it and returned it to Barth, asking to see more of his work.[12] Barth was to send him more all right, but not for three years until in 1955 he had completed *The Floating Opera.*

In the meantime, during the spring of 1952 he received his M.A., and during the summer he went on to study for a Ph.D. in the aesthetics of literature. Since 1951 he had been working as a Junior Instructor for the Department of Writing, Speech and Drama, teaching composition courses to freshmen; now he had the chance to teach more complex matters to a night-school class of adults: expository, descriptive, argumentative, narrative, and imaginative writing, critical reading, logic, analysis of beliefs and propaganda.[13] He also tutored high school and prep school students in grammar, English, American and world literature, composition, and ancient and American history. He studied for the doctorate and taught from the summer of 1952 through the summer of 1953, but at last the cost of maintaining a family while going to school became too much for him. With a first son, John, having been born on October 14, 1952, and with a third child due on January 21, 1954 (it was to be his last child, a boy, Daniel), he applied for a position in the English department at The Pennsylvania State University, was accepted, and began teaching freshman composition there in the fall of 1953.

He also began to come out of a writing slump that he had been in since finishing *Shirt of Nessus* a year and a half earlier. Partly he had been without fictional ideas; partly he had been without the time to write after so much studying and teaching. But now he had decided to stop preparing for the doctorate and had arranged to teach those courses at Penn State that gave him the most free time, remedial English, for example, and prescriptive grammar (one thinks of Jacob Horner). More important than his new leisure time, however, was a new idea he had recently thought of and was eager to develop.[14]

He called the project *Dorchester Tales,* intending to write one hundred stories, mostly bawdy, about the inland shores of Maryland and their history. (The title refers to Dorchester County on the Eastern Shore, in which Barth's home town, Cambridge, is the county seat.) Barth never completed the plan of one hundred tales and most of the fifty he did complete he later destroyed, but a few of the better ones he later put in *The Sot-Weed Factor*, and for this reason the fall of 1953, when he started the *Dorchester Tales,* can also be considered as the start of his professional writing career. Ebenezer Cooke, the hero of *The Sot-Weed Factor*, was in some of the stories, as were other characters Barth later used in that novel: John Smith, Pocahontas, and Mary Mungummory the traveling whore of Dorset County. One story that Barth carried over almost exactly into *The Sot-Weed Factor* was "The Invulnerable Castle," and another, "The Song of Algol," he published on its own in the *Kenyon Review* as "Landscape: The Eastern Shore."[15]

Barth worked on the *Dorchester Tales* until the fall of 1954 when he happened upon the photograph of that old showboat, *The Floating Theater,* and decided to write *The Floating Opera* instead. As we have seen, its conversational manner was similar to that which Sterne had used in *Tristram Shandy,* but again as we have seen, Barth did not pick it up from Sterne as much as he did from the Brazilian novelist Machado de Assis. Some translations of that writer's work had recently been published, *Epitaph of a Small Winner, Bras Cubas,* and *Dom Casmurro*, and Barth came across them during one of his periodic browsing trips to a room in the Penn State Library where new fiction was displayed.[16] *Dom Casmurro* he especially liked, and some elements of its plot he developed in a quite different way in *The Floating Opera*. The narrators of both novels are lawyers, and each becomes involved in a love triangle, the product of which is a child whose father is not definitely known. They consider suicide, describe the day on which they intended to do it, how at night they went to the theater, and how the sight of the child that was perhaps theirs stopped them. They even think of life as an opera, but the difference here is a mark of the difference between the novels: Dom Casmurro's opera is the serious musical kind, his image drawn out and farfetched; Todd Andrews's opera is the floating showboat kind, his image tossed off and fetching.

Barth started work on the novel in January of 1955; three months later he sent it to the agent Lurton Blassingame, to whom he had years before sent *Shirt of Nessus,* and Blassingame sold the book to Appleton-Century-Crofts, the sixth publisher he approached. The story of Barth's dealings with Appleton has been chronicled in chapter 1; no need to repeat it here. What can be added to the record is that Barth felt somewhat held back by the number of publishers the book went to before it was accepted: he could not get a salary increase at Penn State until he published. Otherwise he was not particularly put off by his initial difficulty in having a book published. "I never took it for granted that my work was marketable," he wrote to this writer on March 1, 1970, "and still don't." At any rate, during the summer of 1955 he did the revision that Appleton wanted, and then in October he began *The End of the Road,* which like *The Floating Opera* he finished in three months.

Almost immediately, in early 1956, he began *The Sot-Weed Factor,* planning to complete it in three months as he had the prior two novels, actually working on it for close to three years. Besides the enormous amount of research the book required and its monumental length, there were other reasons for his writing to slow. He was discouraged by the poor sales of *The Floating Opera,* published in 1956, and the equally poor sales of *The End of the Road,* published in 1958 by a different company, Doubleday. That *The Floating Opera* was nominated for a National Book Award did help his spirits for a time, but after all it did not win, and anyway there was a further problem, more severe than the rest, the old problem that had forced him to leave graduate school at Hopkins and come to Penn State to teach: his lack of money.

His initial 1953 salary at Penn State had been low. By 1957 it wasn't much better. "The Barth family is honestly and absolutely out of money. Pretty desperately so," he wrote to his department chairman on January 6 of that year.[17] He was in debt, he said. Reprint money from his first novel and advance money from his second, if either materialized at all, weren't about to materialize for some months yet, so he couldn't borrow on the strength of them. Was there any way that he could get a raise in pay? Failing that, was there no way to fire him and then rehire him so that he could collect his retirement fund? His situation was hopeless, he concluded, unless the department raised his salary at least a little, which the department did. But by 1958 he needed help again, so he applied to the Penn State research fund and was granted $250 to go to Maryland

on research for *The Sot-Weed Factor*. In that year he also applied
to the Guggenheim Foundation for money to let him take a leave of
absence from Penn State in order to write; he was refused. He continued on *The Sot-Weed Factor*, finishing it in March of 1959. By
now he was teaching courses in creative writing and humanities
along with those in composition, and by the end of the year his
salary was more comfortable. In 1960, *The Sot-Weed Factor* was
published by Doubleday, not a financial success, just as his other
novels had not been, although it did increase his literary reputation.
And in June of that same year, after setting aside the novel *The
Seeker* or *The Amateur*, which he had been working on since April
of 1959, he began *Giles Goat-Boy*, the novel that *was* to be a financial
success (prepared for in part by the huge critical success of *The Sot-
Weed Factor* when it came out in paperback in 1964).

But the publication of *Giles Goat-Boy* was to be six years away,
and in the meantime he was still determined to get a leave of
absence to write full time. In 1961 he once again applied for a
Guggenheim fellowship, and once again was refused. In the meantime he had applied as well to Penn State for a sabbatical leave. The
application form asked him to "Describe benefits to self and University that are expected from leave," and he answered, character-
istically dry, "I intend to become wise and sophisticated, also cultured. These are useful attributes in fiction writers and university
teachers." On a separate sheet, he wrote a justification of his leave
that is hard to resist quoting in full.

All the other fiction-writers have been to Europe except me and a
couple of middle-aged Japanese novelists. But I've never been even
to Chicago. My novels are getting crankier and crankier: the New
York Sunday Times said of THE SOT-WEED FACTOR that it was almost
as laborious to read as it must have been to write, and even after all
that labor the reviewer didn't understand what I was talking about.
Pretty soon I'll be writing far-out stories like ALICE IN WONDERLAND
or else another one of those exposés of academic life. The former
can't be done again, and the latter oughtn't to have been in the first
place. What's more, as I get promoted to more interesting courses I
don't have nearly as much time to write as I did back in the days of
English Comp 0. Then I wrote two novels in one year; nowadays I
can't get around to reading that many. If I don't get a leave soon I
bet I'll stop writing altogether—a prospect which some reviewers
may face calmly, but not I. Even Lewis Carroll went to Russia once,

now that I think of it. And look how Hemingway bats around. In fact at the present time every writer I know personally, good and bad, published and unpublished, has either just returned from Europe or is there now or is intriguing for another Guggenheim. Sometimes the experience leaves them unchanged, sometimes it is the ruination of them and sometimes the making; anyhow going abroad seems to be something a U.S. storyteller has to get done with, like losing his chastity, before he can grow up, and I've put it off too long already.

The request was granted. From January to June of 1963, he left work on *Giles Goat-Boy* to have a look at Europe with his wife and three kids in a Volkswagen bus, ingeniously rigged out for a Spartan journey on very little money. They lived for a while in a rainy Spain, then toured. He came back to Penn State in July, took up writing *Giles* and teaching again, and remained at both until September of 1965 when he left Penn State to teach at The State University of New York at Buffalo. His reason for leaving Penn State, he wrote to his chairman, was that "I've worked twelve or thirteen years here and no years anywhere else, and feel the need of a change despite my suspicion that I may be best off where I am." There were reasons to stay at Penn State, he admitted: "the esteem I have for my friends and colleagues in the Department, the pleasure of working under your chairmanship, and my appreciation of the ways in which you, the Department, the College, and the University have made it possible for me to write as well as teach." But Buffalo was offering him a full professorship, plus a third less classroom time for somewhat more salary, and although Penn State would probably have matched the offer, it seemed time to move along. (The night before he went, a friend joked to him, "The examined life is worth leaving.")

Buffalo he liked for his own special reasons: "The lake's polluted. The elms are blighted. The weather is gothic. The place is full of the phosphorescence of decay."[18] There he saw *Giles Goat-Boy* published by Doubleday in 1966 and put on the best-seller charts. There he began *Lost in the Funhouse* in early 1966, finished it in February of 1968, saw it published in September by Doubleday and nominated for a National Book Award, which again he did not receive.* To bring the record more to date: in autumn 1969, he and

---

* When *The Funhouse* was submitted to Doubleday, Barth's editor, Anne Freedgood, was so impressed that she later said she would have recommended

his wife having separated, he took up residence at his summer home on Lake Chautauqua in southwestern New York state, working on a new, long novel provisionally titled *Letters,* commuting to Buffalo a couple of times weekly to teach at the university.

That so far is the general pattern of Barth's life (to 1969 at any rate, more about it later)—certainly not so dramatic as the life of a Hemingway or a Mailer, but perhaps more true to his profession. A writer's job, after all, is to write. Mostly there is time for little else,

---

it for publication even if an unknown had written it (11 December 1969). Barth felt good about it also. He told an interviewer, "Most books, you forget when you're finished, put them away, go on to something else. But I keep thinking about this one. I'm very pleased with it." Still, he did not think people would take to it right away, and he was fairly sure that the book would be murdered by the newspaper critics (Douglas M. Davis, "The End Is a Beginning for Barth's 'Funhouse,'" *National Observer,* 16 September 1969, p. 19). But just one serious shot was fired at it, and that was from Webster Schott ("One Baffled Barth in Search of a Book," *Life,* 18 October 1968, p. 8), who had not taken to *Giles Goat-Boy* either. Most other reviewers frankly admitted that they were not quite sure what Barth was up to in this book and that their lack of understanding was perhaps more their fault than Barth's. So their reviews were almost uniformly characterized by tender-toed judgments: they gave a little praise and held back a little praise and altogether seemed to wish they had an easier way to make a living.

Fortunately, *The Sot-Weed Factor* and *Giles Goat-Boy* had made Barth's reputation sufficiently strong that the mixed and uncertain reviews did not affect too seriously the book's selling power. Six months after its publication in September of 1968, close to 20,000 copies of the hardback edition had been sold; and when the book came out as an Avon paperback in 1969, sales of that edition were ready to go to 100,000. Grosset then brought the book out in a different paperback edition, higher priced than Avon's and better bound, Grosset's theory being that *Lost in the Funhouse* was a special, high-quality book that required equally special handling.

The Funhouse could have been even more special. Prior to its publication, Barth suggested to Doubleday that the pieces he had written for performance on tape might be best published in their proper medium—perhaps they could be recorded on a disc or a tape and sewn into the binding. "But the publisher scared me when he said yes (these guys really *believe* McLuhan), and I backed right down. I was—and am—instinctively conservative in these matters. I didn't want to look gimmicky." Print is stable, after all, and "when you're confronted with a wide range of technical possibilities, I believe the best reaction is a radical limitaton of means" (Douglas M. Davs, "The End Is a Beginning for Barth's 'Funhouse,'" p. 19).

and that little else is usually spent deliberately resting from one day's labor at the desk in order to be fresh for the next day's labor. He cannot afford hangovers and the life style that hangovers represent.

Nor can he afford distractions from his work. One is reminded of a photograph in which Barth is hunched over a desk at home, ears plugged, writing; and next to the photograph is the caption, "With my earplugs in, neither my daughter's daydreams nor the decline of the West matters any more—except as grist for the mill."[19] One is reminded too of the chore lists Barth used to (and still does) pin on a bulletin board in his home—meticulous lists, strictly enforced, with no chance of some forgotten or neglected errand interfering with his work schedule. The schedule itself Barth once described to an interviewer:

> Like Thomas Mann, I suppose I find an orderly life appealing to balance a disorderly—some might say disordered—imagination. I usually teach and write on alternate days. A writing day starts about 8 a.m. and ends at 3 or 4 p.m. The first couple of hours are spent revising the previous day's work; the rest composing. Ten long hand pages is a very good day's work; sometimes a whole day is spent belaboring a single paragraph, and sometimes, of course, nothing will happen at all. I'm inclined to measure by the month and year.[20]

Such measurement requires extreme discipline, the discipline that enables a man to keep writing a book like *Giles Goat-Boy* for over five years, a discipline that in this case has made for some rather brilliant fiction, but an outwardly quiet life.

Yet while his life has not the drama of Hemingway's, it does have drama of a special sort: what Hugh Kenner has ascribed to Samuel Beckett's novels, the drama of "a man in a room writing things out of his head while every breath he draws brings death nearer."[21] In 1965, in connection with that poll which ranked *The Sot-Weed Factor* among the twenty best American novels since 1945, Barth wrote a piece for *Book Week* called "Muse, Spare Me." It was a discussion of how he felt about writing, but what appeared in print was not the complete text of what he wrote. Originally the piece had been called "Publish or Perish": he cut the first half and changed the title before publishing it, and the portion he cut can be found along with those other manuscripts of his on file at the Library of Congress. It is the mate to his discussion of how he felt about writing: a discussion of how he felt about living. And it displays a drama in his mind that more than compensates for any lack of drama in his actions.

"My birthday this year, thirty-fifth of my life, happened to fall on the fortieth day after Easter, celebrated in Christendom as Ascension Day," he began. Ascension Day is traditionally observed by "beating the bounds," by going around the old boundaries of the parish, marking and preserving them. And he decided that the gods were telling him to do much the same: to mark off and assess the first half of his life in preparation for the second. His appraisal was not pleasant.

"Formerly the questions were Who am I? and What if anything am I here for?" he went on. "Now that the grim returns are in, the question is likely to become Shall I keep going anyway? Disabused of sustaining innocence about one's goals and oneself, by what means, on what terms, shall one persist?" His answer was that one should not persist—suicide either literal or figurative is the only valid course. If literal, then one's troubles are over. If figurative, then one starts the second half of his life as though it were really a start and not merely a continuation. Yet after this metaphoric death and rebirth, one is liable to make as many mistakes as he did before, his new self no improvement over the old.

> Ideally it'll be a surer, abler fellow, neither a repetition nor a
> repudiation of the man who died, but a transcension of him: a router
> of pretenders, a giver of laws, a sire of heirs, no longer a seeker but
> a founder; even, in rare cases, a savèd spirit. On the other hand, it
> may be a zombie. But most often, one observes, it's a chap merely
> more reticent, less ambitious, more responsible, less theoretical, more
> conservative, less magnanimous, more competent, less lively, more
> weighty, less attractive, than the one we used to know; no certainer
> of the answers, but less interested in the questions.

In short, one gets older, more tired, and what one hoped would be a change for the better turns out to be little change and not much better.

It is not surprising that he himself should feel about life that way, Barth noted.

> I see through the paradoxical lenses of an ambitious nihilist: a black
> pessimist afflicted with the itch to dream up Beauty if he can, but

unable to "believe in" it; a fellow altogether committed to fictioning (however inept at it), but unable to take either literature or anything else seriously for more than a moodslength—not even the Tragical View, to which by temperament he inclines.

And, he said, he continues to write because the urge is like an itch that wants scratching, because he is still alive, has not killed himself, and thus has to find some way of killing the time. Although he happens to write comically, behind the comedy is the idea that there are only different ways to lose, that things always turn out badly.

> Chuckle, curse, weep or shrug your way to the gallows; drag your heels or run; you'll get there soon in any case, and the trap won't fail to spring. Should you choose to sing a song en route, for whatever reason, and know how to sing in tune, chances are you'll sing that way, whether anyone's listening or not. If you know how to tell stories, chances are you'll tell the best you know as well as you can—since it doesn't matter in the long run anyhow.

At least storytelling has this merit, along with listening to music, performing it, composing it: one is taken out of one's self for a brief time, transported somewhere mystically, and for a while, mostly while one is off, things are bearable.

The first half of the essay ends near there; the second half (published as "Muse, Spare Me") turns from his attitude toward life and concentrates on his image of the storyteller. He used to think of writers like himself as laughing Cassandras, convinced that they alone had the truth, and a dismal truth, but that no one was understanding them. But the image seemed vain, and instead he came to prefer that of the Florentine assassins alluded to in Canto XIX of Dante's *Inferno*, who postpone being buried alive by drawing out their confessions to a priest.

> The beauties of this image are its two nice paradoxes: the more sins he has to confess, the longer retribution is delayed, and since he has nothing to lose anyhow, he may well invent a few good ones to hold the priest's attention.[22]

What is wrong with that image, however, is that the audience is captive, duty-bound to hear him; that the teller saves himself merely by talking, not by entertaining; that his subject matter is perverse autobiography, his sins and his imagined sins.

So finally he thought, and still thinks, of himself in terms of

Scheherazade. "The whole frame of those thousand nights and a night speaks to my heart, directly and intimately—and in many ways at once, personal and technical." The sultan, the story goes, is so disenchanted with life and love that each night he marries a virgin and in the morning has her killed. But when Scheherazade, an expert in all kinds of fiction, offers herself to him, she puts off her morning execution by spinning a tale "artfully continued, involuted, compounded, and complicated through a thousand and one nocturnal installments, during the invention of which she also bears three sons by her imperious audience." In the end, when her inspiration has died, the sultan grants her life, and they live happily. "But not ever after; only until they all are taken by the Destroyer of Delights, whereafter, we're specifically told, 'their houses fell waste and their palaces lay in ruins . . . and [other] kings inherited their riches'—including *The Thousand and One Nights.*"

She remains Barth's image of the storyteller for many reasons. He is interested technically in the frame-story: a fictional situation in which a character tells a story to one person or a group; in which, that is, a story is framed by the story of how it came to be told, a technique not unlike to a lesser extent the one that is here employed. Well-known examples are the *Decameron* where young ladies and gentlemen hiding in a country villa from the Black Plague amuse themselves with clever yarns, and *The Canterbury Tales* where pilgrims on the road to Becket's tomb entertain each other telling stories. But to Barth the best example is that of Scheherazade. "Her tales are told at night: an inestimable advantage, for the whole conception, despite its humor, is darker, more magical and dreamish than Boccaccio's or Chaucer's." She herself has special "prerequisites for her taletellerhood." She has talent; she is a master of fictional traditions; she gives up her virginity, her innocence, for her career; she must always keep yarning, and continue outdoing her previous work.

> The story of deflowered Scheherazade, yarning tirelessly through the dark hours to save her neck, corresponds to a number of things at once, and flashes meaning from all its facets. For me its rich dark circumstances, mixing the subtle and the coarse, the comic and the grim, the realistic and the fantastic, the apocalyptic and the hopeful, figure, among other things, both the estate of the fictioner in general and the particular endeavors and aspirations of this one, at least, who can wish nothing better than to spin like that vizier's

excellent daughter, through what nights remain to him, tales within tales within tales, full-stored with "description and discourse and rare traits and anecdotes and moral instances and reminiscences . . . proverbs and parables, chronicles and pleasantries, quips and jests, stories and . . . dialogues and histories and elegies and other verses . . ." until he and his scribblings are fetched low by the Destroyer of Delights.[23]

The tone here is a good deal more optimistic than in the portion that he cut. But there is the same concern about time passing, and death coming, and what to do with oneself. A remark from the cut portion sums up the general theme of both portions.

> That one declines to terminate one's ridiculous existence . . . surely doesn't mean that one is "affirming life," and just as one may persist in living by a kind of default, so one may work as hard and well as one can, at writing or whatever, despite the fact that there's no final reason to, simply because there's no final reason *not* to, either, and the itch wants scratching.

It would be a mistake to believe that such a remark is Barth's only and last word about himself. He is not that simple, and like another of his favorite storytellers, Proteus, he is not that easily grasped. Very likely he did mean what he wrote at the time he wrote it. For one thing, the black sections of the essay—"Self knowledge is seldom good news"; "Everything gets worse."—are echoed all through *Giles Goat-Boy*, the novel Barth was preparing to finish when he wrote the essay. Then too, the essay came after five years of work on *Giles*, a drain of energy that would deplete anyone. It also came after ten years of little recognition, enough to make someone of his accomplishment fairly bitter, although he himself has never acknowledged that. But years have passed since then, and the particular emotional crisis that the essay demonstrates appears to have been resolved. "Some statements aren't for all time," he says. "People change their minds."[24] Certainly the essay does not give an adequate view of another side of him: the side that likes to brew and keg beer and hunt deer with a bow and arrow (as he used to), or to ski and sail and drink with friends and talk with students and go to football games and play drums in a jazz band and watch shooting stars (as he still does).

> I don't work as many hours as I used to, and when I'm through for the day, I fool around the house, fixing things, using my hands. There was a time when I felt guilty if I took off a Wednesday afternoon to ski—the slopes are less crowded then. So I promised myself I'd work on my free Saturdays to make up for the Wednesday skiing. But all that happened was I didn't write on either day and felt twice as guilty. Not anymore, though. Like today I didn't get much done at all. I went to Buffalo last night to hear a poet read and there was a party afterward that I came home late from. So I was tired when I got up this morning and decided to use the day for errands. Getting snow tires put on my car and things like that.

He says that on a rainy Wednesday afternoon (November 5, 1969), standing at a kitchen counter in his home in Lake Chautauqua, slicing cheese and pepperoni onto plates, spooning pepper salad next to the cheese, uncapping two bottles of beer. Twelve hours later he will be doing the same thing, and in between he and the present writer will have talked all afternoon in his living room (books piled at one end, a butcher's block at the other), gone to Italian supper up the road, driven to Buffalo to hear another poet read, talked some more (this time in a corner bar), dropped in at a student party, and driven back late at night to the lake. But almost from the beginning he will have said:

> One thing that hardly needs telling is that however you judge my work is fine with me. If there's a book of mine you don't like, or something about my fiction that bothers you, write it down. Don't feel that you have to hold back. Of course the other thing that hardly needs telling is that my private life is private and I wouldn't want you to write anything really personal about me.

He has good reason to discourage people who want to write about him rather than about his work. They take up his time and put him on the spot and interfere with his thoughts about his writing. That is one reason he has granted this particular interview:

> I hope you meant what you said. That when I'm asked facts about my work and personal questions about myself I can refer them to you. People come and want me to check their bibliographies, or else they want to know how I got the idea for one of my books. Some questions I enjoy, but that sort I'd prefer to forward to you.

People bother him in all sorts of ways, sometimes comic.

> They come into my house and look at the books on my shelf and try
> to figure what kind of person I am from what I read. What they
> don't understand is that I get sent most of these things in the mail
> and I just shove them on the shelf anywhere they'll go.
>   There's a guy in Washington, D.C., who keeps calling me. The
> guy is always drunk and he always phones about two in the morning
> when you guess that a phone call means the country has been
> bombed, or something worse. I have no idea how he got my number.
> "Mr. Barth," he says, "I want to tell you I think your novel *Second
> Skin* is the best damn novel I ever read." And I keep telling him,
> "Thanks very much, but I didn't write *Second Skin*. Jack Hawkes
> did." Well, after a couple of calls like this, one night for the fun of
> it I told the guy how to get in touch with Jack Hawkes. And a little
> later I heard from Jack about this guy who phoned him in the middle
> of the night and said, "Mr. Hawkes, I just got to tell you I think your
> novel *The Sot-Weed Factor* is the best damn novel I ever read."

On the other hand, many people are determined not to bother him
and determined that no one else bother him either. His agent,
Lurton Blassingame, his present editor, Anne Freedgood, his former
editor, Timothy Seldes, all do their best to keep intruders away from
Barth, and they make sure they themselves say nothing about him
without considering his best interests.

He is thankful for the time they buy him. "A man has to keep
working," he once said.

> No matter how magnificent a talent or how prolific a writer is, it's
> unlikely that more than one or two of his books is going to be read
> a little while later. I have great respect for Horace's notion that you
> ought to spend about nine years on a book—seven years writing it
> and two years polishing it. The great writers of antiquity seldom had
> a big shelf of books like Henry James by the time they died. Virgil,
> for instance, wrote three things; Ovid wrote about four, maybe;
> Homer, two; and I think a man would be pleased if, like Cervantes,
> he ended up with one that was really splendid and about which he
> could imagine it might still interest anybody two generations later.[25]

So Barth has to keep working, and whatever else he does must come
second. He may feel less compulsion to work than he once did;
nevertheless the compulsion he does feel is yet quite strong, and
what he said years ago still holds true. "When a manuscript is

coming well, I'm too satisfied to take anything else seriously, and when it's coming badly, I'm too despondent to."[26]

In November of 1969, at any rate, it is coming well (though there will be what he calls "intractable problems" later on). He sits deep in a chair in his living room, his long legs stretched out, his head pressed back against the chair, a glass of beer in his hand. Behind is a large picture window through which one can see a dark lawn easing down to a sailboat in drydock on a beach and past that to the lake whitecapped by the wind. He is talking about the new novel he is working on, *Letters:* how it is a sort of frame tale, how its form will perhaps be based on a logarithmic spiral that occurs everywhere in nature ("certain sea shells, if expanded infinitely, would become the galaxies"), how the characters from his other books may appear in it along with Andromeda, Medusa, and Napoleon, how the War of 1812 will perhaps be in it too, and how the center will be based on classical material, a story "Perseid" located about five-sevenths of the way through (a perseid being a star that shoots out of the constellation Perseus). He does not want to talk very long about the book: writers have been known to talk a story to death before they write it. But while he does talk about it, his eyes look about as special as eyes can get, off somewhere, and the whole scene—the lake, the boat, the beer, him talking about his work—seems about as complete a picture of him as one can get. What is missing, of course, is him as he sits hunched over a desk, scratching words onto paper, but then nobody gets to see him do that.

9

Perseus in the Vortex, 1972

When you start you have everything to
say, and later you don't want to repeat
yourself. That's my whole aesthetic—
echoing myself without repeating myself.
(John Barth in conversation)[1]

As things turned out, *Letters* was not to be Barth's next work after
all. He had been thinking about that project, making notes for it
since finishing *Lost in the Funhouse* in 1968, and by 1969 had finally
settled on certain aspects of the novel's form and subject matter. It
would have, for example, seven main characters, or more properly,
correspondents, one of which would be Ambrose from *Lost in the
Funhouse* and *The Seeker* or *The Amateur,* the novel he had
worked on from April of 1959 to June of 1960 and then had set aside
in favor of *Giles Goat-Boy.* Indeed, part of *The Amateur* would
appear in *Letters,* and along with that, Barth planned to add two
center pieces, what he called "core texts," which would be attributed
to two characters in the novel and which, unlike the subject matter
of the novel as a whole, would be overtly based on myth.[2]

These two core texts were themselves the result of notes which
he had been making since 1965—not on *Letters*—instead on a group
of mythic figures who for a long time now had been fascinating him:
Odysseus, Perseus, Menelaus, and Scheherazade. The Menelaus
material he had already turned into one of the fictions in *Lost in the
Funhouse,* "Menelaiad," about how Menelaus wrestling with Proteus
on the beach at Pharos had been turned into Proteus telling the
story of Menelaus. The Odysseus material he did not yet know what
to do with, nor for the moment Scheherazade, but Perseus had more
and more begun to occupy his imagination—his notes on that figure
were ending up longer than those he had made on Menelaus, which

themselves had been quite long—and by the late spring of 1969 he had finally decided to stop work on the body of the novel and start with Perseus at the center.[3]

There were several reasons for his increased interest in that figure. One was, as he later said, his recent concern "with stories about people who turn into their own stories or into the sound of their own voices."[4] Both these situations he had already used in "Menelaiad," where Proteus survives in the voice of Menelaus and where, when that voice goes, he will yet continue as that character's story. He had used a variant of that theme in another *Funhouse* story, "Echo," taking up the title character where the Greek myth left her, disembodied, capable only of echoing in her voice what other people say, passing her through one more stage so that in this new story of her she has lost her own voice too, repeating what others say as before, but only in *their* own voices.

But now he saw another chance to work this kind of trans-formation, changing people not so much into their voices, although to a degree that would be involved, but this time, as the Greeks did, making them into stars. "You'll remember there's a group of five constellations which rise together late in the evening in the fall of the year in northern latitudes," he would later say as well. "These five constellations all have to do with Perseus": Perseus who cut off the head of the Gorgon, Medusa, and now holds it in the sky; Andromeda, his wife; her parents, Cepheus and Cassiopeia; and the winged horse, Pegasus, born from the decapitated body of Medusa. "I love the notion of those constellations cycling through the skies every night as a kind of continually repeating narrative," he said. And if his imagination was to lead him to persist in finding new ways to turn people into stories, here was a good one: "those con-stellations which rotate, which cycle, which repeat their stories."[5]

There was in the very way he phrased that statement an indi-cation of another reason for his interest in these mythic figures and their stars. Since 1965, roughly at the same time he had begun making notes on Perseus, he had begun reading regularly Martin Gardner's column, "Mathematical Games," in *Scientific American*. This in turn had led him to one of Gardner's books, *The Second Scientific American Book of Mathematical Puzzles and Diversions*, and in both places he had found information about the medieval mathematician Fibonacci, best known for his introduction to the west of the Hindu-Arabic decimal system and for a classic mathematical sequence in which each of the numbers is the sum of the two that precede it:[6]

1, 1, 2, 3, 5, 8, 13, 21, 34, 55, 89,   etc.

This sequence traces the growth of a logarithmic spiral, and as Gardner noted, logarithmic spirals are manifold in nature, "in the coil of the nautilus shell and snail shells, in the arrangements of the seeds of many plants, such as the sunflower and the daisy, the scales of the pine cone, and so on. *Epeira,* a common variety of spider, spins a web in which a strand coils around the center in a logarithmic spiral."[7] The pattern of scales on a pineapple, the arrangement of certain leaves and branches around a stalk, the swirl of various kinds of tendrils, these as well tend to be based on logarithmic spirals. But the particular occurrence of this pattern which most interested Barth, or rather a correspondence of them, was that between the chambered nautilus sea shell and the spiral galaxies. "If you took that logarithmic spiral which explains the chambered nautilus," he said, "and kept unwinding the thing, you would end up with a spiral galaxy like the one in Andromeda" among the constellations clustered around Perseus.[8] That correspondence was enough to give Barth the ground metaphor for his story about Perseus and its action: Perseus in the sky explaining how once in middle years he had crashed in the desert at Libya and waking to find himself in a spiral-shaped temple had suspected he was in heaven, only to discover he was in something very like a sea shell.

There he would find a series of low-relief murals depicting his earlier adventures, an idea Barth explains he got from Virgil, "the first book of the *Aeneid,* a scene that simply raises my hair every time I read it." In that first book, Aeneas comes to Dido's Carthage. Made invisible by his mother, Venus, he tours the city and sees a group of frescoes which tell the story of the Trojan War. He begins to recognize his friends, and then he sees himself. The importance of that scene is that Aeneas is trying to find out who he is. "That's one of the reasons why one likes Aeneas more than Odysseus," Barth remarks, and the idea of someone looking at images of himself, trying to determine who he is by examining who he's been in order to find out who he's got to be, was sufficiently appealing to him that, as he says, "I stole it."[9]

Just the situation. Not its theme. That he had already come upon on his own. In the same way that he had more and more become preoccupied with stories about people who turn into their stories, so since 1965 he had become intrigued with the idea of people who in middle age look over the first half of their lives in preparation for the second. His first major explication of that theme was actually not in a story at all but in the unpublished part of that essay, "Muse, Spare Me," which he had written for *Book Week* on the occasion of that magazine's 1965 poll in which *The Sot-Weed Factor* had been voted among the twenty best American novels since 1945. He was thirty-five that year, he wrote, an age conventionally considered a mid-point, and he had looked over what had come before in hopes that he might transcend it all, suspecting though that what was yet to come, instead of being ampler and better, would only be more of the same and likely much worse. The characters in *Lost in the Funhouse* had for the most part been imbued with these thoughts as well. The spermatozoon, the story which tells its story, the hindmost Siamese twin, Menelaus, these and several others, all try to account for their present condition by looking at what produced it, and then make predictions about what is to come. Art and life blend. How one is to get through the middle of this sentence, this story, this life, etc., is the question that is finally proposed.

Now, however, by adapting that scene from Virgil, Barth saw an opportunity to treat this theme in a fuller, more expansive (indeed quite optimistic) way than he had ever done before. What accounted for the difference was that, unlike those of Aeneas, Perseus's stories go around in a spiral, and that change from the original situation was all Barth needed to make the story work. Form became content, structure meaning: Perseus, reviewing the events of his life, discovers in their very format the secret of renewal. If the second half of life must be a continuation of the first, it still can be, if striven for, a movement outward and upward, not just recapitulation but recycling, and the drama of his story is that striving.

But to make that spiral pattern a total force within the story, not just a detail in one incident in the plot or a metaphor the truth of which the hero recognizes, Barth had to use it as the basis of his presentation, to make the plot itself a spiral, and the consequence of that technique is that the order of the incidents is somewhat hard to follow, though their relationship is clear enough if taken out of context and considered chronologically. In that new order, young Perseus first does all his hero work, beheads Medusa, rescues Andromeda from the sea monster, Cetus, petrifies his enemies, and settles down to rule Mycenae. There his reign is uneventful. He takes each night to boring captive listeners with the story of his life. Finally, in middle age, his children grown and restless, his marriage on the rocks, himself bored stiff, convinced that it is he now who is petrifying, he sets out to retrace his youth and ends up in ironic, even burlesque imitation.

His trouble is self-centeredness, a turning in on himself instead of out. Indeed he says as much about himself when he goes again for directions from the three gray ladies whom he'd tricked once in his youth and, contrary to instructions, is prepared to trick again. "Perseus!" they exclaim, bereft of the eye he once had stolen from them. "Not at all," he replies, "Self-centered Perseus is my enemy as much as yours."[10] He doesn't mean it, though, or recognize its truth, and just as these three catch him out and dump him from the high point of his "hubris" (p. 97), nearly drowning him (they're flying on Pegasus at the time), so other duplicated tasks turn out disastrously until he does. His instructions for his second start are given to him by a hooded woman in Athene's temple. Whereas before he'd snuck up on Medusa, guided by her reflection on his shield, now his mode of operation must be, "on the one hand, direct instead of indirect—no circuities, circumlocutions, reflections, or ruses—on the other, rather passive than active: beyond a certain point I must permit things to come to me instead of adventuring to them" (pp. 93–94).

There's a touch of mysticism here, reminiscent of the climax of *Giles Goat-Boy*. To use a metaphor that is frequent in this story, if you think too much about achieving things like orgasm, say, they just won't come. Be honest. Go straight forward instead of around. Let what happens happen. It takes him quite a while to learn his lesson, though. Having nearly drowned, he almost dries out in the desert, wakes up to review the spirals in his temple, is impotent with a priestess named Calyxa (an impotence that is typical of his present life. As she says, "You worry too much. . . . The more you think of sex as a performance . . . the more you'll suffer stage fright on your opening nights" [pp. 70–71]), watches art catch up to life until the tableaux of his past are ended, finally achieves some measure of union with Calyxa, and unaware that their "full fillment" (p. 111) signifies other achievements yet to come, sets out to resume his efforts at renewal.

For a time, he still is unsuccessful. He continues his retracement, going to Joppa where he'd rescued Andromeda and where she now has left him for another. There he meets her aged father, Cepheus, wandering pointless in his garden. "Seems to me I've been here forever," the old man tells him. "I make a kind of circuit of our fields, I guess; rotate like my crops; after a while one's much like another" (p. 114). It's the sort of condition that Perseus himself will be in if he doesn't find himself and where he's going. He confronts Andromeda, and as too many times before, they argue. She tells him that she doesn't love the new man she is with. She only consoles herself with him. "It was I she'd loved—Perseus the man, not gold-skin hero or demigod—and wedded we, till I had by lack of heart-deep reciprocity murdered marriage and love alike. 'You never *did* love me,' she charged, 'except as Mythics might mere mortals' " (p. 124). That same self-centeredness again, and rather than see her truth, Perseus replies in cutting fashion, only to hate the man who speaks that way to her: "his last words, as I put him to death promptly and forever on hearing me speak them" (p. 124).

It's the climax and the turning point. The hooded woman who counseled him in Athene's temple appears now in the doorway. She it was who rescued him from drowning. She it was whom he had based his fame on in the first place, Medusa the Gorgon, come back now and in another way, no more with snakes for hair and a glance that petrifies, at least not necessarily. If the man who looks at her uncowled is her true love, the two of them will turn ageless as the stars and be together for all time. If the man is not, she herself will be regorganized and he himself quite likely petrified. There's a boon to be gained but with a risk, and for the first time, Perseus is open, selfless, and direct. He says good-bye to all that he has been, commits himself to all that she has done for him, strides over sill, and as he puts it, "embraced eyes-shut the compound predications of commitment—hard choice! soft flesh!—slipped back mid-kiss her problematic cowl, opened eyes" (pp. 125–126), and the two of them are stellified.

He now narrates his tale from heaven. "Good evening," he begins, his head coming up over the horizon. He's in the stars now, explaining how he got there. It's not clear who he's talking to just yet, presumably all those looking up at him, but the tale he tells is in a spiral, as if he himself were looking down at it. He starts it out a little past mid-way in his second series of adventures, just after he had passed out in the desert and awakened in his spiral temple, ministered to by Calyxa. There the two of them looked over the tableaux of his life to date, so that what in effect the narrative becomes here is a story within a story, Perseus in the sky telling his audience how he told Calyxa how he came to be in the temple which involves him telling her everything that came before. That in turn involves "a very special technical problem in double exposition," as Barth says, for all the time Perseus is explaining to Calyxa the events upon the murals, he is explaining to his audience his relationship with Calyxa as well, working it all out so the climax of the principal exposition (the murals in his temple) coincides with the climax of the second exposition (his relationship with Calyxa) just in time to precipitate climax of the story along its straight time line (his leaving the temple, confronting Andromeda, and committing himself to the New Medusa).[11] It's a narrative structure a little like the one Barth had used earlier in "Menelaiad" where seven tales within tales each progressed to the point where the climax of one triggered the climax of another and so on to the number of seven, somewhat in the manner of those chains of orgasm that Calyxa in this story remembers back to.

The simile is natural enough. As Barth says, "When you begin to talk about dramatic structure, you get inextricably involved in sexual metaphors."[12] The simile is appropriate enough as well, for if in *Lost in the Funhouse* art and life had been a reflection of each other, so here sex and life work the same. The meaning of Perseus's experience is dependent upon his attitudes toward the women in his life: Andromeda whom he ignored, brooding too much about himself, Calyxa whom he craved only as "a mere adorer, not a fellow human" (p. 125), the New Medusa whom he committed himself totally to and, understanding the risk, gave of himself completely. Even so, the first two women now are not ignored. Andromeda is a constellation beside him as he holds Medusa; and Calyxa, perhaps most wonderfully—she with the spiriferate navel that matched up with the windings of his temple walls, she with the name suggestive of that calyx outer whorl, or sepals, at a flower's base—is now a jewel in one of the manacles on one of Andromeda's wrists, a spiral nebula.

Lest the reader miss the dramatic viewpoint of this story, Barth provided several clues to give him bearings. The title, "Perseid," for example (the form of which is in keeping with Barth's recent habit as in "Menelaiad" and "Anonymiad" of imitating ancient titles like the *Iliad* and *Aeneid*), means literally a shower of golden meteors which flashes out across the sky from the constellation Perseus every August. Then too, at the start, having risen and said "Good evening," Perseus explains how "Nightly, when I wake to think myself beworlded and find myself in heaven, I review the night I woke to think and find myself vice-versa" (p. 59), that is, not in heaven as he is now but in his spiral temple. There are similar examples: Perseus explaining how when he left the temple he "cloaked out on the shore and watched the stars wheel, not so many then as now, making stories from their silent signs and correspondences" (pp. 100–101); Cepheus retelling the story of how Perseus rescued Andromeda and married her, saying "I can start the story anywhere; it goes right along, you'll see, hangs together like a constellation if you know the stars, how to read them" (p. 114). Most important, close to half-way through his own story, Perseus starts to wrap up his relation with Calyxa, describing "her back's small small" and "her lean little buttocks," and a new surprising speaker suddenly replies, "No need to go on about small smalls and lean little buttocks" (p. 95).

It's Medusa, her head coming up over the horizon now as well, to whom Perseus replies, "Sorry, love, and good evening." The remainder of the story is directed in particular to her. The ending is their nightly present tense, a brilliant dialogue, mannered and alliterative (but as the hero, punning, says, "I'm high on letters" [p. 126]):

> Now listen and believe me, if there's any truth in words: it wasn't
> you who discovered your beauty to me, but I who finally unveiled it
> to myself. And what I saw, exactly, when I opened my eyes, were

two things in instantaneous succession, reflected in yours: the first
was a reasonably healthy, no-longer-heroic mortal with more than
half his life behind him, less potent and less proud than he was at
twenty but still vigorous after all, don't interrupt me, and grown
too wise to wish his time turned back. The second, one second after,
was the stars in your own eyes, reflected from mine and rereflected
to infinity—stars of a quite miraculous, yes blinding love, which
transfigured everything in view. Perhaps you find the image trite; I
beg you not to say so. (Pp. 132–133)

The image is hardly trite, but their achievement is hardly total
either. They may be immortal, their love the same, but like the two
lovers on Keats's Grecian urn, they are doomed to be in composition
but never complete, to catch occasional sparkling glimpses of each
other but never to meet full face and never to reach full fillment as
Perseus managed with Calyxa. The ending is optimistic, then, which
is not typical of Barth, but as one might expect from him, not
totally so. For Perseus, though, it is sufficient.

The case is otherwise with a relative of his. Toward the end of
his narrative, he asks Medusa, "What ever happened to Cousin
Bellerophon?" and she replies, "That's another story" (p. 129).
Indeed it was: the next one Barth would write. Having finished the
"Perseid," he had sent it to Anne Freedgood, his editor at Doubleday,
and she had liked it greatly but had pointed out that its novella
format made it too long to be published in a magazine and too short
to be a book. The best way to make use of it, she told him, was to
write some others like it and bring them out as a group.[13] The
"Perseid," in fact, was later published in a magazine but only in a
shorter version (in *Harper's* in October of 1972), but her economic
point was nonetheless a good one, and it coincided with Barth's new
interest in the novella form. Just as an eighteenth- or a nineteenth-
century composer would want to try out all the different forms, he
later said, so after his experience with short and long novels and
short fiction he was moved to work some more in this one. It gave
him the chance "to imagine conceits that could only be worked out
in the space of ninety or a hundred pages rather than the shorter
constipated space of the absolute economy of the short story or the
more expansive and sectioned space of the novel." At the same time
it set him the formal task "of writing a story that would be long
enough to be of novella size but impossible to section, a continuous

kind of narrative." Any writer, he went on, would understand what he meant, what a beautiful thing it could be to set yourself a formal task.[14]

In this case, the task involved the mythic hero, Bellerophon, and Pegasus, the flying horse. Barth came naturally to them. His standard source for information on Greek myth had all along been Robert Graves's double-volume study of the subject, and there at the end of Graves's section about Perseus he had come across a note detailing how alike the myths of Perseus and Bellerophon were.[15] The one had killed Medusa with the help of winged sandals; the other had used a winged horse, born from the body of Medusa, to kill the monster, Chimera. Graves went on to note further parallels, how they both had the same source in ancient history, how details of both showed up on the same ancient vases, but for Barth the point was already made, and he saw a use for it. For one thing, he had by now decided that the collection of novellas he was planning would have three sections, and the idea of the three-part Chimera with its head of a lion, body of a goat, and tail of a serpent gave him a convenient title for the book as well as a unifying metaphor, what he would later in another context call "a beastly fiction . . . full of longeurs, lumps, lacunae, a kind of monstrous mixed metaphor" (p. 308), in keeping with the sort of outrageous mannered fiction he was now engaged in. For another, he had by now decided too that, having written a story about a hero who was genuine, he would follow it with a story about a hero who was false, and what better character to pick on than Bellerophon, who was enough like Perseus for his failings to stand out.[16]

The only problem was that when in the fall of 1969 Barth began to write this story he himself began to fail, the first major case of writer's block that he had ever had. To be sure, in the early 1960s he had talked about a block in relation to his failure to complete *The Seeker* or *The Amateur*, but that had not been a block in the normal sense of not being able to write but rather a situation in which a project had turned out less rich than he had hoped and needed to be dropped. Now the words just wouldn't come. He labored with them until the end of the summer of 1970 when he realized that his difficulty with the story was analogous to the problems Bellerophon was having with his horse, that his own non-flights of language, his stops and starts, were the proper technique of his story, and with that "the problem solved itself, the story came out in a burst."[17]

The tactic was to begin the story much as he had "Perseid" with Bellerophon speaking directly to his audience, but while Perseus is a constellation, Bellerophon is a bundle of letters afloat in a Maryland marsh. He too (much like Perseus, he explains) had done all his hero work, in this case slayed the Chimera, and settled in a slump in middle age, turned in on himself, unconcerned with those around him, determined to retrace his golden youth. But whereas with Perseus the problem had been impotence, both real and metaphoric, the problem with Bellerophon is leadenness, a lack of several kinds of levitation, both physical and spiritual (he and Pegasus can't get off). In time they do, however, but Bellerophon makes them fly too high, trying for Olympus as if he were immortal. A gadfly, sent by Zeus, stings Pegasus and tumbles Bellerophon from his pride. Pegasus goes on to constellated heaven. Bellerophon lands in a thorn bush, in the myth at least, and wanders (as Graves notes) about the earth, lame, blind, lonely, and accursed, avoiding the paths of men until he dies.[18] In this story of him, though, he hits that marsh, turned into the muddled printed pages of his life, reprinted somehow in the pages of this section of the book.

Barth changed that end from the one that Graves supplied because it was his custom, as he said, to make as many of the aspects of the fiction metaphors for the content as he could ("not only the 'form' of the story, the narrative viewpoint, the tone, and such, but, where manageable, the particular genre, the mode and medium, the very process of narration—even the fact of the artifact itself"),[19] and so it seemed to him a good conceit to make this story about a hero's life that failed itself a failure, to turn him overtly and self-consciously into the muddled story of his life. The technique was not really new to him. In several of the fictions in *Lost in the Funhouse*, he had already used failed art as a metaphor for life, paradoxically producing in the bargain a group of successful failures as if to dispute his point. But they had all been comparatively short while this was to be a novella, in time the longest in the book, at least four times as long as anything in *The Funhouse*, and it gave him the chance to imagine the biggest, most outrageously successful failure he had so far tried, a marvelous chance to play. Now he had room—

not only for editorial intrusions similar to passages in *Lost in the Funhouse* which he echoed here:

> Storytelling isn't my cup of wine; . . . my plot doesn't rise and fall in meaningful stages but winds upon itself like a whelk-shell or the snakes on Hermes's caduceus: digresses, retreats, hesitates, groans from its utter et cetera, collapses, dies. (P. 196; see p. 96 in *Lost in the Funhouse*)

He also had the scope to include the plot and structure of the story as it would ideally have appeared, based as it would have been on the tidal pattern of the Maryland marsh that Bellerophon is floating on: First Flood, First Ebb, Second Flood, Second Ebb, the first half depicting the first half of his life, his rise and fall from greatness, the second half depicting the second half of his life, his flight toward heaven and his tumble. In addition the structure would have been in imitation of the story-within-a-story pattern of the "Perseid," proceeding

> with unostentatious skill to carry forward the present-time drama (my quest for literal immortality) while completing the plenteous exposition of my earlier adventures—a narrative difficulty resolved by the simple but inspired device of making the second half of my life recapitulate ironically the first, after the manner of the *Perseid*, but with the number five (i.e., threes and twos) rather than seven as the numerical basis of the structure, and a circle rather than a logarithmic spiral as the geometric motif. (P. 142)

A circle because, unlike Perseus, Bellerophon never does transcend himself, merely repeats himself rather than recycles; a story-within-a-story, because Bellerophon, while addressing the reader from his pages floating in the marshes, is explaining how he once rehearsed the story of his life to his youthful Amazon mistress, Melanippe, and that in turn involved him telling her how he once had told the earlier story of his life to his spouse, later his children, and later still a group of students at the University of Lycia. Complex as it is, the scheme is not much different, except in particular detail, from that of the "Perseid," and one sees no reason why it should not have worked, except that somewhere along the line, as in his life, it didn't.

Specifically what went wrong involved a seer named Polyeidus, a character proper to the classic version of the myth and here made into a shape-change, a figure familiar enough in Barth but now a little different inasmuch as his specialty isn't animals or people so much as documents. The "Perseid," it seems, isn't a novella written by John Barth. It's a document that Polyeidus turned into on the occasion of Bellerophon's fortieth birthday to instruct him in the proper renewal of his life. As further examples, he turned into the twenty-two stages of the ideal mythic hero's progress (these again from Lord Raglan's *The Hero*) and the circular pattern of the hero's life (from Joseph Campbell's *The Hero with a Thousand Faces*). He was able to make use of them because, in addition to his documentive, imitative capabilities, he can also borrow from the future, bringing back books and writing before they have been invented and using them as his medium. This prophetic borrowing is an absolute requirement of the plot. After all, given the time of the story, writing doesn't exist, but since Barth's central conceit is that Bellerophon turns into the written story of himself, he needed a logic in the plot to make that transformation possible. The gadfly who stings Pegasus and dumps Bellerophon at the end is Polyeidus in another form as well, and having accomplished his gadfly function, he changes to himself again, conversing with Bellerophon as they drop in a dialogue that imitates the conversation between Perseus and Medusa at *their* end. How to keep from being killed, they ask each other. The answer is that Polyeidus can turn them into a document of Bellerophon's life, and in that form the two of them can plummet safely. Which they do, and the thematic point is double, not just the one already established (that Bellerophon's story turns out as muddled as his life) but another which exists in relation to the first as cause does to effect (Bellerophon, setting out to imitate the pattern of the ideal mythic hero's life, ends up a mere imitation of that pattern's subject, derivative, uninspired, inauthentic, demonstrating all the proper attributes but not possessing them).

Perseus was his own man finally. Bellerophon is only an imitation Perseus, his life a fiction. Indeed a forgery: he isn't even himself, for earlier he had been responsible for the death of his brother, Deliades, and now it turns out that in the shock of the accident that killed him plus an attendant crack upon the head, he himself lost memory and identity. It wasn't Deliades who was killed but his brother, demigod Bellerus. He himself is Deliades

thinking he's Bellerus. He's assumed the role of the brother he has
killed, and Bellerophon (the new name that he goes by) doesn't
mean Bellerus the killer, as he supposes, rather the killer of Bellerus.
It's another instance of how he is an imitation. He is no mythic
hero, nor was meant to be, and he would have been better off to be
himself, to enjoy the ordinary (which is not to say inferior) success
that by middle age he had managed. As he tells a group of students
at the university,

> the final proof, if any is needed, of my fraudulent nature is that on
> the eve of my fortieth birthday, when your typical authentic mythic
> hero finds himself suddenly fallen from the favor of gods and men, I
> enjoy the devotion of my wife, the respect of my children, the esteem
> of my subjects, the admiration of my friends, and the fear of my
> enemies—all which argues the protection of Olympus. (P. 234)

That speech is an echo of what his wife had told him earlier, that
his best work might not be his most spectacular, that far from being
behind him it might lie ahead or actually be in progress:

> I mean the orderly administration of your country, your family, and
> yourself over the long haul; the patient cultivation of understanding
> into wisdom; the accumulation of rich experience and its recycling
> in the form of enlightened policy, foreign, domestic, and personal—
> all those things, in brief, which make a man not merely celebrated,
> but great; not merely admired, but loved. (P. 140)

These he already has. What more could he want? Indeed the
example of Perseus shows how the recognition of these values can
assure success. But Bellerophon, by denying that he is human, by
trying for more than he should expect rather than working to im-
prove the quality of what he's got, ends up that hero's opposite, no
star at all, but floating in those marshes, all washed up.

Polyeidus turns into other documents as well, a spurious letter,
for example, from someone who purports to be Napoleon, long
deposed but still alive in 1971, writing from the Lake Chautauqua
region of New York to his counterpart, deposed, insane King Charles
the Third, somehow still alive, exiled in Maryland. The letter involves a proposal for what he calls "the New, the Second Revolution,
an utterly novel revolution" (p. 244), and in those terms is a
description of Barth's original idea for the *Letters* project, the pub-

lication of which he once planned to coincide with America's bicentennial. As he said, "I'm surrounded by students who speak about such things as the Second Revolution; and so the notion of second revolutions, second cycles, recycling one's life, all these things came together in the . . . narrative ecology of *Chimera*."[20] Napoleon and his utterly novel revolution end up being the persona and brainchild of someone named Jerome Bray who in 1971 is writing to Todd Andrews, the director of something called the Tidewater Foundation, for money to continue work on a revolutionary novel, the creator of which will be a Polyeidus-like computer into which Bray has fed

> all the 50,000-odd entries in "Thompson's *Motif-Index of Folk Literature*," the entire stacks of Lilydale's Marion Skidmore Library plus a reference work called *Masterplots*, elements of magical mathematics with such names as Golden Ratio and Fibonacci series, and . . . a list of everything in the world that came in sevens. Thus equipped, the machine was to analyze the corpus of existing fiction . . . , induce the perfect form from its "natural" approximations, and reduce that ideal to a mathematical model, preliminary to composing its verbal embodiment. (P. 250)

Later Bray changes the basic number from seven to five, inasmuch as half the sum of one and the square root of five produces a number traditionally called the Golden Ratio (1.61803 . . .), which is the ultimate reduction of the Fibonacci sequence and itself a kind of ideal number. This he uses as the basis for perfecting the structure of the Freitag Triangle, a geometric figure relating to the typical rise and fall of dramatic action in a story (reproduced once in *Lost in the Funhouse* [p. 95] and here again [p. 251]), turned in on itself in the form of a kind of logarithmic spiral and intended as the ideal structure for his revolutionary novel. The project is as derivative, heartless, and uninspired as Bellerophon's own life, and indeed the result is another failed version of his story, used here by Barth not for the chance to play more with complexity but for its solid dramatic function, the example it gives to Bellerophon of how not to go about things.

Polyeidus turns into one other document that has interest here, a lecture that Bellerophon reads to his students, itself a lecture that John Barth gives in the future on this story. He explains how in his thirtieth year some readers of *The Sot-Weed Factor* remarked that the adventures of its hero followed in some detail the pattern of the ideal mythic hero as discussed by Lord Raglan, Joseph Campbell, and several other comparative mythologists; how that similarity had not been intentional but that he had next set out consciously to use that pattern as the ironic basis for the structure of *Giles Goat-Boy*, some fictions in *Lost in the Funhouse*, and the "Perseid." That special use of the pattern gave him a chance to address some current thematic concerns of his: "the mortal desire for immortality, for instance, and its ironically qualified fulfillment—especially by the mythic hero's transformation, in the latter stages of his career, into the sound of his own voice, or the story of his life, or both. I am forty" (p. 199). It also allowed him to go about writing from what he thought was the proper imitative angle, away from realism, which in the long run points toward mythic archetypes, instead toward the archetypes directly. "To the objection that classical mythology, like the Bible, is no longer a staple of the average reader's education" and consequently is without effect on contemporary sensibility, he replies, "hum, I forget what, something about comedy and self-explanatory context." He then goes on to quote at length from Robert Graves's summary of the story of Bellerophon and explains how the myth attracted him because of its relation to several pet motifs of his: "the sibling rivalry, the hero's naïveté, the accomplishment of labors by their transcension . . . ; the Protean counselor (Polyeidus means 'many forms'); the romantic triangle; et cetera" (pp. 201–202). And finally he explains about his writer's block and how he used it as the central tactic in this story.

Again this has a proper place. If the problem is to relate myths to daily life, one way to solve it is to show how the theme of this myth is related to Barth's own life. If failed art is the metaphor, one way to dramatize it is by violating the traditional storyteller's precept of showing, not telling, by intruding in the story to explain what the story is about, thus implying that the story itself does not do what it should. Finally if Barth at forty finds himself in a condition analogous to that of Bellerophon at forty, looking over the first half of his life in an effort to go on with the second, one way to incorporate that thematic correspondence is to come in roughly halfway through this story (and in the original conception more or less halfway through this book) to recount a history of his career to date and then show how he built upon it to go on. Thus throughout this story there are plot summaries of *The Floating Opera* and *The End of the Road*, references to *The Amateur, The Sot-Weed Factor*, and *Giles Goat-Boy*, imitations of various passages in *Lost in the Funhouse* and the books that came before it, quotations from the "Perseid," not to mention allusions to such Barth characters as Ebenezer Cooke, Harold Bray, Harrison Mack, Giles Stoker, Henry Burlingame, Todd Andrews, and several others. Layer upon layer, the import is the same, recycling, how to use what has already been done in order to go on.

While Bellerophon fails, Polyeidus has his own form of success. Falling, he plots how he will turn into this story of Bellerophon and then "grow narratively on in death like hair and fingernails until I comprehended the entire Bellerophonic corpus and related literature" (p. 301). Since he will not be Bellerophon's story exclusively, since it will only be one aspect of himself, he will yet be free to operate in some other aspects, and one of those is the next story intended for *Chimera*, a story which, like Polyeidus himself, borrows fiction from the future to establish a tradition in the past and in doing so goes beyond that tradition to establish something new. The last five words of Bellerophon, after he has railed against the condition in which he finds himself, are "It's no *Bellerophoniad*. It's a   ". The blank is conspicuous, presumably representing the moment when he and Polyeidus hit, turned into the story the reader has just finished. But it serves another function too, for in Barth's original arrangement of these stories, the reader then flipped the page and found another story which indeed was no "Bellerophoniad" but a "Dunyazadiad," yet one more document which Polyeidus in his many aspects had become.[21]

The story is one that Barth had been thinking of since at least 1965 when he'd begun making notes on Odysseus, Perseus, Menelaus, and Scheherazade. But his interest in Scheherazade, rather than in writing a story about her, had gone back to long before then, to 1949 when he had taken a job filing books in the classics stacks and the stacks of the Oriental Seminary at the Johns Hopkins University library. There he had come across those massive oriental tale cycles, *The Ocean of Story*,[22] *The Panchatantra*, many others, and, most important, *The Thousand and One Nights*, the framed story-teller of which, Scheherazade, had occupied him greatly ever since. She was his favorite woman in the world, he later said, "the capital storyteller, one of the original liberators of her sex," and he saw in her situation a perfect example of publish or perish.[23] Indeed he used the phrase as the title for that unpublished essay (the first part of "Muse, Spare me") that he wrote in 1965, detailing the meanings of her storytelling plight, relating them to himself.

Now in 1971, the "Bellerophoniad" at last complete, he saw a way to use her. The "Bellerophoniad" itself had taken him more than a year and a half during which, in addition to his writer's block, he had been divorced, had remarried, gone on leave from Buffalo to Boston, and now looking ahead to a teaching year at Buffalo again, he wanted to make this story short (in time the shortest in the book) and one which he could finish in a season (which he did, at Lake Chautauqua in the summer of 1971). Aside from the pleasure he would have in working at last with Scheherazade, there was as well the felicity he noted that this Persian-based material would jar somewhat with the Greek nature of the other stories and thus reinforce the monstrous, mixed-metaphor notion that the book's title, *Chimera*, represented.[24]

The immediate problem was how to write a story about Scheherazade that would be innovative, new, and fresh. To take the elements of her story directly from their source, treat them ironically perhaps, and tell them from her point of view (as he had done with Perseus and Bellerophon) would indeed be repetition, not the renewal this book argued for, and if the progress of its stories was to be in keeping with its theme, he would have to find a new approach. The one he settled on was to make the story not about Scheherazade but her sister, Dunyazade. In the original, Scheherazade each night takes her sister with her to the bedchamber of the King. After the King has had his will with Scheherazade, shortly before he goes to sleep, Dunyazade asks Scheherazade for a story and then at daybreak interrupts her prior to the climax, thus keeping the King in suspense, staying his hand just long enough for Scheherazade, in Barth's words, "to win his heart, restore his senses, and save the country from ruin" (p. 14). The three of them together represented to him a kind of story-teller's allegory, "Dunyazade, the one who primes the pump, the King, the absolute critic, and Scheherazade who must publish or perish night after night after night."[25] At the end, she asks the King for her life, not on the basis of her literature but on the basis of their children, and the King grants her request, not for the children but the stories. He marries her, and "in effect gives her tenure," as Barth says. "She never tells another story." Dunyazade marries the King's younger brother, who started the process, who has been doing the same thing, going to bed with a virgin every night and killing her in the morning, and the story ends with the four of them going into their separate bed-chambers. Now what fascinated him, Barth said, was Dunyazade. With the entire literary tradition, the entire erotic tradition as well, under her belt, what does she do with her husband on her wedding night? "Make love in exciting new ways? There are none. Tell him stories? He's heard them all. Where does she go from there? What does she do next?" The answer was, for Dunyazade and Barth, to tell the story of the stories, to detail the secret circumstances of their origin and the special motives for their telling, something never done before, hence new, and innovative too inasmuch as this new telling builds upon and takes for granted the tradition that led up to it.

Scheherazade, it seems, looking to stop the King from raping a virgin every night and killing her in the morning, sought counsel first in political science and psychology. When none of these and more proved useful, at last she turned to folklore and mythology, seeking in them a theme or way with words which, like a magic spell, would work a miracle. There were thousands of tales about treasures that nobody could find the key to. In her case, she had the key but couldn't find the treasure. It was as if, she said, she and Dunyazade and the King were all characters in a fiction, and in this fiction she was trying to find a key to change the King to a gentle loving husband.

> Now, no matter what way she finds—whether it's a magic spell or a magic story with the answer in it or a magic anything—it comes down to particular words in the story we're reading. . . . And those words are made from the letters of our alphabet: a couple-dozen squiggles we can draw with this pen. This is the key . . . ! And the treasure, too, if we can only get our hands on it! It's as if—as if the key to the treasure *is* the treasure! (P. 8)

No sooner has she said these words than a genie appears from nowhere, looking and talking suspiciously like Barth. He's light-skinned, tall, spectacled, bald, and forty. He's managed to complete, he later says, "two-thirds of a projected series of three *novellas,* longish tales which would take their sense from one another in

several . . . ways" (p. 28), some of which have here been mentioned, more to come. The two he's finished "have to do with mythic
heroes, true and false." The third is "Dunyazadiad," which he's only
part way through and which involves the theme of the key to the
treasure being the treasure, words which he has just set down when
he appeared to them. His project, he explains, is both artistically
and personally "to learn where to go by discovering where I am by
reviewing where I've been—where we've *all* been" (p. 10). And he
likens it to a kind of snail in the Maryland marshes "that makes his
shell as he goes along out of whatever he comes across, cementing
it with his own juices, and at the same time makes his path instinctively toward the best available material for his shell; he carries
his history on his back, living in it, adding new and larger spirals
to it from the present as he grows." The trouble is that he now
moves at that snail's pace and, instead of spirals, moves in circles.
He's quit reading and writing. He's lost track of who he is. His
name's just a jumble of letters; "so's the whole body of literature:
strings of letters and empty spaces, like a code that I've lost the key
to" (pp. 10–11).

Now, though, he is perked because at last he's face to face with
the woman of his dreams, Scheherazade, perked even more because
the bulk of her story hasn't come to pass yet, she hasn't so far thought
of, much less started, her scheme of distracting the King with nightly
tales, hence he can be of service to her. All he need do is supply her
from the future with her stories from the past, which he does and
in the process solves his own dilemma, going forward by going back,
"to the very roots and springs of story" (p. 28). In the process too,
he and Scheherazade discuss the niceties of story structure, compar-
ing writing and reading, telling and listening, to different ways of
making love, noting "the similarity between conventional dramatic
structure—its exposition, rising action, climax, and dénouement—
and the rhythm of sexual intercourse from foreplay through coitus
to orgasm and release" (pp. 24–25). The metaphor is one which
has peculiar relevance to the present subject matter, involving as it
does the issues of mutual relations between the sexes, liberation,
and equality.

> Narrative, in short, . . . was a love relation, not a rape: its success
> depended upon the reader's consent and cooperation, which she
> could withhold or at any moment withdraw; also upon her own
> combination of experience and talent for the enterprise, and the

author's ability to arouse, sustain, and satisfy her interest—an ability
on which his figurative life hung as surely as Scheherazade's literal.
(P. 26)

In any case, the scheme works out, Scheherazade tells her stories,
saves herself and the country's virgins, it's now her wedding night.

Dunyazade's too. She's been telling the story of those stories to
her husband on their bed. Scheherazade, however, hates men so
much she's arranged to trick both her husband and her sister's
husband into agreeing to be tied, whereupon she and Dunyazade
plan to amputate their husbands' sex. That is the present action of
the story, Dunyazade with the knife. Her husband now explains that
he never killed all those virgins he's supposed to have, he only made
it seem that way. Actually they are all away and safe, and that
because the virgin he began with convinced him of his mistake.
Her arguments involved what she called the Tragical View of Sex
and Temperament, a phrase and theory which earlier in *Chimera*
Calyxa had explained to Perseus, and Melanippe to Bellerophon.
Granted that perfect equality between men and women isn't possible
any more than perfect equality on other terms, it nevertheless is
still worth striving for. "To pursue it ardently, against the grain of
things as they were, was in all likelihood to spoil one's chances for
happiness in love; *not* to pursue it, on the other hand, once one had
seen it clearly to be the ideal, no doubt had the same effect" (p. 45).
Since everything leads to the same dark place, better to embrace.
"Treasure me, Dunyazade, as I'll treasure you!" the King, tied down,
explains to her. "Nothing *works!* But the enterprise is noble; it's full
of joy and life, and the other ways are deathy. Let's make love like
passionate equals!" And she replies, "You mean *as if* we were equals.
. . . You know we're not. What you want is impossible." To which
the King responds, "Despite your heart's feelings? . . . Let it be
as if! Let's make a philosophy of that *as if!*" The night is almost over.
She's almost overcome. "Good morning, then! Good morning!"
(pp. 53–54).

It's a fitting end for this book of "Good evening" and "Good
night," a kind of heightened climax to so much re-turning and
confusion. What remains is a last brief section of this story, a kind
of coda even to the book, in which the storyteller (Barth presumably) explains his love for the story of Scheherazade and how if he
could write a story as beautiful it would be about little Dunyazade

and her bridegroom who pass a thousand and one nights in one dark night and then go out in the morning to greet sister and brother in the forenoon of a new life. "Dunyazade's story begins in the middle; in the middle of my own, I can't conclude it," he goes on, "but it must end in the night that all good mornings come to" (p. 55). The Arab storytellers understood this. They didn't end their tales "happily ever after" but rather with a reference to the Death that will eventually overtake all. Life becomes sweeter the more one comes to its end: a conclusion which is tragical, yet not, for death in that sense is what gives life its meaning. Without one there wouldn't be the other. The key to living is to live, to loving love, to writing write, all one and the same and all the treasure.

In the best of all worlds, for, as must be clear by now to any who have read this book, its format is not the one that is here described. The original *Chimera* began with the "Perseid" and its spiral. "Good evening" were its first words, "Good night. Good night" its last. "Bellerophoniad" was next with a punning emphasis on the last part of its title: an imitation of the "Perseid," "Good night," "Good night" its first words, a miserable failure from start to end. Both were forms of Polyeidus as was the "Dunyazadiad" which came next with its "Good morning" end. Various motifs built up throughout, the key to the treasure, for example (pp. 73, 255), and the spiral which Perseus went up through, which Bellerophon tried to achieve but never did ("how to open my life's closed circuit into an ascending spiral, like the sand-collars on the beach, like the Moon-shells that I put to my ear for answers" p. 241), and which the Barth-like visitor in the final story used as his emblem. There Scheherazade gave to him a spiral earring for his lady in imitation of the spiral snail-shell metaphor he had earlier used. "He accepted it joyfully, vowing to spin from it, if he could, as from a catherine-wheel or whirling galaxy, a golden shower of fiction" (pp. 18–19), and he in turn brought back to her a ring with the spiral patterns of ram's horns and conches.[26]

Various overt thematic statements were built upon as well. "I thought to overtake with understanding my present paragraph as it were by examining my paged past, and thus pointed, proceed serene to the future's sentence" (p. 81). Perseus says that first, and Bellerophon, privy to the "Perseid," repeats these words exactly in his story (p. 176). The Barth-like character in "Dunyazadiad" changes the figure somewhat but not the sense. "He wished neither to repudiate nor to repeat his past performances; he aspired to go beyond them toward a future they were not attuned to and, by some magic, at the same time go back to the original springs of narrative" (p. 10). There are many similar cumulative images and quotations, and the result is a group of novellas which twist upon themselves as does a spiral but which, again as does a spiral, eventually come out artistically and thematically on top.

What changed *Chimera's* pattern was that Barth's editor at Doubleday had in the meantime gone to Random House where Barth for various reasons eventually went as well. She thought the book was brilliant, but she did think too that "Dunyazadiad" was the best piece in it, the easiest, most sentimental and agreeable, one especially suited to lead a reader into the others, in contrast with the "Perseid," which however good was quite literally involuted. Barth balked at the suggestion for a time but finally agreed, and the stories were rearranged, "Dunyazadiad" coming first, "Perseid" second, and "Bellerophoniad" third. There were some accidental happy effects, he noted. In keeping with the image of the spiral, each story was now roughly one and one-half times the length of its predecessor, and the first two were almost equal in length to the third.[27] The basically similar tale-within-a-tale structure of the stories remained the same: Barth telling the reader what Dunyazade told her husband, Perseus telling Andromeda what he told Calyxa, Bellerophon telling Melanippe what he told Philonoë. A few relations among the tales remained about the same as well: the constellations which Perseus and his company become are ones which Bellerophon in time stares up at; the Amazon culture which Dunyazade's husband helps to found is the source for the Amazon Melanippe, whom Bellerophon in part tells his story to. But there was no sense of progression, no sense of obstacles overcome, of victories achieved (failed Bellerophon ends the book now, after all, not wisened Dunyazade)—perhaps most important, no sense of Polyeidus as the unifying medium. Perseus isn't really a constellation narrating his story from the sky, after all. He's a character in a story that Polyeidus has taken the form of, the central conceit of which is a constellation telling its story. That is the only basis on which Barth can mix metaphors and have a constellation refer to its paged past and future's sentence. Perseus isn't speaking there, it's Polyeidus.[28] Before, the tone of one story had led naturally to the next,

climaxing in the relative simplicity of "Dunyazadiad" with its synthesis that follows complexity. Now with that story first, the two
remaining seem apart from it, not only in subject but in tone, related
solely to themselves. Indeed the very meaning has been changed:
from the final optimism of Dunyazade's acceptance to the closing
pessimism of Bellerophon's befuddlement. And Barth at last couldn't
help feeling that the arrangement of the stories would have been
better as he'd planned. "Have you done any reading on the various
forms a book can take?" he asked. "The difference between the
arrangement of a book that one ideally has in one's head as opposed
to the way it actually is in print?"[29] And a visitor would have the
feeling that just as Barth had once changed the ending to *The Floating Opera* in accordance with his publisher's wishes, only in time to
change it back to the original, so something like that would eventually happen in this case as well.

The reviewers didn't see any mar in the design, however. They
almost uniformly praised it, though few of them claimed to understand it. Unconsciously or otherwise, they wrote of it in metaphors
appropriate to the spiral and constellation motifs, noting that it
"may dazzle posterity," "spins talkingly out," "twists in and out and
back on itself," that it was a "whirling vortex," "a swirl of ancient
rhetoric and modern slang," "a shower of gold," etc.[30] Its commercial success, as might be expected for such a special book, was not
as great as *Giles Goat-Boy*, but then the success of that book itself
was unexpected and not typical. *Chimera*'s sales were about the
same as *Lost in the Funhouse*, however, 17,000 hardbacks sold in
the first year and an initial paperback sale of 85,000.[31] More significant, after having been nominated for a National Book Award two
times before in connection with *The Floating Opera* and *Lost in the
Funhouse*, Barth finally this time won it, sharing the 1972 fiction
honors with John Williams.

That same year he went on leave again from Buffalo, this time
to teach at Boston University during the academic year of 1972–
1973, and following that he went to the university where he had
begun, Johns Hopkins, teaching in the Writing Seminar and in a
building, Gilman Hall, where years before he had stacked books
and browsed through the Oriental Seminary collection. *Letters* was
not to be ready, he thought, for the 1976 bicentennial celebration as
he'd hoped, but then that publication deadline had not been crucial
to his enterprise, only appropriate to it, and anyway, as he so often

noted, he tended to measure in the long run, not by the month or even the year.

There was the irony that one interviewer noted, that in returning to Johns Hopkins University where he had once been a student he was recycling his life as Perseus and the Barth-like character in "Dunyazadiad" had done, and that was appropriate to a writer for whom art and life were inextricably related, who had more and more in recent years begun to think of his work as a gnomon, which he understood to be a geometric term for a figure adding to a pre-existing figure, enlarging its size without changing its shape—another version of the spiral. Returning to the scenes of his youth, he had begun rereading his books to recover his past ("like looking at an album of photographs from fifteen years ago," he said), and he was "at least as much pleased as embarrassed to recognize a melodious apprenticeship, an energetic innocence." Perhaps when he was ninety he would be as grave as Sophocles at ninety.

"More likely, Zeus willing," he said, "I'll be writing comedy in my eighties as Thomas Mann did, and die laughing."[32]

The record, of course, is not yet complete. Not simply because Barth continues working, but because *Chimera*, by its very literal derivative nature (having been born from another work, *Letters*, which itself is not yet finished), cannot be considered as a convenient stopping place in Barth's career. If he had written no more after *Lost in the Funhouse*, it and the books that led up to it would still have had a logic and direction as a group that left us feeling satisfied. But *Chimera*, however good on its own, seems because of its manner and its message of recycling more a transition than a synthesis, and as a consequence any chronicle of Barth's fiction must at this point seem to end, as Hemingway would say, without a "wow."

On the beach of his desolation, the nameless minstrel of "Anonymiad" once described a kind of book he had in mind.

> Whimsic fantasy, grub fact, pure senseless music—none in itself would do; to embody *all* and rise above each, in a work neither longfaced nor idiotly grinning, but adventuresome, passionately humored, merry with the pain of insight, wise and smiling in the terror of our life—that was my calm ambition. (P. 198)

So too Barth's. The accepting, optimistic nature of *Chimera* indicates a major shift of tone in him, away from the restrictiveness of nihilism toward a more open and measured view of things. "Scheherazade was right to think love ephemeral," we are told in "Dunyazadiad." "But life itself was scarcely so, and both were sweet for just that reason—sweeter yet when enjoyed as if they might endure" (p. 39). That *as if* occurs often in the book, indeed in Barth's work generally, mostly in the form of masks. The difference is that in the earlier fiction his characters put on masks to face intolerable situations whereas now they mask the situations themselves. It is a movement outward instead of in, active instead of passive, a kind of charge instead of a retreat, and it marks a change in direction toward the sort of fiction Barth's nameless minstrel aspired to. Maybe *Letters* or whatever other fiction Barth engages in will demonstrate quite different matters. That is a part of the joy of watching an artist's career progress, the suspense and the resolution. For now at least, we can say (as did Barth himself when in the "Publisher's Disclaimer" to *Giles Goat-Boy* he invented an editor, B, who wrote a profile of Barth's fiction) that

> he turns his back on what *is the case*, rejects the familiar for the amazing, embraces artifice and extravagance; washing his hands of the search for Truth, he calls himself "a monger after beauty," or "doorman of the Muses' Fancy-house." In sum, he is in a class by himself. . . ; whether a cut above or a cut below, three decades ahead or three centuries behind, his . . . readers must decide. (P. xiii)

Notes

Foreword

1. Robert Scholes, "George Is My Name," *New York Times Book Review,* 7 August 1966, p. 1.
2. Leslie Fiedler, "John Barth: An Eccentric Genius," *New Leader* 44 (13 February 1961): 23.
3. Granville Hicks, "The Up-to-Date Looking Glass," *Saturday Review* 51 (28 September 1968): 32.
4. *The Floating Opera* (Garden City, N.Y.: Doubleday, 1967), pp. 6–7. More complete bibliographic information is provided in the text and notes to chapter 1.
5. "Heroic Comedy," *Newsweek* 68 (8 August 1966): 82.

Chapter 1

1. Judith Golwyn, "New Creative Writers," *Library Journal* 81 (1 June 1956): 1497. The stories were "Parnassus Approached," "Fox-Island Incident," and "Lilith and the Lion." The tale-cycle was *Dorchester Tales.* Along with the master's novel, *Shirt of Nessus,* they are discussed in chapter 8.
2. John Enck, "John Barth: An Interview," *Wisconsin Studies in Contemporary Literature* 6 (1965): 7.
3. Ibid., p. 10.
4. Golwyn, "New Creative Writers," p. 1497.
5. Alan Prince, "An Interview with John Barth," *Prism* (Sir George Williams University, Spring 1968): 47. When Barth wrote *The Floating Opera,* those works by Assis that he knew best were *Epitaph of a Small Winner* and *Bras Cubas* in addition to *Dom Casmurro,* the last of which is discussed further in chapter 8.
6. The quotation is only in the original edition, currently available in an Avon paperback, p. 241. Subsequent references are either to this edition or the revised edition by Doubleday (1967).
7. John Barth to D.M. (5 November 1969).
8. Barth's agent, Lurton Blassingame, to D.M. (20 May 1969). A more sparse account of these transactions is in the preface to the revised edition of *The Floating Opera,* along with other information about the novel's history.
9. Art Myers, "Life's But a Showboat Drifting By," *Washington Post and Times Herald,* 26 August 1956, p. E6.
10. Ibid. See also Stanley Edgar Hyman, "John Barth's First Novel," *New*

Leader 48 (12 April 1965): 21; Richard Schickel, *"The Floating Opera,"* *Critique* 6, no. 2 (1963): 65, 67.

11. Barth's "Prefatory Note to the Revised Edition" of *The Floating Opera.* Even with "the original and correct ending" restored, Barth still was not to avoid criticism. A reader for *Publishers' Weekly* (6 March 1967) took exception to the prefatory note, called it "rather petulant," and added "it is to be hoped that Mr. Barth is now happy with his creation"; sometimes a writer cannot win.

12. *Publishers' Weekly* 191 (6 March 1967): 73.

13. Enck, "John Barth: An Interview," p. 7.

Chapter 2

1. John Barth to D.M. (5 November 1969); Barth's preface to the revised edition of *The Floating Opera* (1967); Judith Golwyn, "New Creative Writers," *Library Journal* 81 (1 June 1956): 1497. There has been some confusion about the book's exact title. It is *The End of the Road* in the first edition, but *End of the Road* in an early paperback edition. In later ones, paper and hardback, the initial definite article has been returned, and this most recent version is used here. It is also the one Barth put on the front page of the novel's typescript, which is on file at the Library of Congress. See chapter 8 for a reproduction of that page.

2. Barth's agent, Lurton Blassingame, to D.M. (20 May 1969). Unless otherwise indicated, all other information about the publishers and *The End of the Road* comes from this source.

3. Barth's Doubleday editor, Timothy Seldes, to D.M. (11 December 1969).

4. Barth's Doubleday editor, Anne Freedgood, to D.M. (11 December 1969).

5. John Barth to D.M. (5 November 1969).

6. Appleton-Century-Crofts to D.M. (17 March 1969); Anne Freedgood to D.M. (20 March 1969).

7. "A Study in Nihilism," *Time* 72 (21 July 1958): 80.

8. Taliaferro Boatwright, "Jacob Horner Came Out of His Corner, and Then—," *New York Herald Tribune Book Review,* 20 July 1958, p. 3. See also Paul Pickrel, "Unlucky Jake," *Harper's* 217 (August 1958): 87, who says that *The End of the Road* has "far more freshness, more wit and invention, and more intellectual life of its own than most recent American fiction."

9. David Kerner, "Psychodrama in Eden," *Chicago Review* 13, no. 1 (Winter-Spring 1959): 59–60.

10. George Bluestone, "John Wain and John Barth: The Angry and the Accurate," *Massachusetts Review* 1, no. 3 (May 1960): 588. This array of enthusiastic critics is typical of how *The End of the Road* was received, but it does not represent the full spectrum of opinion. For example, when the book finally appeared in England in 1962, some British reviewers were very unimpressed, and one in particular found it "neither very interesting nor convincing." He even felt that, considering the greatness of *The Sot-Weed Factor* which by then had been published, this lesser novel by Barth should have been sup-

pressed. "Strife and Struggle," *Times Literary Supplement,* 28 September 1962, p. 757.

11. Alan Prince, "An Interview with John Barth," *Prism* (Sir George Williams University, Spring 1968): 57.

12. Bluestone, "John Wain and John Barth," p. 586.

13. When in 1967 *The Floating Opera* was published by Doubleday in a revised edition, *The End of the Road* and Barth's third novel *The Sot-Weed Factor* (1960) appeared along with it, also revised. As was discussed in chapter 1, the revisions in *The Floating Opera* are substantial, affecting the book's style and theme. The revisions in *The End of the Road* and *The Sot-Weed Factor,* on the other hand, affect only style. In the case of *The Sot-Weed Factor,* they amount to about fifty pages of matter here and there cut out. In the case of *The End of the Road,* they are so minimal as barely to be detected, an occasional word or sentence having been cut or amended. In spite of its little difference from the first edition, the revised edition is nevertheless the authorized one and is thus used as the source for all quotations. Complete citation for the noted passage is as follows: *The End of the Road,* rev. ed. (Garden City, N.Y.: Doubleday, 1967), p. 41. Subsequent references will be only to page numbers and will be found immediately after quotations.

14. John Enck, "John Barth: An Interview," *Wisconsin Studies in Contemporary Literature* 6 (1965): 12.

15. Prince, "An Interview with John Barth," p. 57.

16. Ibid., p. 56.

17. Jean Elizabeth Kennard, "Towards a Novel of the Absurd: A Study of the Relationships between the Concept of the Absurd as Defined in the Works of Sartre and Camus and Ideas and Form in the Fiction of John Barth, Samuel Beckett, Nigel Dennis, Joseph Heller, and James Purdy," unpublished dissertation (University of California, Berkeley, 1968), p. 114.

18. Prince, "An Interview with John Barth," p. 54.

Chapter 3

1. Alan Prince, "An Interview with John Barth," *Prism* (Sir George Williams University, Spring 1968): 50–51.

2. John Enck, "John Barth: An Interview," *Wisconsin Studies in Contemporary Literature* 6 (1965): 10–11.

3. Ibid., p. 11.

4. Prince, "An Interview with John Barth," p. 54.

5. Ibid., p. 48.

6. Ibid., p. 52; John Barth to D.M. (5 November 1969).

7. Enck, "John Barth: An Interview," p. 7.

8. Prince, "An Interview with John Barth," p. 49.

9. Lawrence C. Wroth, "*The Maryland Muse* by Ebenezer Cooke," *Proceedings of the American Antiquarian Society* 44 (October 1934): 268–278. In 1731, two Cooke poems (*Bacon's Rebellion* plus a revised version of *The Sot-Weed Factor*) were published together as *The Maryland Muse.* Wroth's biography of Cooke introduces a facsimile of that collection.

10. Philip E. Diser, "The Historical Ebenezer Cooke," *Critique* 10, no. 3 (1968): 49.

11. Wroth, *"The Maryland Muse* by Ebenezer Cooke," pp. 268–278; Diser, "The Historical Ebenezer Cooke," pp. 49–52.

12. Enck, "John Barth: An Interview," p. 8.

13. R.W. Murphy, "In Print: John Barth," *Horizon* 5 (January 1963): 37.

14. As we noted earlier, Barth's novel *The Sot-Weed Factor* was published in 1960 and republished with a slightly revised text in 1967 along with new and revised editions of Barth's two earlier novels, *The Floating Opera* and *The End of the Road.* Barth added a preface to *The Sot-Weed Factor* of 1967, pointing out the parallel that in making changes he had done quite as Cooke had done to his poem *The Sot-Weed Factor* when it was republished in 1730. "The cases differ," he continued, "in that Cooke's objective was to blunt the barbs of his original satire, he having dwelt by then many years among its targets, but mine is merely, where possible, to make this long narrative a quantum swifter and more graceful." He might have added that, although no cut was major or in a block, the cumulative effect of various minor excisions was to shorten the book by almost fifty pages. The revised text is the authorized one, hence it has been chosen here as the source for all quotations as published in hardback by Doubleday. The noted passage is from p. 458; other page numbers are placed within the body of the text and next to the passages to which they refer.

15. Prince, "An Interview with John Barth," p. 51.

16. Ibid., p. 50.

17. Alan Holder, " 'What Marvellous Plot . . . Was Afoot?' History in Barth's *The Sot-Weed Factor,*" *American Quarterly* 20, no. 3 (Fall 1968): 599–600.

18. Brantz Mayer, *Shea's Early Southern Tracts,* no. 2, New York, 1865.

19. Philip Young, "The Mother of Us All: Pocahontas Reconsidered," *Kenyon Review* 24, no. 3 (Summer 1962): 397; included in Young's *Three Bags Full: Essays in American Fiction* (New York: Harcourt Brace Jovanovich, 1972), p. 182.

20. Enck, "John Barth: An Interview," p. 6.

21. Ibid., p. 7.

22. Arthur Cooper, "An In-Depth Interview with John Barth," *Harrisburg Patriot,* 30 March 1965, p. 6.

23. Enck, "John Barth: An Interview," p. 7.

24. Lurton Blassingame to D.M. (20 May 1969).

25. Terry Southern, "New Trends and Old Hats," *Nation* 191 (19 November 1960): 381.

26. Helen Arthur, "The Marathon Adventures of a 17th-Century Englishman," *New York Herald Tribune Lively Arts Section,* 22 January 1961, p. 30.

27. "The Virgin Laureate," *Time* 76 (5 September 1960): 77.

28. "'I' Faith, 'Tis Good," *Newsweek* 56 (29 August 1960): 89.

29. Anne Freedgood to D.M. (20 March 1969).

30. Enck, "John Barth: An Interview," p. 12.

Chapter 4

1. John Enck, "John Barth: An Interview," *Wisconsin Studies in Contemporary Literature* 6 (1965): 14. When the novel was released as a paper-

back in 1964, the phrase "a moral allegory cloaked in terms of colonial history" was printed on the rear cover and attributed to Barth.

2. R.W. Murphy, "In Print: John Barth," *Horizon* 5 (January 1963): 37.

3. John Barth, "Afterword," *The Adventures of Roderick Random* by Tobias Smollett (New York: Signet, 1964), p. 479.

Chapter 5

1. John Enck, "John Barth: An Interview," *Wisconsin Studies in Contemporary Literature* 6 (1965): 8.

2. John Barth, "Afterword," *The Adventures of Roderick Random* by Tobias Smollett (New York: Signet, 1964), p. 479.

3. Enck, "John Barth: An Interview," p. 12; Phyllis Meras, "John Barth: A Truffle No Longer," *New York Times Book Review*, 7 August 1966, p. 22; Alan Prince, "An Interview with John Barth," *Prism* (Sir George Williams University, Spring 1968): 58–59. For the principal theory of archetypes, see vol. 9, part 1 of Jung's collected works, *The Archetypes and the Collective Unconscious* (Princeton: Princeton University Press, rev. ed. 1968); for an excellent example of its literary application, see Philip Young's "Fallen from Time: Rip Van Winkle," *Three Bags Full: Essays in American Fiction* (New York: Harcourt Brace Jovanovich, 1972), pp. 204–231.

4. Meras, "John Barth: A Truffle No Longer," p. 22.

5. Lord Raglan, *The Hero. A Study in Tradition, Myth, and Drama* (London, 1936), pp. 178–179.

6. Prince, "An Interview with John Barth," p. 59.

7. "Cover-letter to the Editors and Publisher," *Giles Goat-Boy* (Garden City, N.Y.: Doubleday, 1966), p. xxiii. Subsequent references are to this edition; the page numbers are provided next to relevant quotations. For the sake of completeness, it should be noted that somewhat different portions of this novel, called "Test Borings," were published in *Modern Occasions*, ed. Philip Rahv (New York: Noonday Press, 1966), pp. 247–263. Barth has described them as "three fragments written as trial-starts for *Giles Goat-Boy* before its hero, attitude, and viewpoint were clearly conceived" (the remark is from an early prospectus Barth wrote for the book, on file at the Library of Congress, Manuscript Division).

8. John Barth to D.M. (5 November 1969).

9. Ibid.

10. Anne Freedgood to D.M. (20 March 1969). She later said: "We taped a reading Barth gave of the introduction to *Giles*, the part where he pretends that various editors have looked at the book and are making their criticisms of it. And we ran that tape to a group of salesmen. The passages are full of trade jokes and no one around here could write a book report for three weeks without identifying himself with one of Barth's invented editors. The salesmen loved the tape so much they were ready to go out and promote the book into every store in the country" (11 December 1969).

11. Anne Freedgood to D.M. (28 March 1975); Robert Scholes to D.M. (20 January 1975).

12. Webster Schott, "A Black Comedy to Offend Everyone," *Life* 61 (12 August 1966): 10.

13. W. Balliett, "Rub-a-Dub-Dub," *New Yorker* 42 (10 December 1966): 234.

14. Robert Garis, "What Happened to John Barth?," *Commentary* 42, no. 4 (October 1966): 89, 92.

15. Richard Poirier, "Wescac and the Messiah," *Book Week,* 7 August 1966, p. 1.

16. Saul Maloff, "Heroic Comedy," *Newsweek* 68 (8 August 1966): 81.

17. Robert Scholes, "George Is My Name," *New York Times Book Review,* 7 August 1966, p. 1.

18. Prince, "An Interview with John Barth," p. 58.

19. Meras, "John Barth: A Truffle No Longer," p. 22.

20. Joseph Campbell, *The Hero with a Thousand Faces* (Cleveland: World Publishing Co., 1956), p. 30.

21. Saul Maloff, "Heroic Comedy," p. 82.

22. Schott, "A Black Comedy to Offend Everyone," p. 10.

Chapter 6

1. "Tanker Sinks Fishing Boat; 47 Saved, One Is Missing," *New York Times,* 14 July 1969, p. 1.

2. Alan Prince, "An Interview with John Barth," *Prism* (Sir George Williams University, Spring 1968): 61.

3. Douglas M. Davis, "The End Is a Beginning for Barth's 'Funhouse,'" *National Observer,* 16 September 1969, p. 19; Prince, "An Interview with John Barth," p. 61.

4. Davis, "The End Is a Beginning for Barth's 'Funhouse,'" p. 19; Prince, "An Interview with John Barth," p. 61.

5. Prince, "An Interview with John Barth," p. 46.

6. "Autobiography" was first published in *New American Review* no. 2 (New York: New American Library, 1968), pp. 72–75. It was later published, along with similar stories, in Barth's *Lost in the Funhouse* (Garden City, N.Y.: Doubleday, 1968). A 1969 Bantam paperback of *Lost in the Funhouse* is the same as the original hardcover edition except for "Seven Additional Author's Notes." But unless otherwise indicated, all quotations are taken from the Doubleday original. The noted passage is from p. 36; subsequent page numbers are within the text beside the quotations to which they refer. Barth wrote the additional notes for *Lost in the Funhouse* after it had come out in America. He included them in the British hardcover and then in the American paperback, and he wrote them reluctantly, he said, as a response to some critics who charged that several details in his stories were deliberately obscure.

7. Robert Graves, *The Greek Myths* (Baltimore: Penguin, rev. ed. 1960), vol. 1, pp. 286–288.

8. Davis, "The End Is a Beginning for Barth's 'Funhouse,'" p. 19.

9. Ibid.

10. King Prajadhipok's visit to the United States in 1931 was much publicized. The narrator of "Petition" is just partly exaggerating when he writes: "The magazines proclaim the triflingest details of your daily round; society talks of nothing else but your comings and goings; a word from you sends government officers scurrying, reroutes express-trains, stops presses, marshals

the finest medical talents in the nation" (p. 59). The King had come to the United States for an operation that would remove a cataract from his left eye; and when the operation was performed successfully on May 10, 1931, at Ophir Hall in White Plains, New York, the fact was considered important enough to merit space on the front page of the following day's *New York Times.* Ophir Hall, incidentally, was not a hospital but a mansion where the King was a guest.

11. Tony Tanner, "No Exit," *Partisan Review* 86, no. 2 (1969): 294.

12. John Barth to D.M. (5 November 1969). The manuscripts of "Ambrose His Mark" and "Water-Message" along with a letter from Barth to *Esquire,* all on file at the Library of Congress, Manuscript Division, explicitly relate these stories to *The Seeker* or *The Amateur.*

13. Ambrose Lightship is well known; its fascinating history is not. In 1823, a small ship equipped with a beacon was first stationed twenty-two miles outside New York harbor as a guide to ocean traffic. Later, in 1908, the name of the lightship then in use was made Ambrose, and it remained so for all later ships. Lobster-red, held in place by a 7800-pound mushroom anchor, manned by a crew of sixteen that stayed on board for weeks at a stretch, the lightships often risked being run down. Vessels of every size, from cruisers to liners, went by at an interval of one every seven minutes, and during fog it was absolutely necessary for them to pass as close as possible to Ambrose in order to get their direction straight for the harbor. Surprisingly, the lightships were struck just four times in fifty-nine years. They were never bothered by World War II German submarines which frequently torpedoed nearby ships, littering the water with oil and wreckage, but that in itself is not surprising— since the lightships were in effect attracting targets for the U-boats, it would have been foolish to sink such unintended help. Finally, on August 23, 1967, the tradition of Ambrose Lightship ended. The sixth Ambrose, in service since 1952, was replaced by a permanent, four-legged tower and restationed off the coast of New England. For more information about Ambrose Lightship, see Homer Bigart, "Ambrose Lightship Blinks Her Last Lonely Signal," *New York Times,* 24 August 1967, pp. 1, 75.

14. Davis, "The End Is a Beginning for Barth's 'Funhouse,'" p. 19.

15. John Barth to D.M. (5 November 1969).

Chapter 7

1. Alan Prince, "An Interview with John Barth," *Prism* (Sir George Williams University, Spring 1968): 60.

2. Bruce Jay Friedman, "Those Clowns of Conscience," *Book Week,* 18 July 1965, pp. 2, 7. See also Friedman's introduction to *Black Humor,* a 1965 anthology he edited for Bantam Books.

3. Prince, "An Interview with John Barth," p. 57.

4. Richard Kostelanetz, "The Point Is That Life Doesn't Have Any Point," *New York Times Book Review,* 6 June 1965, pp. 3, 28, 30.

5. Arthur Cooper, "An In-Depth Interview with John Barth," *Harrisburg Patriot,* 30 March 1965, p. 6.

6. Robert Scholes, *The Fabulators* (New York: Oxford University Press, 1967). Scholes feels that there are a great many fabulators presently at work,

but for reasons of space he limits himself to six who "illustrate the range and vigor of modern fabulation" (p. 13). In addition to Barth, they are Durrell, Vonnegut, Southern, Hawkes, and Murdoch.

7. John Enck, "John Barth: An Interview," *Wisconsin Studies in Contemporary Literature* 6 (1965): 7.

8. Prince, "An Interview with John Barth," p. 57.

9. Scholes, *The Fabulators*, p. 12.

10. Philip Young, *Ernest Hemingway: A Reconsideration* (University Park: The Pennsylvania State University Press, 1966), pp. 43–48.

11. "Help! A Stereophonic Narrative for Authorial Voice," *Esquire* 72 (September 1969): 108–109.

12. John Barth to D.M. (5 November 1969).

13. Prince, "An Interview with John Barth," pp. 55–56.

Chapter 8

1. Arthur Cooper, "An In-Depth Interview with John Barth," *Harrisburg Patriot*, 30 March 1965, p. 6. The following two quotations are from the same source.

2. Mopsy Strange Kennedy, "Roots of an Author," *Washington Post Potomac*, 3 September 1967, p. 17.

3. Ibid., p. 18.

4. Ibid., p. 19.

5. Barth's 1953 letter of application to teach English at The Pennsylvania State University (on file in the Rare Book Room at Penn State).

6. Cooper, "An In-Depth Interview with John Barth," p. 6.

7. Alan Prince, "An Interview with John Barth," *Prism* (Sir George Williams University, Spring 1968): 44.

8. Ibid., p. 45.

9. Ibid., pp. 44–45.

10. John Barth to D.M. (5 November 1969).

11. John Barth, "Lilith and the Lion," *Hopkins Review* 4 (Fall 1950): 49–53.

12. Lurton Blassingame to D.M. (20 May 1969).

13. Barth's 1953 letter of application to teach English at The Pennsylvania State University.

14. John Barth to D.M. (5 November 1969).

15. Ibid.; "Landscape: The Eastern Shore" appeared in *Kenyon Review* (Winter 1960): 104–110.

16. John Barth to D.M. (4 February 1970).

17. This and subsequent correspondence, either in the form of letters to his Penn State English department chairman or applications for various grants, are on file at the Rare Book Room of the Penn State library.

18. Saul Maloff, "Heroic Comedy," *Newsweek* 68 (8 August 1966): 82.

19. John Barth, "My Two Muses," *Johns Hopkins Magazine* 12, no. 7 (April 1961): 13.

20. Cooper, "An In-Depth Interview with John Barth," p. 6.

21. Hugh Kenner, *Samuel Beckett* (Los Angeles: University of California Press, 1968), p. 62.

22. John Barth, "Muse, Spare Me," *Book Week*, 26 September 1965, p. 28.

23. Ibid., p. 29.

24. John Barth to D.M. (5 November 1969).

25. Cooper, "An In-Depth Interview with John Barth," p. 6.

26. Barth, "My Two Muses," p. 9.

Chapter 9

1. Israel Shenker, "Complicated Simple Things," *New York Times Book Review*, 24 September 1972, p. 36.

2. John Barth to D.M. (12 March 1975).

3. Ibid.

4. John Barth to an audience at The University of Iowa (13 March 1971).

5. Ibid.

6. Barth to D.M. (12 March 1975).

7. Martin Gardner, "About Three Types of Spiral and How to Construct Them," in "Mathematical Games," *Scientific American* (April 1962), p. 158. See also "The Multiple Fascinations of the Fibonacci Sequence," in "Mathematical Games," *Scientific American* (March 1969), pp. 116–120, an article that appeared at the time Barth was preparing to write the "Perseid."

8. Barth to an audience at The University of Iowa (13 March 1971).

9. Ibid.

10. John Barth, *Chimera* (New York: Random House, 1972), p. 96. Subsequent quotations are from this edition and cited within the body of the text.

11. Barth at The University of Iowa (13 March 1971).

12. Ibid.

13. Anne Freedgood to D.M. (28 March 1975).

14. Barth at The University of Iowa (13 March 1971).

15. Robert Graves, *The Greek Myths* (Baltimore: Penguin, rev. ed., 1960), vol. 1, p. 244.

16. Barth to D.M. (12 March 1975).

17. Shenker, "Complicated Simple Things," p. 37; Barth to D.M. (12 March 1975); Barth at The University of Iowa (13 March 1971).

18. Graves, *The Greek Myths*, vol. 1, p. 254.

19. Barth, *Chimera*, p. 203, an expanded version of what he had earlier explained at The University of Iowa (13 March 1971).

20. Shenker, "Complicated Simple Things," p. 37.

21. Barth to D.M. (12 March 1975).

22. See John Barth, "The Ocean of Story," in *Directions in Literary Criticism: Contemporary Approaches to Literature,* ed. Stanley Weintraub and Philip Young (University Park: The Pennsylvania State University Press, 1973), pp. 1–6. Essentially an analysis of this longest of all tale cycles, the piece has certain fictive overtones inasmuch as it details the story of how Barth came to be interested in the cycle, and builds to a muted though nonetheless emotional conclusion which is reminiscent of those footnotes to literature he sees Borges primarily engaged in.

23. Barth at The University of Iowa (13 March 1971).

24. Barth to D.M. (12 March 1975).

25. Barth at The University of Iowa (13 March 1971).

26. Actually Barth makes no mention of the spiral design of these ram's horns and conches. Presumably he thought that the emphasis in context would be heavyhanded and that the reader by this point would recognize the pattern on his own. In any case, the idea for the detail once again came from Martin Gardner, who had provided illustrations of these spirals in "A Discussion of Helical Structures, from Corkscrews to DNA Molecules," in "Mathematical Games," *Scientific American* (June 1963), pp. 151, 152.

27. Barth to D.M. (12 March 1975); Anne Freedgood to D.M. (25 March 1975).

28. Indeed, in his foreseeing capacity, Polyeidus threatens to become "Harold Bray" and his non-fiction counterpart, Napoleon; he's already turned into a lecture by John Barth and could just as easily turn into John Barth himself; in his infinite capabilities he is potentially everything, both fact and fiction. That distinction itself now makes no sense. Art and life are the same. They *are* Polyeidus. If John Barth wrote these stories, so did Polyeidus *as* John Barth. Everything is imaginary, the embodiment of one mind, a Platonic conception of the world that Barth first toyed with in *The Sot-Weed Factor* when Ebenezer Cooke, toward the end, began to suspect that everything which had happened to him was a dream; a concept he did more with in *Giles Goat-Boy* when Giles, on the run in the campus library, asks a receptionist for directions—she looks up from a very large book that she is reading, almost as if he is exactly the figure she expects to see just then, and that because the book she is reading is the book that he is in, fiction and life having come together at that moment. A similar concept runs through *Lost in the Funhouse*, particularly in "Menelaiad" where all those stories within stories are really the product of one mind, Proteus, who has turned into Menelaus and his story. It is a distinctly non-Aristotelian, non-realistic philosophy which Barth, with his addiction to the notion of *as if*, finds especially appealing and which serves as the rationale for the kind of fantastic, fabulistic fiction he is working with. "It's an ancient idea. It's as old as Greek drama, anyhow," Barth says—"to play on the fact that this is a play that you're watching. And Shakespeare does it constantly: 'All the world's a stage,' et cetera. *The Tempest* is the example *par excellence*: the master of illusion uncloaking his illusions on one level while maintaining them on another. . . . And that's not decadence or mere gimmickry: it's a way of getting certain kinds of things expressed. Borges makes the remark that those moments in literature when the characters within a work begin to comment on, or be aware of, the fiction that they're in, disturb us because such moments remind us of the fiction that *we're* in. A Schopenhauerian idea, which seems to me to be unexceptionable," "Having It Both Ways: A Conversation between John Barth and Joe David Bellamy," *New American Review*, no. 15 (New York: Simon and Schuster, 1972), p. 143.

29. Barth to D.M. (12 March 1975).

30. *Playboy* (October 1972), p. 26; Leonard Michaels, *New York Times Book Review*, 24 September 1972, p. 1; *Publishers' Weekly* (31 July 1972), p. 68; *Times Literary Supplement*, 26 July 1974, p. 783; *Life* (6 October 1972), p. 28.

31. Anne Freedgood to D.M. (25 March 1975).

32. Shenker, "Complicated Simple Things," p. 37.

Bibliography

Fiction by John Barth

"Lilith and the Lion." *Hopkins Review* 4 (Fall 1950): 49–53.

The Floating Opera. New York: Appleton-Century-Crofts, 1956; revised edition Garden City, N.Y.: Doubleday, 1967.

The End of the Road. Garden City, N.Y.: Doubleday, 1958; revised edition 1967.

"The Remobilization of Jacob Horner." *Esquire* 50 (July 1958): 55–59. (Condensed version of chapter 6 of *The End of the Road*)

"Landscape: The Eastern Shore." *Kenyon Review* 12, no. 1 (Winter 1960): 104–110.

The Sot-Weed Factor. Garden City, N.Y.: Doubleday, 1960; revised edition 1967.

"Ambrose His Mark." *Esquire* 59 (February 1963): 97, 122–124, 126–127. (Included in *Lost in the Funhouse*)

"Water-Message." *Southwest Review* 48 (Summer 1963): 226–237. (Included, with small revision, in *Lost in the Funhouse*)

Giles Goat-Boy or, The Revised New Syllabus. Garden City, N.Y.: Doubleday, 1966.

"Night-Sea Journey." *Esquire* 65 (June 1966): 82–83, 147–148. (Included in *Lost in the Funhouse*)

"Test Borings." *Modern Occasions.* Ed. Philip Rahv. New York: Noonday Press, 1966, pp. 247–263. (Trial-starts for *Giles Goat-Boy*)

"Lost in the Funhouse." *Atlantic* 220 (November 1967): 73–82. (Included in *Lost in the Funhouse*)

"Autobiography: A Self-Recorded Fiction." *New American Review,* no. 2. New York: New American Library, 1968, pp. 72–75. (Included in *Lost in the Funhouse*)

Lost in the Funhouse. Garden City, N.Y.: Doubleday, 1968.

"Petition." *Esquire* 70 (July 1968): 68, 70–71, 135. (Included in *Lost in the Funhouse*)

"Title." *Yale Review* 57 (Winter 1968), 213–221. (Included in *Lost in the Funhouse*)

"Help! A Stereophonic Narrative for Authorial Voice." *Esquire* 72 (September 1968): 108–109.

"Dunyazadiad." *Esquire* 77 (June 1972): 136–142, 158, 160, 162, 164, 166, 168. (Included, somewhat longer, in *Chimera*)

Chimera. New York: Random House, 1972.

"Perseid," *Harper's* 245 (October 1972): 79–96. (Included, somewhat longer, in *Chimera*)

Non-Fiction by John Barth

"My Two Muses." *Johns Hopkins Magazine* 12, no. 7 (April 1961): 9–13.

"Afterword." *The Adventures of Roderick Random* by Tobias Smollett. New York: Signet, 1964, pp. 469–479.

"Muse, Spare Me." *Book Week*, 26 September 1965, pp. 28–29.

"A Gift of Books." *Holiday* 40 (December 1966): 171. (Brief praise of Borges's *Labyrinths*)

"Censorship—1967: A Series of Symposia." *Arts in Society* 4 (1967): 294.

"The Literature of Exhaustion." *Atlantic* 220 (August 1967): 29–34.

A Tribute to Vladimir Nabokov. In *Nabokov: Criticism, Reminiscences, Translations and Tributes*. Ed. Alfred Appel, Jr., and Charles Newman. Evanston: Northwestern University Press, 1970, p. 350.

"A Tribute to John Hawkes." *Harvard Advocate* 104 (October 1970): 11.

"The Ocean of Story." *Directions in Literary Criticism*. Ed. Stanley Weintraub and Philip Young. University Park: The Pennsylvania State University Press, 1973, pp. 1–6.

Writer's Choice. Ed. Rust Hills. New York: McKay, 1974. (Brief note preceding "Lost in the Funhouse," pp. 1–2)

Recordings by John Barth

John Barth Reads from Giles Goat-Boy. New York: CMS Records, 1968. (LP Disc: 551)

Prose Readings by John Barth. New York: McGraw-Hill, 1970. ("Test Borings" plus slight commentary) (Tape: cassette 81575, reel-to-reel 75988)

Two Narratives for Tape and Live Voice. New York: McGraw-Hill, 1970. (Tape: cassette 81673; reel-to-reel 78162)

Reviews

The Floating Opera

Adelman, George. *Library Journal* 81 (August 1956): 1789.

"Comic Opera." *Omaha World-Herald,* 13 January 1957, sec. G, p. 29.

Cooper, Madison. "Chockfull of Curiosities." *Dallas Morning News,* 14 October 1956, part 5, p. 15.

———. "First Novel Inspired by Famous Showboat." *Springfield Sunday Republican,* 12 August 1956, sec. C, p. 12.

Freedley, George. *Morning Telegraph* (New York), 28 August 1956, p. 2.

Harding, Walter. "Needless Vulgarity in Novel." *Chicago Sunday Tribune Magazine of Books,* 21 October 1956, p. 14.

Hicks, Granville. "Doubt Without Skepticism." *Saturday Review* 48 (3 July 1965): 23.

Hogan, William. "A Bookman's Notebook—Life Is a Showboat, A Young Author Finds." *San Francisco Chronicle,* 28 August 1956, p. 19.

Hyman, Stanley Edgar. "John Barth's First Novel." *New Leader* 48 (12 April 1965): 20–21.

Kirkus 24 (15 June 1956): 417.

Los Angeles Mirror and Daily News, 20 August 1956, part 2, p. 2.

Mandel, Siegfried. "Gaudy Showboat." *New York Times Book Review,* 26 August 1956, p. 27.

Myers, Art. "Life's But a Showboat Drifting By." *Washington Post and Times Herald,* 26 August 1956, p. E6.

Prescott, Orville. "Books of the Times." *New York Times,* 3 September 1956, p. 11.

Rubin, Louis D., Jr. "Novels of the Eastern Shore and War." *Baltimore Evening Sun,* 27 August 1956, p. 16.

Schickel, Richard. "An 'Opera' Afloat." *Milwaukee Journal,* 30 December 1956, part 5, p. 4.

The Floating Opera (rev. ed.)

Bradbury, Malcolm. *Guardian Weekly,* 10 October 1968, p. 14.

Graham, K. *Listener* 80 (3 October 1968): 26.

Price, R.G. "New Novels," *Punch* 255 (2 October 1968): 487.

Publishers' Weekly 191 (6 March 1967): 73.

Times Literary Supplement, 10 October 1968, p. 1161.

Wall, Stephen. *Observer,* 29 September 1968, p. 26.

The End of the Road

Bluestone, George. "John Wain and John Barth: The Angry and the Accurate." *Massachusetts Review* 1 (May 1960): 582–589.

Boatwright, Taliaferro. "Jacob Horner Came Out of His Corner, and Then—." *New York Herald Tribune Book Review,* 20 July 1958, p. 3.

Bradbury, Malcolm. "New Novels." *Punch* 243 (10 October 1962): 540.

Coleman, John. *Queen* 221 (London, 18 September 1962): 27–28.

"Fiction by Tyndarous." *John O'London's* 7 (27 September 1962): 4.

Hicks, Granville. "Doubt Without Skepticism." *Saturday Review* 48 (3 July 1965): 23–24.

Kerner, David. "Psychodrama in Eden." *Chicago Review* 13 (Winter-Spring 1959): 59–67.

Kirkus 26 (15 May 1958): 362.

LaHaye, Judson. *Best Sellers* 18 (1 August 1958): 165.

Pickrel, Paul. "Unlucky Jake." *Harper's* 217 (August 1958): 87.

Raven, Simon. "A Lemon for the Teacher." *Spectator,* 21 September 1962, p. 410.

Richardson, Maurice. "Upper Crusts." *New Statesman* 64 (21 September 1962): 370.

"Strife and Struggle." *Times Literary Supplement,* 28 September 1962, p. 757.

"A Study in Nihilism." *Time* 72 (21 July 1958): 80.

Wermuth, Paul C. *Library Journal* 83 (1 September 1958): 2319–2320.

The End of the Road (rev. ed.)

Publishers' Weekly 191 (26 June 1967): 64.

The Sot-Weed Factor

Arthur, Helen. "The Marathon Adventures of a 17th-Century Englishman." *New York Herald Tribune Lively Arts Section,* 22 January 1961, p. 30.

Baines, Nancy. *Cape Times* (Capetown, South Africa), 29 November 1961, p. 12.

Barker, Shirley. "History Is Still Good Fiction." *Saturday Review* 43 (26 November 1960): 21–22. (Brief mention)

"The Black Humorists," *Time* 85 (12 February 1965): 94–96. (Brief mention)

Dientsfrey, Harris. "Blended Especially for a Heady Smoke." *Book Week,* 15 March 1964, p. 18.

Fiedler, Leslie A. "John Barth: An Eccentric Genius." *New Leader* 44 (13 February 1961): 22–24.

Fuller, Edmond. "The Joke Is on Mankind." *New York Times Book Review,* 21 August 1960, p. 4.

Harding, Walter. "An Historical Novel to End All Historical Novels." *Chicago Sunday Tribune Magazine of Books*, 21 August 1960, p. 5.

Hicks, Granville. "Doubt Without Skepticism." *Saturday Review* 48 (3 July 1965): 23–24.

Hyman, Stanley Edgar. "The American Adam." *New Leader* 47 (2 March 1964): 20–21.

"I' Faith, 'Tis Good." *Newsweek* 56 (29 August 1960): 88–89.

"Invitation to Escape." *Times Literary Supplement*, 27 October 1961, p. 765.

King, Francis. "Smog of the Spirit." *New Statesman* 62 (13 October 1961): 524–525.

Kirkus 28 (15 June 1960): 462.

McLaughlin, Richard. "The Sot-Weed Factor." *Springfield Sunday Republican*, 25 September 1960, sec. D, p. 4.

Observer, 10 October 1965, p. 22.

Robie, Burton A. *Library Journal* 85 (15 September 1960): 3099.

Shrapnel, Norman. *Manchester Guardian*, 31 October 1961, p. 7.

Southern, Terry. "New Trends and Old Hats." *Nation* 191 (19 November 1960): 381.

Sutcliffe, Denham. "Worth a Guilty Conscience." *Kenyon Review* 23 (Winter 1961): 181–184.

"The Virgin Laureate." *Time* 76 (5 September 1960): 77.

Walsh, William J., S.J. *Best Sellers* 20 (15 September 1960): 200–201.

The Sot-Weed Factor (rev. ed.)

Bannon, B.A. *Publishers' Weekly* 190 (14 November 1966): 111.

Choice 4 (June 1967): 418.

Peterson, C. *Books Today* 4 (8 January 1967): 9.

Giles Goat-Boy

America 115 (26 November 1966): 706.

Arimond, John. "Revelation or Hoax?" *Extension* (October 1966): 54.

Balliett, W. "Rub-a-Dub-Dub." *New Yorker* 42 (10 December 1966): 234.

Beagle, Peter S. "John Barth: Long Reach, Near Miss." *Holiday* 40 (September 1966): 131–132, 134–135.

"Black Bible." *Time* 88 (5 August 1966): 92.

Booklist 63 (15 November 1966): 363.

Brooks, Peter. *Encounter* 28 (June 1967): 71–75.

Burgess, Anthony. *Spectator*, 31 March 1967, p. 369.

Byrd, Scott. "*Giles Goat-Boy* Visited." *Critique* 9, no. 1 (1966): 108–112.

Choice 3 (October 1966): 632.

Corbett, E.P. *America* 115 (17 September 1966): 290.

Corke, H. *The Listener* 77 (30 March 1967): 437.

Davis, D.M. *National Observer* 5 (1 August 1966): 19.

Donoghue, Denis. "Grand Old Opry." *New York Review of Books* 7 (18 August 1966): 25–26.

Featherstone, Joseph. "John Barth as Jonathan Swift." *New Republic* 155 (3 September 1966): 17.

Fremont-Smith, Eliot. "The Surfacing of Mr. Barth." *New York Times* 115 (3 August 1966): 39M.

Fuller, E. *Wall Street Journal* 46 (9 August 1966): 12.

Goldman, Albert. "*Giles Goat-Boy,* 'egghead omnibus.'" *Vogue* (15 August 1966).

Green, M. *Manchester Guardian,* 6 April 1967, p. 11.

Harding, W. *Books Today* 3 (31 July 1966): 3.

———. *Library Journal* 91 (August 1966): 3762.

"Heroic Comedy." *Newsweek* 68 (8 August 1966): 81–82.

Hicks, Granville. "Crowned with the Shame of Men." *Saturday Review* 49 (6 August 1966): 21–23.

Johnson, B.S. *Books and Bookmen* 12 (April 1967): 60.

Kirkus 34 (1 June 1966): 550.

Kitching, J. *Publishers' Weekly* 189 (23 May 1966): 81.

Klein, Marcus. "Gods and Goats." *Reporter* 35 (22 September 1966): 60–62.

Levitas, G. *Book World* 1 (17 September 1967): 15.

MacNamara, D. *New Statesman* 73 (31 March 1967): 442.

Maddocks, M. *Christian Science Monitor* 58 (4 August 1966): 11.

Malin, Irving. *Commonweal* 85 (2 December 1966): 270.

McColm, Pearlmarie. "The Revised New Syllabus and the Unrevised Old." *Denver Quarterly* 1 (Autumn 1966): 136–138.

Merril, J. *Fantasy and Science Fiction* 32 (March 1967): 20.

Morse, J. Mitchell. "Fiction Chronicle." *Hudson Review* 19 (Autumn 1966): 507–514.

National Observer 5 (29 August 1966): 17.

O'Connell, Shaun. "Goat Gambit at the University." *Nation* 203 (5 September 1966): 193.

Petersen, C. *Books Today* 4 (20 August 1967): 13.

Poirier, Richard. "wescac and the Messiah." *Book Week,* 7 August 1966, pp. 1, 12.

Publishers' Weekly 191 (26 June 1967): 68.

Samuels, Charles T. "John Barth: A Buoyant Denial of Relevance." *Commonweal* 85 (21 October 1966): 80–81.

Saturday Review 50 (30 September 1967): 47. (Brief mention)

Schlueter, P. *Christian Century* 83 (21 September 1966): 1149.

Scholes, Robert. "George Is My Name." *New York Times Book Review*, 7 August 1966, pp. 1, 22.

Schott, Webster. "A Black Comedy to Offend Everyone." *Life* 61 (12 August 1966): 10.

Shapiro, J.L. *Best Sellers* 26 (1 October 1966): 231.

Shuttleworth, M. *Punch* 252 (5 April 1967): 504.

Stuart, Dabney. "A Service to the University." *Shenandoah* 18 (Autumn 1966): 96–99.

Tanner, Tony. *Partisan Review* 34 (Winter 1967): 102.

Teachers College Record 68 (November 1966): 185.

Times Literary Supplement, 30 March 1967, p. 261.

Virginia Quarterly Review 43 (Winter 1967): viii.

"Year of the Fact." *Newsweek* 68 (19 December 1966): 117. (Brief mention)

Lost in the Funhouse

Adams, Phoebe. *Atlantic* 222 (October 1968): 150.

Appel, Alfred, Jr. "The Art of Artifice." *Nation* 207 (28 October 1968): 441.

Ardery, P.P. *National Review* 20 (3 December 1968): 1230.

Axthelm, Pete. "Tiny Odyssey." *Newsweek* 72 (30 September 1968): 106, 108.

Carruth, Hayden. "Barth's *Lost in the Funhouse:* Reality's Essence Explored in Unconventional 'Fictions.'" *Philadelphia Inquirer Book News*, 6 October 1968, p. 7.

Cassill, R.V. "The Artist as Art." *Book World*, 15 September 1968, p. 16.

Davenport, Guy. "Like Nothing Nameable." *New York Times Book Review*, 20 October 1968, pp. 4, 63.

Davis, Douglas M. "The End Is a Beginning for Barth's 'Funhouse.'" *National Observer*, 16 September 1968, p. 19. (Includes interview)

"Fable for People Who Can Hear with Their Eyes." *Time* 92 (27 September 1968): 100.

Harding, Walter. *Library Journal* 93 (15 September 1968): 3153.

Hicks, Granville. "The Up-to-Date Looking Glass." *Saturday Review* 51 (28 September 1968): 31–32.

"Just for the Record." *Times Literary Supplement*, 18 September 1969, p. 1017.

Kirkus 36 (1 August 1968): 836.

Murray, J.J. *Best Sellers* 28 (15 October 1968): 282.

Playboy (November 1968): 26, 30.

Publishers' Weekly 194 (29 July 1968): 56.

Richardson, Jack. "Amusement and Revelation." *New Republic* 159 (23 November 1968): 30, 34–35.

Schott, Webster. "One Baffled Barth in Search of a Book." *Life* 64 (18 October 1968): 8.

Tanner, Tony. "No Exit." *Partisan Review* 86, no. 2 (1969): 293–295, 297–299.

Chimera

Adams, Phoebe. *Atlantic* 230 (October 1972): 135.

Allen, Bruce. *Library Journal* 97 (August 1972): 2638.

Best Sellers 33 (1 November 1973): 355.

Booklist 69 (15 November 1972): 274.

Breslin, John B. "A Prospect of Books." *America* 127 (7 October 1972): 265.

Bryant, Jerry H. "The Novel Looks at Itself—Again." *Nation* 215 (18 December 1972): 631–633.

Choice 9 (December 1972): 1288.

Crinklaw, Don. "One Low Voice in Wild Company." *National Review* 24 (13 October 1972): 1136–1137.

Ellmann, Mary. *Yale Review* 62 (March 1973): 468.

Hill, William B., S.J. *America* 127 (18 November 1972): 422.

Kirkus 40 (15 July 1972): 813.

Lehmann-Haupt, Christopher. *New York Times*, 20 September 1972, p. 45.

Locke, Richard. "Sherry's 1,001 Groovy Nights." *Life* 73 (6 October 1972): 28.

"Lost in the Barth House." *Christian Science Monitor*, 20 September 1972, p. 10.

McGrath, Peter. "Trinity Tales." *New Society*, 1 August 1974, p. 304.

Meyer, Arlin G. "Form, Fluidity, and Flexibility in Recent American Fiction." *Cresset* 36 (April 1973): 11–15.

Michaels, Leonard. *New York Times Book Review*, 24 September 1972, pp. 35–37.

"The Narrative Springs." *Times Literary Supplement*, 26 July 1974, p. 783.

Newsweek 81 (1 January 1973): 53. (*Chimera* selected as one of twelve noteworthy fictions of 1972)

New York Times, 20 September 1972, p. 45.

New York Times Book Review, 3 December 1972, p. 74. (*Chimera* selected as one of several noteworthy fictions of 1972)

New Yorker 48 (30 September 1972): 125.

Perkins, Bill. "In One of Three Barth Seems Not So Parched and Plucked After All." *National Observer* 11 (7 October 1972): 21.

Playboy (October 1972): 26.

Prescott, Peter S. "Heroes over the Hill." *Newsweek* 80 (9 October 1972): 108, 110.

Psychology Today 6 (January 1973): 20.

Publishers' Weekly 202 (31 July 1972): 67–68.

———— 204 (13 August 1973): 57.

Sale, Roger. "Enemies, Foreigners, and Friends." *Hudson Review* 25 (Winter, 1972–73): 705–706.

Sheppard, R.Z. "Scheherazade and Friend." *Time* 100 (2 October 1972): 80.

Wood, Michael. "New Fall Fiction." *New York Review of Books* 19 (19 October 1972): 34–35.

Critical Studies

Alter, Robert. "The Apocalyptic Temper." *Commentary* 41 (June 1966): 61–66. (On *The Sot-Weed Factor*)

Altieri, Charles. "Organic and Humanist Models in Some English *Bildungsroman*." *Journal of General Education* 23 (1971): 220–240. (Wilde, Joyce, Barth, principally)

"American Fiction: The Postwar Years, 1945–65." *Book Week*, 26 September 1965, pp. 1–3, 5–7, 18, 20, 22, 24–25.

Barnes, Hazel E. *The Literature of Possibility: A Study of Humanistic Existentialism.* Lincoln: University of Nebraska Press, 1959, p. 380. (Brief mention of *The End of the Road*)

Bean, John C. "John Barth and Festive Comedy: The Failure of Imagination in *The Sot-Weed Factor*." *Xavier University Studies* 10, no. 1 (1971): 3–15.

Bellamy, Joe David. "Algebra and Fire." *Falcon* 4 (1972): 5–15. (Interview)

————. "Having It Both Ways." *New American Review*, no. 15 (1972): 134–150. (Interview, included in *The New Fiction*. Urbana: University of Illinois Press, 1974, pp. 1–18)

Bienstock, Beverly G. "Lingering on the Autognostic Verge: John Barth's *Lost in the Funhouse*." *Modern Fiction Studies* 19 (Spring 1973): 69–78.

Binni, Francesco. "John Barth e il romanzo di società." *Studi Americani* 12 (1966): 277–300.

Bradbury, John M. "Absurd Insurrection: The Barth-Percy Affair." *South Atlantic Quarterly* 68, no. 3 (Summer 1969): 319–329.

Brady, Karen. "Barth Enjoys Teaching Youth; Finds Buffalo Culturally Alive." *Buffalo Evening News,* 3 September 1966.

Bryer, Jackson R. "John Barth: A Bibliography." *Critique* 6, no. 2 (1963): 86–89.

Cooper, Arthur. "An In-Depth Interview with John Barth." *Harrisburg Patriot* 30 March 1965, p. 6.

Decker, Sharon D. "Passionate Virtuosity: The Fiction of John Barth." Unpublished dissertation, University of Virginia, 1973.

Dippie, Brian W. " 'His Visage Wild; His Form Exotick': Indian Themes and Cultural Guilt in John Barth's *The Sot-Weed Factor.*" *American Quarterly* 21, no. 1 (Spring 1969): 113–121.

Diser, Philip E. "The Historical Ebenezer Cooke." *Critique* 10, no. 3 (1968): 48–59.

Enck, John. "John Barth: An Interview." *Wisconsin Studies in Contemporary Literature* 6 (1965): 3–14.

Ewell, Barbara C. "John Barth: The Artist of History." *Southern Literary Journal* (Spring 1973): 32–46.

"Existential Comedian." *Time* 89 (17 March 1967): 109.

Feldman, Burton. "Anatomy of Black Humor." *Dissent* 15 (1968): 158–160.

French, Michael R. "The American Novel in the Sixties." *Midwest Quarterly* 9 (July 1968): 365–379.

Friedman, Bruce Jay. "Those Clowns of Conscience." *Book Week,* 18 July 1965, pp. 2, 7. (Excellent discussion of "Black Humor" with very brief reference to Barth)

Garis, Robert. "What Happened to John Barth?" *Commentary* 42, no. 4 (October 1966): 89–95.

Giachetti, Romano. "L'ombra di Sheherazade: Conversazione con John Barth." *La Fiera Letteraria,* 18 July 1968, pp. 2–3.

Golwyn, Judith. "New Creative Writers—35 Novelists Whose First Work Appears This Season." *Library Journal* 81 (1 June 1956): 1496–1497. (Reprints a letter from Barth)

Graff, Gerald E. "Mythotherapy and Modern Poetics." *Triquarterly,* no. 11 (1968): 76–90.

Gresham, James T. "John Barth as Minippean Satirist." Unpublished dissertation, Michigan State University, 1973.

Gross, Beverly. "The Anti-Novels of John Barth." *Chicago Review* 20 (November 1968): 95–109.

Harris, Charles B. *Contemporary American Novelists of the Absurd.* New Haven: College and University Press, 1972. (Heller, Vonnegut, Pynchon, Barth)

Hassan, Ihab. "The Existential Novel." *Massachusetts Review* 3 (Summer 1962): 795–797. (Short remark on *The End of the Road*)

Hauck, Richard Boyd. "These Fruitful Odysseys: John Barth," in *A Cheerful Nihilism: Confidence and "The Absurd" in American Humorous Fiction.* Bloomington: Indiana University Press, 1971.

Hendin, Josephine. "John Barth's Fictions for Survival." *Harper's* 247 (September 1973): 102–106.

Hill, Hamlin. "Black Humor: Its Cause and Cure." *Colorado Quarterly* 17 (Summer 1968): 57–64.

Hinden, Michael. *"Lost in the Funhouse:* Barth's Use of the Recent Past." *Twentieth Century Literature* 19 (1973): 107–118.

Hirsh, David. "John Barth's Freedom Road." *Mediterranean Review* 2, no. 3 (1972): 38–47. (On *The End of the Road*)

Holder, Alan. " 'What Marvelous Plot . . . Was Afoot?' History in Barth's *The Sot-Weed Factor." American Quarterly* 20, no. 3 (Fall 1968): 596–604.

Janoff, Bruce L. "Beyond Satire: Black Humor in the Novels of John Barth and Joseph Heller." Unpublished dissertation, Ohio University, 1972.

"John Barth: Goat-Boy's Father." *Playboy* (March 1967): 142.

"John Barth Papers." *Quarterly Journal of the Libary of Congress* 26 (October 1969): 247–249.

Jones, D. Allen. "The Game of the Name in Barth's *The Sot-Weed Factor." Research Studies* 40 (1972): 219–221.

Joseph, Gerhard. *John Barth.* Minneapolis: University of Minnesota Press (Pamphlets on American Writers, no. 91), 1970.

Kennard, Jean Elizabeth. "John Barth: Imitations of Imitations." *Mosaic* 3, no. 2 (1970): 116–131.

———. "Towards a Novel of the Absurd: A Study of the Relationships between the Concept of the Absurd as Defined in the Works of Sartre and Camus and Ideas and Form in the Fiction of John Barth, Samuel Beckett, Nigel Dennis, Joseph Heller, and James Purdy." Unpublished dissertation, University of California, Berkeley, 1968.

Kennedy, Mopsy Strange. "Roots of an Author." *Washington Post Potomac,* 3 September 1967, pp. 17–19. (Photographs of Barth's close relatives plus their remarks about his career)

Kiely, Benedict. "Ripeness Was Not All: John Barth's *Giles Goat-Boy." Hollins Critic* 3, no. 5 (December 1966): 1–12.

Kiernan, Robert F. "John Barth's Artist in the Funhouse." *Studies in Short Fiction* 10 (1973): 373–380.

Klein, James R. "The Tower and the Maze: A Study of the Novels of John Barth." Unpublished dissertation, University of Illinois, Urbana-Champaign, 1972.

Klinkowitz, Jerome. *Literary Disruptions. The Making of a Post-Contemporary American Fiction.* Urbana: University of Illinois Press, 1975.

Knapp, Edgar H. "Found in the Barthhouse: Novelist as Savior." *Modern Fiction Studies* 14, no. 4 (1968): 446–451.

Kostelanetz, Richard. "American Fiction of the Sixties," in *On Contemporary Literature.* Ed. with an introduction by Richard Kostelanetz. New York: Avon, 1969, pp. 634–652.

———. "The New American Fiction," in *The New American Arts.* Ed. Richard Kostelanetz. New York: Horizon Press, 1965, pp. 194–236.

———. "Notes on the American Short Story Today." *Minnesota Review* 5 (1965): 214–221.

———. "The Point Is That Life Doesn't Have Any Point." *New York Times*

Book Review, 6 June 1965, pp. 3, 28, 30. (Discussion of "literature of the absurd" with brief reference to *The Sot-Weed Factor*)

Kyle, Carol A. "The Unity of Anatomy: The Structure of Barth's *Lost in the Funhouse.*" *Critique* 13, no. 3 (1972): 31–43.

Lask, Thomas. "Art Is Artifice in Barth Reading." *New York Times,* 21 November 1967, p. 52.

Le Clair, Thomas. "John Barth's *The Floating Opera:* Death and the Craft of Fiction." *Texas Studies in Literature and Language* 14 (1972): 711–730.

Lee, L.L. "Some Uses of Finnegan's Wake in John Barth's *The Sot-Weed Factor.*" *James Joyce Quarterly* 5 (Winter 1968): 177–178.

"The Logical and the Lost" *Esquire* 50, no. 1 (July 1958): 16. (Editorial remark about "The Remobilization of Jacob Horner")

Loughman, Celeste M. "Mirrors and Masks in the Novels of John Barth." Unpublished dissertation, University of Massachusetts, 1971.

Majdiak, Daniel. "Barth and the Representation of Life." *Criticism* 13 (1970): 51–67.

Mason, Julian D. "Acquisition Notes: The Papers of John Barth." *Library of Congress Information Bulletin* 28 (8 May 1969): 1.

McDonald, James L. "Barth's Syllabus: The Frame of *Giles Goat-Boy.*" *Critique* 13, no. 3 (1972): 5–10.

Meras, Phyllis. "John Barth: A Truffle No Longer." *New York Times Book Review,* 7 August 1966, p. 22. (Includes brief interview)

Mercer, Peter. "The Rhetoric of *Giles Goat-Boy.*" *Novel* 4 (1971), 147–158.

Miller, Russell H. "*The Sot-Weed Factor:* A Contemporary Mock-Epic." *Critique* 8, no. 2 (Winter 1965–66): 88–100.

Morrell, David. "Ebenezer Cooke, Sot-Weed Factor Redivivus: The Genesis of John Barth's *The Sot-Weed Factor.*" *Bulletin of the Midwest Modern Language Association* 8, no. 1 (Spring 1975): 32–47.

Murphy, R.W. "In Print: John Barth." *Horizon* 5 (January 1963): 36–37.

Noland, Richard W. "John Barth and the Novel of Comic Nihilism." *Wisconsin Studies in Contemporary Literature* 7 (1966): 239–257.

Poirier, Richard. "A Literature of Law and Order." *Partisan Review* 36, no. 2 (1969): 189–204.

———. "The Politics of Self-Parody." *Partisan Review* 35 (Summer 1968): 339–353.

Prince, Alan. "An Interview with John Barth." *Prism* (Sir George Williams University, Spring 1968): 42–62.

Rodrigues, Eusebio L. "The Living Sakhyan in Barth's *Giles Goat-Boy.*" *Notes on Contemporary Literature* 2, no. 4 (1972): 7–8.

Rogers, Thomas. "John Barth: A Profile." *Book Week,* 7 August 1966, p. 6.

Rovit, Earl. "The Novel as Parody: John Barth." *Critique* 6, no. 2 (1963): 77–85.

Rubin, Louis D., Jr. "Notes on the Literary Scene: Their Own Language." *Harper's* 230 (April 1965): 173–175.

Schickel, Richard. *"The Floating Opera." Critique* 6, no. 2 (1963): 53–67.

Scholes, Robert. "The Allegory of Exhaustion." *Fiction International* 1 (1973): 106–108.

―――. "Disciple of Scheherazade." *New York Times Book Review*, 8 May 1966, pp. 5, 22.

―――. *The Fabulators.* New York: Oxford University Press, 1967. (Excellent first chapter about the nature of Barth's fiction; lengthy last chapter on *Giles Goat-Boy*)

―――. "Metafiction." *Iowa Review* 1, no. 4 (Fall 1970): 100–115.

Shenker, Israel. "Complicated Simple Things." *New York Times Book Review*, 24 September 1972, pp. 35–38. (Interview)

Shimura, Masao. "Barth to America Bungaku no Dento." *Eigo Seinen* 117 (1971): 414–416. (Barth and the tradition of American literature)

―――. "John Barth, *The End of the Road*, and the Tradition of American Fiction." *Studies in English Literature* (English Literary Society of Japan, 1971): 73–87.

Slethang, Gordon E. "Barth's Refutation of the Idea of Progress." *Critique* 13, no. 3 (1972): 11–29.

Smith, Herbert F. "Barth's Endless Road." *Critique* 6, no. 2 (1963): 68–76.

Sommavilla, Guido. "Il cinismo cosmico di John Barth." *Letture* 24 (1969): 98–110.

Stark, John O. *The Literature of Exhaustion.* Durham, N. C.: Duke University Press, 1974. (Borges, Nabokov, and Barth)

Stubbs, John C. "John Barth as a Novelist of Ideas: The Themes of Value and Identity." *Critique* 8, no. 2 (1966): 101–116.

Sugiura, Ginsaku. "Imitations-of-Novels—John Barth no Shosetsu." *Eigo Seinen* 115 (1969): 612–613.

Tanner, Stephen L. "John Barth's Hamlet." *Southwest Review* 56 (1971): 347–354.

Tanner, Tony. "The Hoax That Joke Bilked." *Partisan Review* 34 (Winter 1967): 102–109.

Tatham, Campbell. "John Barth and the Aesthetics of Artifice." *Contemporary Literature* 12 (1971): 60–73.

―――. "The Gilesian Monomyth: Some Remarks on the Structure of *Giles Goat-Boy*." *Genre* 3 (1970): 364–375.

―――. "The Novels of John Barth." Unpublished dissertation, University of Wisconsin, 1968.

Tharpe, Jac. *John Barth: The Comic Sublimity of Paradox.* Carbondale: Southern Illinois University Press, 1974.

Thomas, Jesse James. "The Image of Man in the Literary Heroes of Jean-Paul Sartre and Three American Novelists: Saul Bellow, John Barth, and Ken Kesey—A Theological Evaluation." Unpublished dissertation, Northwestern University, 1967.

Tilton, John W. *"Giles Goat-Boy:* An Interpretation." *Bucknell Review* 18, no. 1 (1970): 93–119.

Trachtenberg, Alan. "Barth and Hawkes: Two Fabulists." *Critique* 6, no. 2 (1963): 4–18.

Vine, Richard. *John Barth: An Annotated Bibliography.* Harrisburg, Pa.: Scarecrow Press, 1976.

Waldmeir, Joseph J. "Only an Occasional Rutabaga: American Fiction Since 1945." *Modern Fiction Studies* 15 (1969): 467–481.

Weixlmann, Joseph N. "Counter-Types and Anti-Myths: Black and Indian Characters in the Fiction of John Barth." Unpublished dissertation, Kansas State University, 1973.

———. *John Barth: An Annotated Bibliography.* New York: Garland, 1976.

———. "John Barth: A Bibliography." *Critique* 13, no. 3 (1972): 45–55.

Index

192   *Index*

Hero, The, 60, 152
Hero with a Thousand Faces, The,
  60, 152
Hicks, Granville, xv
History, use of, xvi, xvii, 27, 31–32,
  33, 36–37, 39–44, 45, 57
Homer, 138
Hoover, J. Edgar, 70
Horace, 138
Hughes, Howard, 70

Iliad, 147
Innocence, xvii, 32, 37, 44, 49–50, 51,
  52, 53, 54–55, 65, 95, 101, 104–5,
  107, 110, 115, 135, 164
"Invulnerable Castle, The," 127

James, Henry, vii, 138
*John Barth: The Comic Sublimity of
  Paradox,* xv
Johns Hopkins University, 123, 124,
  125, 128, 156, 163, 164
Joseph, Gerhard, xv, 5
Joyce, James, xvii
Juilliard School of Music, 123
Jung, Carl, 60–61, 72, 170 n. 3
  (ch. 5)

Kafka, Franz, xvii
Keaton, Buster, 72
Keats, John, 148
Kennard, Jean, 24
Kennedy (Joe, John, Robert, Jacque-
  line), 70
Kenner, Hugh, 132
Kostelanetz, Richard, 98
Khrushchev, Nikita, 70

Lake Chautauqua, N.Y., 131, 137,
  153, 157
"Landscape: The Eastern Shore," 127
Letters, 131, 139, 140, 153, 163, 164,
  165
Library of Congress, 77, 96, 102, 115–
  20, 132, 172 n. 12
Life, 68, 79, 131
"Life-Story," 93, 105, 111
"Lilith and the Lion," 108, 125
Literary Guild, 67
Literature of the Absurd, 98–99
"Literature of Exhaustion, The," 116

"Lost in the Funhouse," 87–88, 89,
  90–91, 92, 96, 108
Lost in the Funhouse, xv, xvii, 80–96,
  98, 99, 101, 105, 111, 112, 113,
  114, 116, 120, 123, 130–31, 140,
  141, 143, 146, 150, 151, 155, 156,
  163, 164, 175 n. 28; publication
  history, 171 n. 6

Mailer, Norman, 131
Malden, Md., 31, 34, 46, 122
Man without Qualities, The, 102
Mann, Thomas, 132, 164
Marx, Karl, 31
Maryland Muse, The, 35, 168 n. 9
Masterplots, 154
"Mathematical Games," 141
Mayer, Brantz, 41, 42
McCarthy, Joe, 70
McLuhan, Marshall, 131
"Menelaiad," 91, 93, 94–95, 96, 108,
  140, 141, 146, 147
More, Henry, 31, 39
Motif-Index of Folk Literature, 154
Murdock, Iris, 172–73 n. 6
"Muse, Spare Me," 116, 132, 134–36,
  143, 157
Musil, Robert, 102
Mysticism, xvii, 71, 72, 76, 78, 79,
  97, 134, 144
Myth, xvi, xvii, 56–58, 60–64, 66,
  83, 94, 107, 114, 116, 140, 141,
  149, 150
Myth of the Birth of the Hero, The,
  60
Mythotherapy, 22–25, 102–7

Napoleon, 139, 153, 154
National Book Award, xv, 128, 130,
  163
New York Times Book Review, 68,
  69, 129
Newton, Sir Isaac, 31, 39
"Night-Sea Journey," 91, 92, 96, 101
Nihilism, xvii, 1, 3, 13, 16, 19, 25,
  26, 28, 82, 99, 101–2, 105, 133–
  34, 136, 143, 165
Novel of Ideas, 15–16, 47–48, 100

Ocean City, Md., 87
"Ocean of Story, The," 174 n. 22